God's Merciful Love

The Old Testament

God's Merciful Love

*Educational and
Theological Advisors*

*Rev. Richard M. Hogan
Rev. John M. LeVoir
Mary Jo Smith*

Image of God Series
Grade Six

Image of God, Inc.
Brooklyn Center, MN 55430

God's Merciful Love

The Old Testament

Donna May   James M. May

IGNATIUS PRESS   SAN FRANCISCO

Nihil obstat: Mark B. Dosh
            Censor Librorum

Imprimatur: † John R. Roach, D.D.
            Archbishop of St. Paul and Minneapolis
            July 22, 1991

Excerpts from the English translation of *The Roman Missal* © 1973, International Committee on English in the Liturgy, Inc. (ICEL); excerpts from the English translation of *Rite of Penance* © 1974, ICEL. All rights reserved.

Scripture selections are taken from the *New American Bible with Revised New Testament*, © 1986 by the Confraternity of Christian Doctrine, Washington, D.C., and are used with permission. All rights reserved.

Text of "Canticle of Brother Sun" (page 35) is from Lawrence Cunningham, *Saint Francis of Assisi*, Harper and Row, Publishers, Inc. © 1981.

Cover art: Scala/Art Resource, N.Y.
K 38962 Michelangelo. Centro della volta.
Creation of Adam (detail). Vatican, Sistine Chapel.

Illustrations: Barbara Harasyn

For additional information about the Image of God program: 1-800-635-3827

Published 1992 by Ignatius Press, San Francisco
© 1992 Image of God, Inc.
All rights reserved
ISBN 978-0-89870-336-8
Manufactured by Toppan Printing Co., LTD
Manufactured in Hong Kong on January 2, 2010
Job # 09-11-208
in compliance with the
Consumer protection Safety Act

Photo Credits
6 The Crosiers, Gene Plaisted, OSC (Bethel United Church, Louisville, KY). 10 Catholic News Service (CNS), from *L'Osservatore Romano*. 11 Prof. Emeritus Ansgar Sovik. 24 The Crosiers (St. Raphael Church, Crystal, MN). 29 *Left*, Bill Pritchard, CNS. *Center*, Joel M. LaVallee, CNS. *Right*, Kenneth Murray, CNS. 30 Ansgar Sovik. 34 The Crosiers (St. Bridget Church, Minneapolis, MN). 44 The Crosiers (Holy Spirit Church, St. Paul, MN). 48 CNS/KNA-Bild. 68 The Crosiers (Sacred Heart Church, Winona, MN). 79 Ansgar Sovik. 89 The Crosiers (Blessed Sacrament Church, La Crosse, WI). 91 (Hebron, Tomb of the Patriarchs.) 104 The Crosiers (St. Bernard Church, Madison, WI). 111 Ansgar Sovik. 117 The Crosiers (St. Bridget Church, Minneapolis, MN). 120 The Crosiers (St. Luke Lutheran Church, St. Paul, MN). 132 The Crosiers (Kirk in the Hills, Bloomfield Hills, MI). 148 Ansgar Sovik. 161 The Crosiers (St. Matthew Lutheran Church, St. Paul, MN). 164 The Crosiers (Sacred Heart Church, Freeport, MN). 172 The Crosiers (St. Joseph Cathedral, La Crosse, WI). 174 The Crosiers (Messiah Episcopal Church, St. Paul, MN). 176 Ansgar Sovik. 193 Ansgar Sovik. 199 The Crosiers. 218 The Crosiers (St. Ita Church, Chicago, IL). 228 The Crosiers (Kirk in the Hills, Bloomfield Hills, MI). 238 The Crosiers (St. Mark Episcopal Church, Minneapolis, MN). 240 The Crosiers (House of Hope Church, St. Paul, MN). 245 The Crosiers (Hennepin United Methodist Church, Minneapolis, MN). 247 The Crosiers (Hamline Methodist Church, St. Paul, MN). 249 The Crosiers (House of Hope Church). 252 The Crosiers (St. Gregory Church, Chicago, IL). 255 The Crosiers (Kirk in the Hills, Bloomfield Hills, MI). 259 The Crosiers (House of Hope Church). 264 The Crosiers (House of Hope Church). 269 The Crosiers (St. Mary's Home, St. Paul, MN). 272 *Top*, Michael Collopy, *Bottom*, Christopher M. Riggs, *The Catholic Advance* (Wichita, KS). 277 The Crosiers (Kirk in the Hills, Bloomfield Hills, MI). 290 The Crosiers (Sacred Heart Church, Winona, MN). 304 The Crosiers (Kirk in the Hills, Bloomfield Hills, MI). 310 The Crosiers (Kirk in the Hills). 323 The Crosiers. 324 The Crosiers (Steve Pauley's family). 329 CNS (1979 photo). 332 The Crosiers. 346 The Crosiers. 351 *Left*, Art Institute of Chicago (French altarpiece, 15th cent.). *Right*, The Crosiers. 352 The Crosiers (St. Joseph Church, Kalamazoo, MI). 353 The Crosiers (St. Joseph Church, Kalamazoo, MI). 363 Art Institute of Chicago (French altarpiece, 15th cent.).

Contents

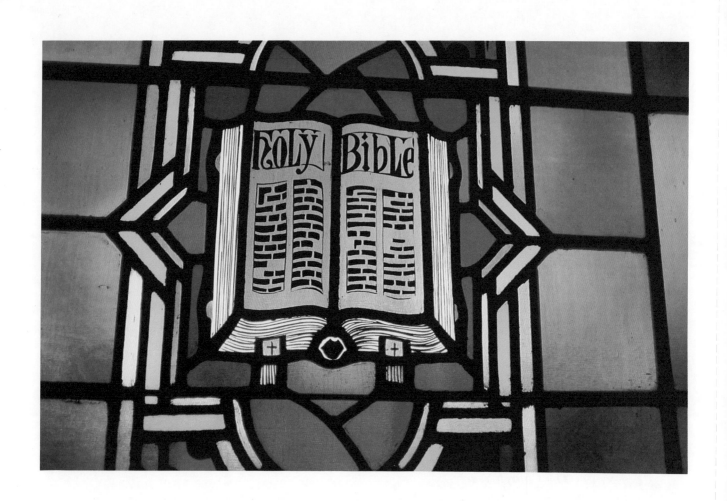

Learning about the Bible

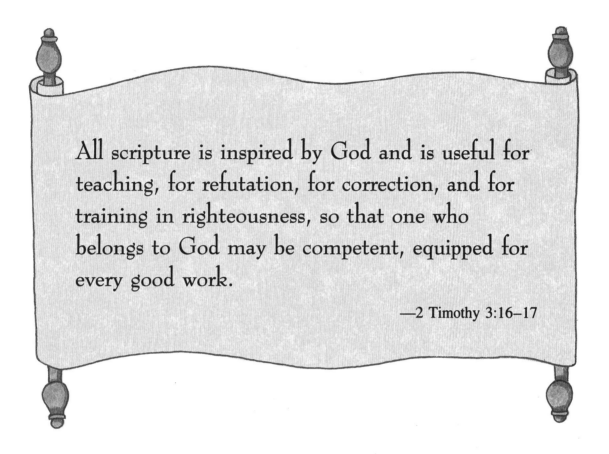

All scripture is inspired by God and is useful for teaching, for refutation, for correction, and for training in righteousness, so that one who belongs to God may be competent, equipped for every good work.

—2 Timothy 3:16–17

Divine Revelation

God the Father, in His infinite mercy and love, sent His Son, Jesus Christ, to the world to reveal the Truth. To *reveal* means to make something known that was not known before. Christ revealed to us truths that we could never have known in any other way. Divine revelation teaches us about God. It is the hidden truths God chose to reveal about Himself. Moreover, because we are made in God's image, when God tells us about Himself, He is also telling us about ourselves.

The Role of the Church

While on earth, Jesus knew that, following His passion, death, and resurrection, He would return in glory to the right hand of His Father in heaven. But not wishing to leave us orphans, He established the Church on earth. Saint Paul tells us that "It is he [Christ] who is the head of the body, the church" (Col 1:13). Pope Pius XII (*Mystici Corporis* 67) explains the teaching in this way: ". . . the unbroken tradition . . . from the earliest times teaches that the Divine Redeemer [Christ] and the Society which is His Body [the Church] form but one mystical person." Pope John Paul II quotes Saint Augustine when he teaches that "Christ and the Church are one single mystical person". This *mystical person* continues Christ's work to reveal the Truth. Since its foundation, almost two thousand years ago, and today, and for all earthly time to come, the Church continues to reflect on Divine Revelation and to restate it for each generation to understand. Jesus completed His work while He was with us on earth. Saint John the Evangelist was most likely the last eyewitness to record the events of Jesus' life. Therefore, Divine Revelation ended with the death of Saint John (c. A.D. 100). But the Church continues to reflect on and interpret the entire word of God for each new age.

REVIEW QUESTIONS

The questions marked with an asterisk (*) ask about a basic concept of our Faith.

*1. What did God the Father send His Son, Jesus Christ, to the world to reveal?

*2. What is Divine Revelation?

3. What does Divine Revelation teach us?

*4. Who is Christ's mystical person on earth?

5. Why did Christ establish the Church?

6. How does the Church continue Christ's work to reveal the truth?

7. Who was most likely the last eyewitness to record the work of Jesus?

Sacred Tradition

Sacred Tradition is the "handing down" from generation to generation of all that Christ has revealed. Tradition is preserved under the guidance of the Holy Spirit in the Church. The word *tradition* comes from the Latin word *tradere*, "to hand over". The first recorded statement of Sacred Tradition is the Bible. Our word *Bible* comes from the Greek word *biblion*, which means "book". The Bible is our most important book. It is, in a way, a history of what God has done in our world. It is God's proclamation. It is a book that tells us who God is and who we are as images of God.

Sacred Tradition, however, also includes such things as the Apostles' Creed, the writings of the Fathers of the Church (such as Saint Augustine, Saint Jerome, Saint Gregory the Great, and Saint Ambrose), the Church's divine liturgy, and the decrees of the Church.

Sacred Scripture

The Bible is not a single book but rather a collection of 73 books separated into two major divisions: the Old Testament and the New Testament. The *Old Testament* contains 46 books all written before Christ was born (B.C.). The *New Testament* contains 27 books written after Christ was born (A.D., an abbreviation of the Latin *anno Domini*, "in the year of our Lord"). Together the books of the Old and New Testaments, the Bible, are referred to as *Sacred Scripture*.

Divine Inspiration

The books of the Bible were written by many different people. All of them, however, were guided by God, Who is the author of all Sacred Scripture. They wrote down, through their own thoughts and choices, what He wished them to write. This guidance by God is called divine inspiration. God the Holy Spirit inspired the human authors of Sacred Scripture to write God's message to His people.

> Sacred Tradition and Sacred Scripture, then, are bound closely together, and communicate one with the other. For both of them, flowing out from the same divine well-spring, come together in some fashion to form one thing, and move towards the same goal. Sacred Scripture is the speech of God as it is put down in writing under the breath of the Holy Spirit. And Tradition transmits in its entirety the Word of God which has been entrusted to the apostles by Christ the Lord and the Holy Spirit.
> —*Dogmatic Constitution on Divine Revelation* II, 9.

The Magisterium of the Church

Remember that Jesus Christ revealed the truth and is the revelation of God the Father. Since the Church is Jesus' mystical person on earth, the Church alone can guarantee that the revelation of Christ contained in Sacred Scripture and in Sacred Tradition is taught to each successive age. This teaching authority of the Church, given by Christ to the successors of the Apostles (the bishops in union with the Pope), is called the *Magisterium* (from the Latin *magister*, meaning "teacher"). The Magisterium is responsible for teaching Divine Revelation to the people of God.

Once we understand this mystical bond between Christ and His Church, we can easily understand why all Sacred Scripture must be interpreted in light of the Church's teaching authority.

Throughout the Church's history there have been many councils and synods. At these meetings, the bishops of the world, together with the pope, share the responsibility of teaching and guiding the Church. There have been numerous synods, such as the 1990 World Synod of Bishops pictured here. There have been 21 Ecumenical or General Councils of the Church. The first council was Nicaea I, held in the year 325. The most recent Ecumenical Council was Vatican II, which met from 1962 to 1965.

REVIEW QUESTIONS

  *1. What is Sacred Tradition?

   2. Where can the first recorded statement of Sacred Tradition be found?

   3. Why is the Bible the most important book ever written?

  *4. What are the names of the two major divisions of the Bible?

   5. What is another name for the Bible?

   6. What important event marks the beginning of the Old Testament?

   7. What important event marks the beginning of the New Testament?

   8. How do we know that the message in the Bible is God's message to His people?

  *9. What role did the human authors play in the writing of Sacred Scripture?

 *10. Who is the author of the Bible?

  11. In addition to the writings of Sacred Scripture, what are some examples of other things included in Sacred Tradition?

  12. Who guarantees that Divine Revelation, found in Sacred Scripture and Tradition, is taught to each generation?

 *13. What is the Magisterium of the Church?

Qumran, where the Dead Sea Scrolls were discovered in caves.

How Was the Bible Written?

The Old Testament was originally written mostly in Hebrew, with a few parts in Greek. The New Testament was written in Greek. Since then there have been many *translations*, or versions, of the Bible. The original *manuscripts*, handwritten texts, of the books of the Bible have not survived. The earliest surviving manuscripts are known as the Dead Sea Scrolls. They were found in 1947, buried in a cave near the Dead Sea. Many of them date from as early as the second century B.C. That means they were written about two hundred years before Christ was born. Their discovery was important because biblical scholars could then compare the texts they had known with these newly discovered texts. Do you know what they learned? In over a thousand years of copying texts, there were almost no differences! The *scribes*, the people who had copied these books of the Old Testament, had been very careful not to make mistakes. In this effort God had helped them. And so God's message was passed on and continues to be passed on to each generation. Today the Bible can be read in more than two thousand different languages!

The Languages of the Bible

The first book of the Bible is Genesis, and the first sentence in Genesis is: "In the beginning, . . . God created the heavens and the earth." Here we see that sentence written in Hebrew and Greek, the original languages of the Bible texts, and in Latin, according to the translation by Saint Jerome. There are many versions of the Bible in English. In this book we are using the *New American Bible*.

Hebrew: The Old Testament was written mostly in Hebrew. Hebrew is read from right to left.

בראשית א

בראשית ברא אלהים

את השמים ואת והארץ

Greek: The New Testament was originally written in Greek. Here is the first sentence of Genesis, chapter one, written in Greek:

ΓΕΝΕΣΙΣ, ΚΕΦ. α.

Ἐν ἀρχῇ ἐποίησεν ὁ Θεὸς τὸν οὐρανὸν καὶ τὴν γῆν.

Latin: Latin uses the same alphabet as English. The most famous Latin version of the Bible is called the Vulgate. The Vulgate was translated by Saint Jerome from Hebrew and Greek versions.

GENESIS, CAPUT I.

In principio creavit Deus caelum et terram.

English: This is the same passage from Genesis, from the *New American Bible*:

GENESIS, CHAPTER 1

In the beginning, . . . God created the heavens and the earth.

Literary Forms

When you go to the library you find many different types of books from which to choose. You may wish to read, for example, a biography of a famous person or a history book that tells about the American Revolution. Or you may choose a novel or a collection of poems. Biography, history, novel, and poetry are all literary forms. *Literary forms* are different types of writing. The books of the Bible are written in many literary forms. In order to understand God's message found in the Scriptures, it is important to know what literary forms were used to tell this message.

The Books of the Bible and Their Literary Forms

Old Testament Literary Forms

The books of the Old Testament include these literary forms—history, law, prophecy, prayer, and wisdom.

History books. The core of these books is historical. It is important to remember that the human author is writing these books not to teach a history lesson, but to teach a religious truth. The history books include Genesis, parts of Exodus, Joshua, Judges, Ruth, 1 and 2 Samuel, 1 and 2 Kings, 1 and 2 Chronicles, Ezra, Nehemiah, Tobit, Judith, Esther, Lamentations, Baruch, and 1 and 2 Maccabees.

Law books. These books give an account of the various laws and rules that the Jewish people followed. They include Exodus (in part), Leviticus, Numbers, and Deuteronomy.

Prophecy books. These books contain the words of the *prophets*. The word *prophet* comes from the Greek word *prophetes*, which means "one who speaks before others". The prophets, then, were special people or messengers, chosen by God to speak to His people. The prophets include Isaiah, Jeremiah, Ezekiel, and Daniel, as well as Hosea, Joel, Amos, Obadiah, Jonah, Micah, Nahum, Habakkuk, Zephaniah, Haggai, Zechariah, and Malachi.

Prayer book. The Book of Psalms is a prayer book, a collection of songs and poems that are used to worship and praise God.

Wisdom books. These books give insight or common sense about human life and our actions toward each other and toward God. They include Job, Proverbs, Ecclesiastes, Song of Songs, Wisdom, and Sirach.

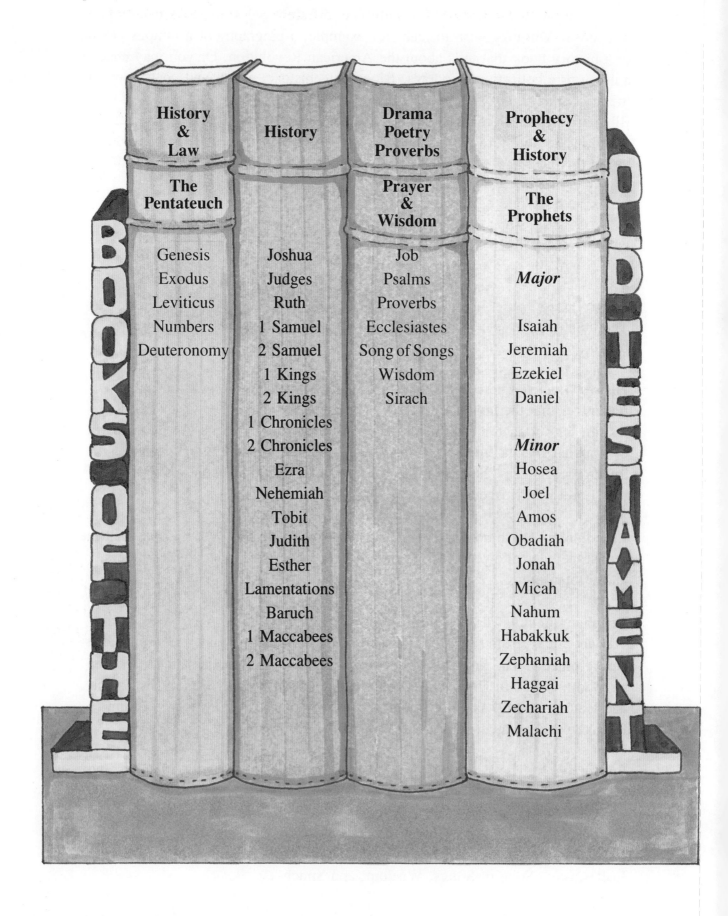

BOOKS OF THE / **OLD TESTAMENT**

History & Law	History	Drama Poetry Proverbs	Prophecy & History
The Pentateuch		Prayer & Wisdom	The Prophets
Genesis	Joshua	Job	*Major*
Exodus	Judges	Psalms	
Leviticus	Ruth	Proverbs	Isaiah
Numbers	1 Samuel	Ecclesiastes	Jeremiah
Deuteronomy	2 Samuel	Song of Songs	Ezekiel
	1 Kings	Wisdom	Daniel
	2 Kings	Sirach	
	1 Chronicles		*Minor*
	2 Chronicles		Hosea
	Ezra		Joel
	Nehemiah		Amos
	Tobit		Obadiah
	Judith		Jonah
	Esther		Micah
	Lamentations		Nahum
	Baruch		Habakkuk
	1 Maccabees		Zephaniah
	2 Maccabees		Haggai
			Zechariah
			Malachi

New Testament Literary Forms

The books of the New Testament include these literary forms—gospel, letters, history, and prophecy.

Gospel. The Gospels are factual accounts of the deeds and words of Jesus Christ. They were recorded by Matthew, Mark, Luke, and John.

Letters. These books of the New Testament are actual letters, or epistles, that were written by several disciples to various Christian communities and to friends. They include the letters written by Saint Paul to the Romans, Corinthians (1 and 2), Galatians, Ephesians, Philippians, Colossians, Hebrews, and Thessalonians (1 and 2), as well as to Timothy (1 and 2), Titus, and Philemon. They also include the epistles written by Saint James, Saint Peter (1 and 2), Saint John (1, 2, and 3), and Saint Jude.

History book. The Acts of the Apostles is the only history book of the New Testament. It is a historical account of the early Christian Church.

Prophecy book. One New Testament book, Revelation, is a kind of prophecy about the end of the world and the fulfillment of the kingdom of God.

The Gospels	Letters (or Epistles)		Church History
Matthew			Acts of the Apostles
Mark	Romans	Titus	
Luke	1 Corinthians	Philemon	**Prophecy Book**
John	2 Corinthians	James	Revelation
	Galatians	1 Peter	
	Ephesians	2 Peter	
	Philippians	1 John	
	1 Thessalonians	2 John	
	2 Thessalonians	3 John	
	1 Timothy	Jude	
	2 Timothy	Hebrews	

1. Name the languages in which the Bible was originally written.
2. What do we mean by literary form?
3. Why is it important to know the literary form of the book in which the human author chose to write God's message?
4. List several types of literary forms used in the Old Testament.
5. List several types of literary forms used in the New Testament.

Concepts of Faith

1. **What did God the Father send His Son, Jesus Christ, into the world to reveal?**
   The Truth.

2. **What is Divine Revelation?**
   The hidden truths that God chose to reveal about Himself.

3. **Who is Christ's mystical person on earth?**
   The Church.

4. **What is Sacred Tradition?**
   The "handing down" from generation to generation of all that Christ has revealed. Tradition is preserved under the guidance of the Holy Spirit in the Church.

5. **What are the names of the two major divisions of the Bible?**
   The Old Testament and the New Testament.

6. **What role did the human authors play in the writing of Sacred Scripture?**
   They were divinely guided by God to write down, through their own thoughts and choices, what God wished them to write.

7. **Who is the author of the Bible?**
   God.

8. **What is the Magisterium of the Church?**
   It is the teaching authority of the Church; the Pope and the bishops of the Church in union with him.

Vocabulary

reveal: To make known something that was not previously known.

Divine Revelation: The hidden truths God chose to reveal about Himself.

mystical person of Christ: The Church.

Old Testament: The first division of the Bible; it includes 46 books written before the time of Christ.

B.C.: Abbreviation of "before Christ".

New Testament: The second division of the Bible; it includes 27 books written after Christ was born.

A.D.: Abbreviation of the Latin *anno Domini*, which means "in the year of our Lord".

Sacred Scripture: The books of the Old and New Testaments; the Bible; the first recorded statement of sacred Tradition.

Magisterium: The teaching authority given by Christ to the Church.

translations: Different versions of the Bible.

manuscript: Handwritten text.

scribes: People who, throughout the ages, copied books.

Vulgate: The most famous Latin translation of the Bible, made by Saint Jerome.

literary forms: Different types of writing.

prophet: A messenger, a person chosen by God to speak to His people.

epistle: A letter.

Living the Lesson

Discuss the following questions with your classmates, family, and friends.

1. You have learned that the Bible is our most important book. How can you use the Bible in your daily life with your family?

2. How can the Bible remind us that we are important to God and to each other?

Prayers

The "Apostles' Creed".

Old and New Testament Relationships

Jesus said that He came to fulfill the law found in the Old Testament, not to destroy it. Therefore, it is important to study the Old Testament as well as the New Testament. We cannot understand Jesus unless we understand what He fulfilled. This worksheet lists some of the prophecies of the Old Testament that Jesus fulfilled in the New Testament. Find both the Old and New Testament Scripture references in your Bible, and then write a short answer that completes the sentence. If you do not know the abbreviation for the book, look it up in the list of abbreviations in your Bible. The first number that follows the abbreviation of the book is the chapter number; the number or numbers after the colon are the verse numbers. For example, "Is 7:14" means the Book of Isaiah, chapter 7, verse 14.

1. Is 7:14; Mt 1:23

Jesus would be born of a virgin and would be called _____.

2. Jer 23:5-6; Mk 11:9-10

Jesus would be a descendant from the house of _____.

3. Mi 5:1; Mt 2:1, 5-6

Jesus would be born in _____.

4. Mal 3:1; Mt 11:10

God sent a _____ to prepare the way for the coming of Jesus.

5. Zec 11:7; Jn 10:11

Jesus would be the good _____.

6. Is 42:7; Jn 8:32

Jesus will open the _____,

and you will know _____, and the truth

will set you _____.

7. Ps 118:22; Mt 21:42

Jesus is the _____ which the builders _____ .

8. Ps 41:10; Jn 13:18

Jesus would be betrayed by a _____ .

9. Ps 22:19; Mt 27:35

What would they do with Jesus' garments? _____ .

10. Ex 12:46; Jn 19:36

Jesus would be killed without His _____ being broken.

Other Names for Jesus

Throughout the Bible, Jesus is given many names. Match each name for Jesus with its correct Scripture reference by placing the letter of the name on the line next to the reference.

1. _____ Is 53:7   **A** Redeemer

2. _____ Rv 19:16   **B** High Priest

3. _____ Is 59:20   **C** Light of the world

4. _____ Is 9:5   **D** Head of the Church

5. _____ Is 11:10   **E** Lamb of God

6. _____ Mal 3:20   **F** Prince of Peace

7. _____ Heb 4:15   **G** King of Kings

8. _____ Heb 2:10   **H** Leader of our salvation

9. _____ Eph 1:22   **I** Sun of justice

10. _____ Jn 8:12   **J** Root of Jesse

Genesis: The Creation of the World and of Man and Woman

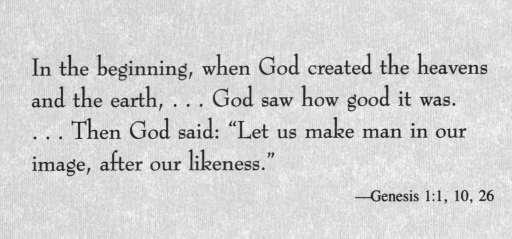

> In the beginning, when God created the heavens and the earth, ... God saw how good it was. ... Then God said: "Let us make man in our image, after our likeness."
>
> —Genesis 1:1, 10, 26

An Introduction to the Book of Genesis

The Pentateuch

The Pentateuch is the name given to the first five books of the Bible. These five books are Genesis, Exodus, Leviticus, Numbers, and Deuteronomy. The word *pentateuch* comes from two Greek words: *penta*, which means "five", and *teuchos*, a container for scrolls. In ancient times, messages were written on rolled pieces of paper called scrolls. A scroll is similar to a book. These five books are very important to the Jewish people because together they form "The Torah", or "The Law", the most important part of the Jewish Bible. It contains the story of the formation of the people of God, including creation, the stories of Abraham and Moses, and the beginnings of the Israelite nation.

The Book of Genesis

Genesis is the name of the first book of the Bible. The word *genesis* comes from the Greek word for "origin" or "birth". This book narrates the origin, or beginning, of the world, the birth of the human race, and the early history of the Hebrew people.

As you look over the first few pages of the Book of Genesis in your Bible, you will notice that there is more than one story, or *account*, of creation. Are you surprised? In fact, there are many stories of creation: most of the ancient peoples from all parts of the world have a story of creation that is part of their culture and tradition. In our present culture, science has its own story to tell about the origin, or beginning, of the world. In science class you may have studied the "Big Bang" theory, which claims that the earth came into existence as the result of an enormous explosion. You may have studied about *evolution*, a scientific theory that claims human beings have developed gradually from a simpler form of life.

So what are we to believe? How are we to know the truth about our beginning? From your reading of the first chapter in this textbook, you may remember several important facts. The writers of the Bible were *inspired* by God. Do you remember what that means? God helped or guided them to write His message through their own thoughts and words. This cannot be said of the other stories of creation that are part of folklore or mythology.

The other important fact to remember is that the books of the Bible were written in several different *literary forms*. History, law, and prophecy are just a few examples. Although the Book of Genesis is classified as a history book, it was written to teach an important religious truth. The Book of Genesis is not primarily concerned with *when* God created the world and man and woman. Nor is it primarily concerned with *how long* creation took. The Bible tells us that God made everything from nothing. The miracle of creation is the same whether it took six days or six years or six million years!

Science and our belief in God need not be in competition with each other. For example, we can learn about the "Big Bang" theory. We can believe, as some scientists do, that the universe began from a huge explosion of gases and matter. But what caused the explosion? And who created the gases and matter? Science does not know the answer. Our faith tells us that God created everything. He is the ultimate source of all knowledge, including all of what science teaches us. Thus, science can help us to understand the development of God's creations. If we remember the important truth that God is the Creator of all things and the source of all knowledge, the teachings of science and the teachings of our Faith will never be in conflict.

REVIEW QUESTIONS

*1. What is the name given to the first five books of the Bible?

2. What does the Pentateuch teach us?

*3. What is the name of the first book of the Bible?

4. In general, what does Genesis talk about?

5. What two important facts should we remember when we read about the story of creation in Genesis?

6. How can the study of science lead us to a better knowledge of God, our Creator?

You are now ready to read the first account of creation found in your Bible. Read Genesis 1:1–31 and 2:1–4, or read the following summary.

A Summary of the First Account of Creation

In the beginning, God created the heavens and the earth out of nothing.

On the first day God said, "Let there be light", and there was light. God saw how good the light was. God called the light "day", and the darkness he called "night".

On the second day God said, "Let there be a dome in the middle of the waters, to separate one body of water from the other." God called the dome "the sky". And he saw that it was good.

Then on the third day God said, "Let the water under the sky be gathered into a single basin, so that the dry land may appear." God called the dry land "the earth", and the basin of water he called "the sea". God saw how good it was. Then God said, "Let the earth bring forth vegetation." And so it happened. God saw how good it was.

Then God said: "Let there be lights in the dome of the sky, to separate day from night. Let them mark the fixed times, the days and the years . . . to shed light upon the earth." And so God made the sun and the moon and the stars. And God saw how good it was on the fourth day.

On the fifth day God said, "Let the water be filled with many living creatures, and on the earth let birds fly beneath the dome of the sky." And so it happened. God saw how good it was, and God blessed them.

Then God said: "Let the earth bring forth all kinds of living creatures: cattle, creeping things, and wild animals of all kinds." And so it happened on the sixth day. And God saw how good it was.

Then God said: "Let us make man in our image, after our likeness. Let them have dominion over the fish of the sea, the birds of the air, and the cattle, and over all the wild animals and all the creatures that crawl on the ground." God created man in his image: male and female he created them; in the divine image he created them. God blessed them, saying: "Be fertile and multiply; fill the earth and subdue it. Have dominion over the fish of the sea, the birds of the air, and all the living things that move on the earth." And so it happened. God looked at everything he had made, and he found it very good. Evening came, and morning followed—the sixth day.

Because God was finished with his work on the seventh day, he rested. He blessed the seventh day and made it holy.

—Adapted from Genesis 1:1–31, 2:1–4

The Seven Days of Creation

1	2	3	4	5	6	7
Light. Darkness.	Upper and Lower Waters.	Land. Sea. Vegetation.	Sun. Moon. Stars.	Birds. Fishes.	Animals. Man and Woman.	God rested.

A Discussion of the First Account of Creation

In this first story, God's creation took place in six days. To *create* means to make something out of nothing. Each creative act was introduced by the words "and God said . . .". During the first three days God prepared the world to receive the work of the next three days. Saint Thomas Aquinas referred to days 4, 5, and 6 as works of *ornamentation*. At Christmas time, when you place ornaments on the Christmas tree, you decorate it. It seems that God wished to decorate or *ornament* His first three days of creation. On day 1, God created the light and the darkness. On day 4, God ornamented the light and darkness with the sun, the moon, and the stars. On day 2, God created the upper and lower waters. Then He filled them with the birds and fishes on day 5. On day 3, God created the land and sea and plants. The earth was now prepared to receive animals and man and woman on day 6. After seeing that all He made was good, God rested on day 7.

The Church teaches us many things from the story of creation. What can we learn about God and about ourselves as images of God from this first account of creation? We come to know ourselves and the world around us. One of the first things we learn is that God existed before everything else. He is the Creator. No one created Him. He was there at the beginning of time. In fact, we know that God always was, always is, and always will be. He is everlasting. He is *eternal*. We cannot imagine how powerful God must be to create everything out of nothing. And how wise He must be! God's design of creation is wonderful. He shaped our world in the first three days and then beautified it during the next three days. He takes care to provide us with every need. *Everything* comes from God, and all that comes from Him is good. How often this phrase is repeated: "And God saw how good it was." In fact, when God created man and woman, the Bible says, "And he found it *very* good." We not only wonder at the power of God through which all things are made and on which all things depend, but we are amazed at His wisdom and goodness. What more can God do to show us His love!

And yet God does do more. "Let us make man in our image, after our likeness." Out of all God's creation, the sun, the moon, the stars, the fish and birds, the plants and animals, only we, male and female, are made in His *image*. What does this word *image* mean? When you look at yourself in the mirror, you see a reflection, a likeness, an image of yourself. Is this what God means? Do we look like God? How can this be? God the Father is a spirit. He does not have a body. Furthermore, each of us is unique. Therefore, to be made in God's image must mean more than to be a physical reflection of God. God is a personal Being with a mind and a will, the power to think and the power to choose. What makes human beings different from God's other earthly creatures is that we, like God, are persons. We are human persons. God created human persons with personal souls. A soul is the spiritual part of a person. Our souls give us the power to think and to choose. We think with our minds, and we choose with our wills. The animals and plants are not persons. They cannot think and choose. Human persons can think and choose.

What is more, God created each of us with a body. Our bodies are given to us by God so that the acts of our minds and wills might be expressed in physical ways. Our bodies are a unique gift to us from God. They should always express God-like actions. Because God created each and every one of us in His image and because He values us beyond measure, we have dignity and worth. We should act according to our dignity. We should never use or mistreat ourselves and others in a way that would offend human dignity. God loves us so much that He shares His very existence with us. As His images, we are called to be like Him. We, too, should love each other as images of God and value the goodness in all of God's creation.

> *I give you thanks that I am fearfully, wonderfully made; wonderful are your works.* —Psalm 139:14

What are our responsibilities as images of God?

God gives us the answer in Genesis 1:28. "God blessed them, saying: 'Be fertile and multiply; fill the earth and subdue it. Have dominion over the fish of the sea, the birds of the air, and all the living things that move on the earth.'"

There are two very important messages in this verse. (1) "Be fertile and multiply"—God invites Adam and Eve to form a family. He invites them to "fill the earth" with more images of God. He invites them to love as He loves. In other words, He asks them to share in the gift of creation by forming families and having children. God asks to share in this responsibility, too. (2) "Have *dominion* over the fish of the sea, the birds of the air, and all the living things that move on the earth." What does this mean? God did not give Adam and Eve the world to use for mere pleasure and enjoyment. He gave them the responsibility to govern the earth, to "subdue it". He gives us the same responsibility. We must use this responsibility wisely. We should take care of all of God's creation. This responsibility is called *stewardship*. God cares for us. As His images, we should do the same for all of His creation.

What is more, God's creation was made for everyone. We should share the good things of the earth with all peoples. God has given us many talents and skills. We are all asked to use our gifts, to give of ourselves, to work toward using the things of the world to benefit others. This creative work will help us to appreciate our own dignity as images of God. By practicing a proper stewardship over the things of the earth, we accept God's invitation to have "dominion", and we love others as God loves them.

REVIEW QUESTIONS

1. In God's act of creation, how are the first three days related to the next three days?
2. What did God do on the seventh day?
3. How did God look upon His creations at the end of the first six days?
4. What did God do after the creation of man and woman?
5. What does the Church teach us about God from the story of creation?
6. What do human persons have that makes them unique, separates them from the animals, and proves that they are made in God's image?
*7. What is a personal soul?
8. How do human persons express their thoughts and choices in a physical way?
9. Why must we respect the dignity of others?
*10. What did God ask Adam and Eve to do after He created them?
11. What did God mean when He asked Adam and Eve to be fertile and multiply?
12. What did God mean when He asked Adam and Eve to have dominion over the earth?

Read Psalm 148 and praise God for His wonderful creation!

The second account of creation is found in Genesis 2:4–25. Read these verses from your Bible, or read the summary printed below.

A Summary of the Second Account of Creation

When the LORD God made the earth and the heavens, he saw that there was no man to till the soil. So the LORD God formed man out of the clay of the ground and blew into his nostrils the breath of life, and so man became a living being.

Then the LORD God planted a garden in Eden, in the east, and he placed there the man whom he had formed. God made many different trees grow that were delightful to look at and good for food. And in the middle of the garden God planted the tree of knowledge of good and evil.

The garden was made where the Tigris and the Euphrates Rivers join with two other streams to form a single river.

Then God took man and settled him in the garden of Eden, to cultivate and to care for it. The LORD God said to man, "You are free to eat from any of the trees of the garden except the tree of knowledge of good and evil. From that tree you shall not eat; the moment you eat from it you are surely doomed to die."

Then God said, "It is not good for the man to be alone." So God created various wild animals and birds, and he brought them to the man to see what he would call them. The man gave names to all the cattle, the birds, and all the wild animals. But none proved to be the suitable partner for the man.

So God cast a deep sleep on the man, and he took out one of his ribs. From this rib God created a woman. When God brought her to the man, the man said, "This one, at last, is bone of my bones and flesh of my flesh; / This one shall be called 'woman', for out of 'her man' this one has been taken."

That is why a man leaves his father and mother and clings to his wife, and the two of them become one body.

The man and his wife were both naked, yet they felt no shame.

A Discussion of the Second Account of Creation

This second account of creation is different from the first. The first story is an exciting drama. The writer seems to be watching the very act of creation. Each creative act is described in detail. The second account is written from a different point of view. It is chiefly concerned with the creation of man and woman. All of God's other creative actions are mentioned to help us understand more about the creation of the human person.

What is God telling us in this second account of creation? God creates man before the rest of His creatures, indicating that they are made for man's sake. How does God make man? God portrays Himself as a potter, Who molds man's body out of clay. Then God "blew into his nostrils the breath of life, and so man became a living being". This "breath of life" is man's *soul*. You may remember from the discussion of the first account of creation that the soul is the spiritual part of a person. The soul gives a person the power to think and to choose. God then places man in the garden of Eden. He provides man with various trees that are "delightful to look at and good for food". One of these trees is the tree of knowledge of good and evil.

What is unique about the tree of knowledge of good and evil? What makes it different from the other trees in the garden? God tells man, "You are free to eat from any of the trees of the garden except the tree of knowledge of good and evil. From that tree you shall not eat; the moment you eat from it you are surely doomed to die." In this chapter of Genesis, Adam does not question God's will. He does not wonder why the fruit of this tree is forbidden. He accepts God's wisdom and love. He does not question God. Adam knows that

God loves him, cares for him, and wishes only what is good for him. In the third chapter of Genesis, we will learn more about the tree of knowledge of good and evil.

In chapter 2, verse 18, God says, "It is not good for the man to be alone. I will make a suitable partner for him." But God does not make woman immediately. He first creates the birds and animals and brings them to Adam to name. Man is given the opportunity to be a part of God's creative act—to show his wisdom and to name God's creatures. But "None proved to be the suitable partner for the man." Adam recognizes that he is unique. Among all of God's creatures there is none like himself. Further, he sees that there is no other human person he can love. He needs to share his love with another human person. As an image of God, he needs to love another human being in a God-like way. Hence, woman is created and is intended to be the full partner of his life. What joy Adam expresses when he says, "This one, at last, is bone of my bones and flesh of my flesh."

How wise and wonderful God is! God allows Adam to feel lonely when he is naming the animals. He was lonely because he didn't have another human person to love. When he meets Eve, he knows the joy of loving another human person. God creates woman so that man and woman will be able to express their love for each other through their bodies. Adam's joy is great, because he knows that, like him, Eve is another image of God. Adam knows his own dignity as an image of God, and therefore he values Eve. Eve also knows her dignity as an image of God, and therefore she values Adam.

This is the reason why Adam and Eve felt no shame, even though they were naked. Shame is an emotion caused by guilt over a willful thought or action that is wrong. Adam and Eve knew what was good. They knew that each one of them was of incredible worth and value. Their actions toward each other reflected this knowledge. They were able to love each other in a God-like way. "That is why a man leaves his father and mother and clings to his wife, and the two of them become one body." God blessed their union and laid the foundation for the sacrament of marriage, which Jesus would later institute.

God's message to us is very clear. All human beings have *dignity*. We have value and worth because we are created in God's image and likeness. When we see and appreciate our own dignity, we can value the dignity of others. We can love others as God loves us. As with Adam and Eve, God gives us His very life, *grace*. Grace is a gift from God that helps us act in a God-like way. Grace helped Adam and Eve to act in a God-like way. Through grace we are capable of acting in a God-like way. We can do what God created us to do. We can love Him and others through Him.

1. How does the second account of creation differ from the first?
2. In the second account of creation, from what did God make the first man?
3. What is the name of the tree from which Adam and Eve must not eat?
4. What did Adam come to understand after he named the animals?
5. Why did God create woman?
6. How did Adam and Eve express their love for each other?
*7. What did God give Adam and Eve so that they could love Him?
8. What does grace help us to do?

Concepts of Faith

1. **What is the name given to the first five books of the Bible?**
   The Pentateuch.
2. **What is the name of the first book of the Bible?**
   Genesis.
3. **What is the personal soul?**
   The personal soul is the invisible, spiritual, and immortal gift from God that gives each human being life.
4. **What did God ask Adam and Eve to do after He created them?**
   To be fertile and multiply and to have dominion over the earth.
5. **What did God give Adam and Eve so that they could love Him?**
   Grace.

Vocabulary

Pentateuch: The first five books of the Bible.

Genesis: The first book of the Bible.

account: Story.

evolution: A scientific theory that claims human beings have developed from a simpler form of life.

literary forms: Different types of writing.

create: To make something out of nothing.

ornament: To decorate.

ornamentation: Decoration.

universe: All of God's creations.

eternal: Everlasting.

image: A reflection; a likeness.

dignity: Value, worth.

dominion: Authority to govern the earth.

stewardship: Responsibility to care for all of God's creations.

grace: God's life. A gift in us that helps us act in a God-like way.

Living the Lesson

1. Make a list of things that you can do to carry out God's invitation to have "dominion" over all the earth. What can you do to take care of the environment (air, water, and land)? What can you do to take care of animals (your pets and other animals)? Discuss these things with your family and friends, and then *do* one of the things you wrote on your list.

2. We have learned that we should always respect one another because we are all made in God's image. How do we sometimes use or mistreat people? How should we act toward one another? What can we do to help those who are mistreated? What can we do to help people in need? Discuss these ideas with family and friends.

3. The creation story teaches us many things about God. Take a look at the world around you. Is creation continuing today? In what ways? Are you a part of God's ongoing creative work? What does our part in God's ongoing creative work teach us about God and ourselves? Discuss these questions with your family and friends.

Psalms of Praise

Psalms that contain praises of God the Creator:

Psalm 8	The Majesty of God and the Dignity of Man and Woman
Psalm 19	God's Glory in the Heavens and in the Law
Psalm 65	Thanksgiving for God's Blessings
Psalm 95	A Call to Praise and Obedience
Psalm 96	The Glories of the Lord, the King of the Universe
Psalm 104	Praise of God the Creator
Psalm 136	Hymn of Thanksgiving for the Everlasting Kindness of the Lord (verses 1–9)
Psalm 139	The All-knowing and Ever-present God
Psalm 147	Zion's Grateful Praise to Her Bountiful Lord
Psalm 148	Hymn of All Creation to the Almighty Creator
Psalm 150	Final Doxology with Full Orchestra

The Canticle of Brother Sun

Most High, omnipotent, good Lord,
To You alone belong praise and glory,
Honor, and blessing. No man is worthy to breathe Thy name.

Be praised, my Lord, for all your creatures.

In the first place for the blessed Brother Sun,
Who gives us the day and enlightens us through You,
He is beautiful and radiant with his great splendor,
Giving witness of Thee, Most Omnipotent One.

Be praised, my Lord, for Sister Moon and the stars
Formed by You so bright, precious, and beautiful.

Be praised, my Lord, for Brother Wind
And the airy skies, so cloudy and serene;
For every weather, be praised, for it is life giving.
Be praised, my Lord, for Sister Water,
So necessary yet so humble, precious, and chaste.

Be praised, my Lord, for Brother Fire, Who lights up the night.
He is beautiful and carefree, robust, and fierce.

Be praised, my Lord, for our sister, Mother Earth,
Who nourishes and watches us
While bringing forth abundance of fruits with colored
Flowers and herbs.

Be praised, my Lord, for those who pardon through Your love
And bear witness and trial.
Blessed are those who endure in peace,
For they will be crowned by You, Most High.

Be praised, my Lord, for our sister, Bodily Death,
Whom no living man can escape.
Woe to those who die in sin.
Blessed are those who discover Thy holy will.
The second death will do them no harm.

Praise and bless my Lord.
Render thanks.
Serve Him with great humility. Amen.

—Saint Francis of Assisi
(translated by Lawrence Cunningham)

God's Design of Creation

God divided His creative work into six days. After each day numbered below, write a short description of what God created on that day. Give the chapter and verse number of the source of your answers. To find the answers, read Genesis 1:1–31 and 2:1–4.

DAY 1 _____

Genesis _____ : _____

DAY 2 _____

Genesis _____ : _____

DAY 3 _____

Genesis _____ : _____

DAY 4 _____

Genesis _____ : _____

DAY 5 _____

Genesis _____ : _____

DAY 6 _____

Genesis _____ : _____

What did God do on Day 7?

_____

Genesis _____ : _____

Original Sin, the First Murder, and God's Merciful Love

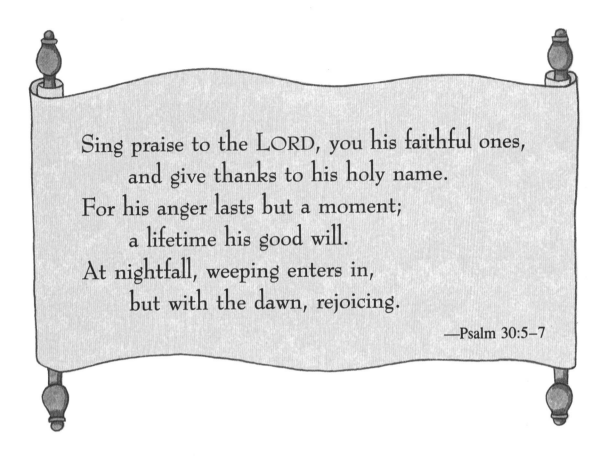

Sing praise to the LORD, you his faithful ones,
   and give thanks to his holy name.
For his anger lasts but a moment;
   a lifetime his good will.
At nightfall, weeping enters in,
   but with the dawn, rejoicing.

—Psalm 30:5–7

Adam and Eve were created in God's image. They were persons with souls. They had minds and wills. They had the abilities to think and to choose in a God-like way. They were given God's life, grace, to help them live as images of God. They lived a life that had no sickness or death. All nature lived in harmony around them. They knew that God loved them.

Adam and Eve loved God. But God wanted to give Adam and Eve a chance to love Him even more. So, in Genesis 2:16–17, God told them: "You are free to eat from any of the trees of the garden except the tree of the knowledge of good and evil. From that tree you shall not eat; the moment you eat from it you are surely doomed to die." Adam and Eve had the freedom to love God and to do as He asked. They were also told how they would harm themselves if they chose not to love God. They knew all of this, and yet they chose to eat the fruit.

Read Genesis 3:1–24, which tells the story of Adam and Eve's sin. The following story is only a summary of chapter 3 of Genesis.

Adam and Eve Sin

Satan, in the form of a serpent, approached Eve and asked her if she really believed that God would allow her to die if she ate the fruit of one particular tree. Then Satan tried to convince Eve that God would not allow her to die. Satan told Eve that God knew that if she ate the fruit of this tree she would be like God and as wise as God. Eve saw that the fruit was delicious; she wanted to be like God and as wise as God. So she took some of the fruit and ate it. Then Eve gave some of the fruit to Adam, who ate it also. As soon as they both had eaten the fruit, they knew that they had sinned. They were ashamed when they saw that they were naked, so they sewed fig leaves together to cover themselves. They tried to hide themselves from God and were afraid to answer Him when He called to them. God said, "You have eaten, then, from the tree of which I had forbidden you to eat!" Adam replied, "The woman whom you put here with me—she gave me fruit from the tree, and so I ate it." God asked Eve, "Why did you do such a thing?" Eve answered, "The serpent tricked me into it, so I ate it."

First, God told the serpent what would happen to him because he had tempted Adam and Eve. Then God spoke to Adam and Eve. They would have to work hard all their lives and could no longer live in the garden of Eden. They would know suffering and death. After this, God showed His merciful love and made leather garments for them to wear.

—Adapted from Genesis 3:1–24

Original Sin

What was the sin that Adam and Eve committed that had such severe effects? Was it the tree and its fruit that caused the sin? What kind of fruit was on the tree? Why did Satan choose the form of a snake?

All of these questions come to mind when we read the story of Adam and Eve and their sin. Before we answer these questions, we should remember what we have learned about the writers who were inspired by God to tell His message.

God allowed the writers to use their own thoughts and experiences to relate His message. At the time this text was written, the writers wished to represent Satan in a way that would suggest to their readers all that was evil and hateful. Many of the pagan gods of the Near East were pictured as serpents. The people who worshiped these serpent gods believed that the gods possessed magical powers of evil. The writers of Genesis wanted to encourage worship of the one true God, so it was natural for them to choose the form of a serpent to represent all that was evil. We, of course, know that snakes are important to the environment and provide a beneficial function in the cycle of nature. It was the Devil, or Satan, who tempted Adam and Eve, not a snake.

Does it matter what kind of fruit was on the tree? No. What matters is that Adam and Eve chose not to love God. Instead, they chose to sin. Sin is an offense against God. Adam and Eve offended God because they chose to believe the devil when he promised them that they could be equal to God. Their pride caused them to sin. They knew that to eat from the tree was wrong, because God had told them. Yet they chose to do it anyway. This is when they sinned. Because it was the first sin, it is called *original sin*.

When Adam and Eve chose to sin, they hurt themselves in three ways. First, they lost God's gift of grace and were not able to share God's life on earth or live with God in heaven. Second, they wounded their abilities to think and to choose. Their minds were "darkened" by sin, and their wills were weakened. Third, they "wounded" their bodies, letting them become subject to suffering and death.

Why were the effects of their sin so severe? We must remember that, before they sinned, Adam and Eve were not exactly like us. They were enlightened by God's grace. Their minds were not darkened, and their wills were not weakened. Their minds and wills could govern their bodies and their feelings. They did not find it as easy as we do to commit sin. This is why the first sin and its consequences were so serious.

Adam and Eve represent the entire human race. They are our first parents. Just as parents pass on to their children certain traits, so Adam and Eve have passed on to us, their children, original sin and its effects. We are all conceived and born with original sin. Our wills are weakened, and our minds are darkened. We cannot easily govern our feelings and emotions. We find it easy to sin. We often act like Adam and Eve when we are tempted to do wrong. How often do we let our pride influence us to choose what is wrong? When our parents tell us to do something, how often do we think, "Who are they to tell me what to do?" "I know what is best for me." "I'll do what I want to do!" And when we are caught in an act of disobedience or in a lie, how often do we blame someone else for our sinful behavior. Just as Eve said, "The serpent tricked me", so we say, "My friends said it was OK." Or just as Adam said, "[Eve] gave me fruit from the tree, and so I ate it", so we often say, "Johnny made me do it." Just as Adam and Eve felt ashamed when they sinned and tried to hide from God, we, too, feel guilty when we sin and often try to "cover up" our mistakes or to hide the truth from our parents.

How are we to know the truth? How do we determine if something is a sin? We can know because God has told us. God has revealed the truth to us through the Scriptures and through the teachings of the Church. It is from these sources that we can know what is right and what is wrong. Then, when it comes time for us to make a choice, we can remember the words of Jesus, spoken in the Garden the night before He died, "Father . . . not my will but yours be done" (Lk 22:42).

God's Merciful Love

God continued to love Adam and Eve after they sinned, as He continues to love us after we sin. In Genesis 3:21, God made leather garments for Adam and Eve to wear. God provided for their needs. The clothing is a sign of His merciful love. By providing clothing for them, God saved them from one of the effects of their sin—suffering from the elements. They must have been grateful to Him for this. Their gratitude drew them closer to God. In this way, God drew good out of evil. This is an example of God's merciful love.

A more important example of God's merciful love can be found in Genesis 3:15–16. God is speaking to Satan when He says, "I will put *enmity* between you and the woman, and between your offspring and hers." The word *enmity* means "hatred" or "hostility". The Church teaches us that the woman mentioned here is Mary. The offspring of Satan are his followers. The offspring of Mary is Christ. This passage says that there will be hostility on the part of Satan toward Christ. In other words, Satan will hate Christ.

This passage, then, is the first promise of a Savior. This promise is a sign of God's merciful love. God loves us so much that He brings good out of the evil of sin. He promises to send us His Son as our Savior. Only the Savior could make up for original sin and all other sins and repair our relationship with God. It is through Jesus that we are drawn closer to God. When Jesus chose to do what His Father asked and suffered death on the Cross, He showed us the meaning of perfect love. By His teachings and example, Jesus shows us who we are and how we should act as images of God.

God's merciful love is expressed also through the sacraments. One of the sacraments Jesus gave us is the sacrament of Baptism. Baptism gives us God's grace, which removes original sin, makes us members of the Church, and allows us to live with God someday in heaven. When we receive the sacraments, the grace we are given restores our friendship with God, draws us closer to Him, and helps us to act as His images.

1. How were Adam and Eve to show their love for God?

2. Why did Adam and Eve choose to eat the fruit from the tree of the knowledge of good and evil?

3. Who is the serpent in this story?

*4. When do we sin?

5. How do we know that something is wrong?

*6. What do we call the first sin?

*7. How did Adam and Eve hurt themselves when they chose to sin?

8. What do we inherit from Adam and Eve?

*9. How are we affected by original sin?

*10. What is merciful love?

11. In what ways did God show His merciful love to Adam and Eve?

12. What does the sacrament of Baptism do for us?

The Story of Cain and Abel

Read Genesis 4:1–10 for the scriptural account of the story of Cain and Abel, or read the following summary, which is based on Genesis 4:1–16 and Hebrews 11:4.

Adam and Eve named their first son Cain. Their second son they called Abel. Abel became a shepherd, while Cain was a farmer. It was the custom in those days to thank the Lord for His goodness and to show love for Him by offering a burnt sacrifice. The best animal of the flock or the best fruits of the harvest were given back to the Lord in this way. Abel, who was a shepherd, brought one of the best lambs from his flock. Cain brought some of the fruit from his harvest. The Lord looked with favor on Abel and accepted his offering. But God did not accept Cain's offering. Perhaps the fruit that Cain offered was not his best produce. Perhaps Cain did not offer his sacrifice in a spirit of love and thanksgiving. Cain became angry with the Lord and jealous of his brother. The Lord asked Cain why he was angry. He told Cain to take control of himself and to rid himself of resentment.

But Cain would not control his anger. He plotted against his brother. Cain said to his brother Abel, "Let us go out in the field." And when they were in the field, Cain attacked Abel and killed him. Later, when the Lord asked Cain where Abel was, he replied, "I do not know. Am I my brother's keeper?" The Lord knew that Cain had murdered his brother. He then told Cain the consequences

THE SACRIFICE OF ABEL

of his terrible sin. Cain would no longer be able to work the field in which he had murdered his brother. He would no longer be able to live with his family. Wherever he went, he would not be a successful farmer. He would, instead, "become a restless wanderer on the earth". Cain said to the Lord: "My punishment is too great to bear." Cain was afraid that, with no family and no home, there would be no one to protect him from harm. So the Lord put a mark on Cain and said, "If anyone kills Cain, Cain shall be avenged sevenfold." Then Cain left the Lord's presence and became a nomad, wandering from place to place throughout the desert.

A Discussion of the Story of Cain and Abel

The story of Cain and Abel can teach us several things. It is a story that illustrates the effects of original sin. One of these effects is that the human person finds it easy to sin. It was difficult for Cain to control his feelings of jealousy and anger. In Genesis 4:7, God says to Cain, "If you do well, you can hold up your head; but if not, sin is a demon lurking at the door: his urge is toward you, yet you can be his master." God is encouraging Cain to do good and warning Cain that it can be easy to sin. The writer of this passage chose to use a demon to represent sin. When we think of a demon, pictures of monsters and evil spirits come into our minds. These can be frightening! Is God trying to scare Cain? Of course not. God is trying to make Cain, and us, understand that there are temptations in our world that can lead to sin. We all have an inclination to give in to these temptations. The temptation to sin can often be very difficult to avoid or to overcome. And yet God gives Cain hope that he can overcome the inclination to sin and be the "master" of sin. God's grace can help all of us to choose to act as images of God. There is never a temptation to sin that is so great that God's grace cannot help us overcome it.

But Cain did not master his feelings of anger—he sinned. He chose to let his feelings influence him so that he did not act as an image of God. These sins increased in their intensity until he murdered his own brother. Cain did not make any effort to change his ways. One sin led to another until Cain totally rejected his brother. He did not love his brother as he should have. In killing Abel, Cain not only ended the life of his brother, but he seriously hurt his relationship with God, and he hurt himself. In sinning, Cain created a world for himself that was very different from the one God wished for him.

God is a loving God, Who cares for all His children. As images of God, we have a responsibility to love and to care for all our brothers and sisters in the world. The answer to the question "Am I my brother's keeper?" is a very definite *yes*, even when we have to master our emotions to care for people.

The story of Cain and Abel also teaches us about *sacrifice*. A sacrifice is an action in which someone or something is offered to God as a sign of love. Offering sacrifice was a religious custom practiced by most ancient civilizations. Ancient peoples, in order to show their love for God, to give thanks, or to praise Him, often offered something precious or valuable, such as prize crops or a spotless lamb. The story of Cain and Abel describes the offering of such sacrifices.

In the letter to the Hebrews (Heb 11:4), we read that it was not what Abel offered, but his faith that made his gift acceptable. Abel's sacrifice was accepted because he offered it with an attitude of faith. Cain's attitude of anger and jealousy showed that he offered his sacrifice with a different spirit.

Abel's sacrifice, pleasing and acceptable in God's sight, *prefigures*, or shows ahead of time, another more important sacrifice. That sacrifice is perfect, holy, and spotless and is offered by God Himself for our redemption, or salvation from our sins. It is the sacrifice of the spotless Lamb of God, Jesus Christ, on the Cross on Calvary. That sacrifice on Calvary—the same sacrifice offered in an unbloody manner—is recalled and presented again every time Mass is celebrated. Jesus offered Himself in love to the Father.

When we attend Mass, we should offer ourselves with Jesus to the Father in a spirit of love and faith. Do we come to Mass with an attitude of sincere faith? Do we make an effort to praise and to adore God with our prayers? Do we thank God for all the wonderful things He has given us? Do we pray and ask Him to help us when we are troubled? Do we tell Him that we are truly sorry for our sins? Or do we just sit in the pew and passively wait for the hour to end? How many times have we grumbled to ourselves, "Why do I have to go to Mass?" "I don't get anything out of church, it's boring." Understanding the meaning of offering sacrifice can help us answer these questions. We offer sacrifice to praise and to adore God, our Creator, to thank Him for His many blessings, to ask Him for help when we are in need, and to show Him that we are sorry for our sins. The choice to worship God, to express our love for Him, is one that is freely made. God will not force us to love Him. If we offer sacrifice with a spirit like Cain's, we may face the consequences of wandering from place to place without the joy and comfort of God's grace. The spiritual riches to be gained by offering ourselves to God in a spirit of sincere faith are beyond all measure.

1. List some of the effects of original sin as illustrated by the story of Cain and Abel.
2. Why was Abel's sacrifice acceptable to God?
3. In what perfect sacrifice can we participate?
4. Why do we offer prayer and sacrifice to God?
5. How did God show His merciful love to Cain?
6. How does God show us His merciful love?

Concepts of Faith

1. **When do we sin?**
   We sin when we know that something is wrong and we choose to do it anyway.
2. **What do we call the first sin?**
   Original sin.
3. **How did Adam and Eve hurt themselves when they chose to sin?**
   (a) They lost God's gift of grace and were not able to share God's life on earth or to live with Him in heaven. (b) They damaged their abilities to think and to choose. (c) They "wounded" their bodies and would experience suffering and death.
4. **How are we affected by original sin?**
   (a) We are born without grace. (b) Our abilities to think and to choose are damaged. (c) Our bodies will experience suffering and death.
5. **What is merciful love?**
   Drawing something good out of evil.

Vocabulary

original sin: The first sin committed by Adam and Eve; with regards to us, it is the sin inherited by all human beings (except Christ and Mary) from Adam and Eve.

enmity: Hatred or hostility.

sacrifice: An action in which someone or something is offered to God as a sign of love.

prefigure: To show ahead of time.

Living the Lesson

1. You have learned that one effect of original sin is that our minds and wills often find it difficult to master our feelings. For example: Suppose that you are walking home from school. You are hungry and really want a candy bar. But you do not have enough money to buy one. You are walking by a store. You know that it would be easy to go into the store and to sneak a candy bar into your bookbag when the clerk isn't looking. You know that it is wrong to steal. But your stomach is growling! What do you do? Discuss this situation with your friends and family. Perhaps you might share a similar situation taken from your own experience.

2. You have learned that when we sin, we not only hurt our relationship with God, but we hurt ourselves and our relationship with others. In other words, sin is not only an action against God, but it is also a social action. Think of an example that would illustrate that sin hurts our relationship with others.

3. In the story of Cain and Abel, when God asked Cain if he knew where Abel was, Cain replied, "I do not know. Am I my brother's keeper?" The Church teaches us that we should be responsible for and care for each other. Discuss the many ways in which we can demonstrate that we are our "brother's keeper".

Prayer

The "Act of Contrition".

"Am I my brother's keeper?"

God, in His goodness and merciful love, has given us the gift of grace to help us to live as images of God. Below are listed some of the ways in which our relationship with God is strengthened. Write a short paragraph describing how each of these opportunities can help you become a better reflection of God.

PRAYING

_____
_____
_____

ATTENDING MASS

_____
_____
_____

RECEIVING THE HOLY EUCHARIST

_____
_____
_____

GOING TO CONFESSION

_____
_____
_____

God's Merciful Love and the Existence of Pain and Suffering

If God loves us so much, then why does He allow pain and suffering to exist? You have learned that one effect of original sin is that we experience suffering and death. Knowing this, however, does not always make it easy to understand or accept.

Some reasons for suffering are easier to understand and accept than others. For example, if a person commits a terrible crime, it is easy for us to understand that that person should be punished for committing the crime by going to jail.

But what about the suffering that is caused by a natural disaster, such as an earthquake, or by an illness, such as cancer? The suffering caused by these examples is not easy to understand or accept. No terrible crime or sin was committed by the people affected. We should never think that God sent an earthquake because the people it affected were bad. God does not punish people for sin by sending illness or disasters. And yet many innocent people suffer from illness or disasters.

And so we ask the question, why does God allow suffering to exist? We will probably never be able to answer this question completely. God does show us, however, that good can be drawn out of evil. Remember, God loves us mercifully. Even the suffering and death of His Son, Jesus, was followed by the Resurrection. Time and time again, God shows us His merciful love.

Read the following story about a disaster. In the space given, write your thoughts about the good that can be drawn from the suffering caused by this disaster.

You have lived next door to your friend, John, since you were in the first grade. Your family and his are more than just good neighbors—you are all good friends. One night, John's house burns down. Luckily, no one is hurt. But the entire house and all the family belongings are destroyed in the fire. Your neighbors have nowhere to live, no clothes, no furniture, nothing.

_____

_____

_____

_____

Noah, the Great Flood, and God's Merciful Love

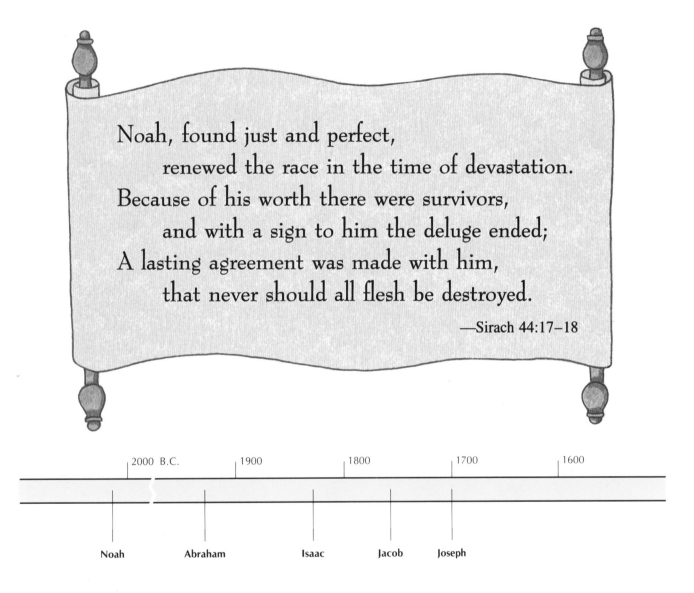

Noah, found just and perfect,
    renewed the race in the time of devastation.
Because of his worth there were survivors,
    and with a sign to him the deluge ended;
A lasting agreement was made with him,
    that never should all flesh be destroyed.

—Sirach 44:17–18

| 2000 B.C. | 1900 | 1800 | 1700 | 1600 |

Noah — Abraham — Isaac — Jacob — Joseph

The story of Noah and the great flood is a story that most of you have heard before. When you were a little child, the story of Noah may have been read to you, along with other favorite Bible stories. You may know a song about Noah, the ark, and the animals. You may have drawn pictures of the animals going into the ark. The story of Noah is enjoyable and easy to remember, almost like a nursery rhyme. If your teacher asked you to retell the story now, what details would you remember about the story?

Now that you are older, it is time for you to read the story of Noah as it appears in the Bible. As with many stories in the Bible, probably more than one writer contributed to the story of the flood. Just as several of you remembered different details of the story, so more than one writer wrote down God's message to us. Archaeologists and others who study ancient times are convinced that a widespread flood or *deluge* did occur in Mesopotamia in approximately 2000 B.C. Ancient stone tablets have been discovered that tell about such a flood. Almost every nation around Israel believed that there once was a great flood. There are, therefore, many versions of the story. Some of the details of the stories are very similar to those found in the Scriptures. Some of the details are different. There is one important detail that should be remembered when we read the biblical story of Noah. The story of Noah was written not only to explain a historical event but, more important, to teach a religious lesson that spoke about God's merciful love and a promise in which all of us would share.

REVIEW QUESTIONS

1. What is a deluge?
2. When and where did the great flood occur?
3. Why was the story of Noah written?

The scriptural reading of the story of Noah has been divided into three sections:

Part I   God warns Noah of the flood and Noah prepares
           for its coming (Gen 6:5–22).

Part II   The Great Flood (Gen 7:6–24, 8:1–22).

Part III   God's covenant with Noah (Gen 9:1–17).

Read Part I: God warns Noah of the flood, and Noah prepares for its coming (Gen 6:5–22).

A Discussion of Genesis 6:5–22

In the first part of the story of Noah, God saw that the people whom He had created in His image had chosen to sin. "In the eyes of God the earth was corrupt and full of lawlessness" (Gen 6:11). "He regretted that he had made man on the earth" (Gen 6:6). In other words, God was sorry because His people had chosen to sin and to hurt themselves by rejecting His care. So God announced the consequences of their sin. He announced that flood waters would cover the earth. Noah, however, had not rejected God's love—"But Noah found favor with the LORD" (Gen 6:8). Because of Noah's attitude of love, God saved Noah, his three sons, Shem, Ham, and Japheth, their wives, and two of every living creature on the earth. Noah must have been very grateful to God for this act of merciful love.

God then gave Noah detailed instructions about how to build an ark and how to gather the animals. Noah must have loved God and had faith in Him, for "He carried out all the commands that God gave him" (Gen 6:22). To build an ark of the size described in the Bible and to gather all the animals into it was no small task! Do you know how big the ark was? The Bible says that the ark was 300 cubits long, 50 cubits wide, and 30 cubits high. That means it was approximately 440 feet long, 73 feet wide, and 44 feet high. Its length was one and a half times the length of a football field; its height was about as high as a four-story building; and its width was slightly more than the distance from the pitcher's mound to homeplate on a baseball diamond.

Would it be possible for one man and his three sons to build such a boat? Would it be possible to gather into the ark two of every kind of animal? It is exciting to think that an ark this huge could have been built. In fact, there are many explorers today who are still searching for the ark. The Church teaches us, however, that, just as with the story of Adam and Eve, it is not important that the details of the story be entirely accurate. The important lesson to remember is that sin is always followed by an effect or a consequence. In this case, the effect of sin was death through the flood. Noah and his family, who chose to love God, to have faith in Him, and to live their lives as images of God, were saved by God's merciful love.

REVIEW QUESTIONS

1. Why did the great flood occur?
2. Why were Noah and his family saved from the destruction of the flood?
3. What lesson should we remember about the choice to sin?

Read Part II: The Great Flood (Gen 7:6–24, 8:1–22).

A Discussion of the Great Flood

In Genesis 7:6–24, the writer describes the great flood. "For forty days and forty nights heavy rain poured down on the earth" (Gen 7:12). The writer describes in detail the extent of the destruction that this deluge worked upon the earth. All the people suffered the consequences of their sins. The ark floated upon the waters for a long time. Although Noah and his family were saved from the flood, they too suffered from its destruction. They must have felt afraid and lonely. Terrible thunderstorms can be frightening. Noah and his family must have been grateful to God that they were safe inside the ark.

The ark is often used as a symbol for the Church. The ark reminds us that the Church and her teachings can protect us from harm. Noah and his family were saved from the dangers of the flood because they chose to think and to act as images of God. They placed their trust in God and listened to Him when He asked them to build the ark. Then, when the rains came, the ark protected them from the terrible storm. In this way, the Church is like the ark. Just as the ark protected Noah and his family from some of the effects of the flood, so the Church can protect us from some of the effects of sin.

We, like Noah, should listen to God and trust in Him. We need to listen to God and to the teachings He gives us through the Church. We need to say "Yes" to God's invitation to think and to act as His images. The Church, like the ark, is strong. Just as the ark was strong enough to overcome the effects of the flood, so the Church is strong enough to overcome all sin and some of its effects. She accomplishes this through the sacraments, which give us *grace*, God's life.

In Genesis 8:1, we read that "God made a wind sweep over the earth, and the waters began to subside." Finally, the ark came to rest on a mountain called Ararat. Noah was anxious to discover if there was dry land, so several times he sent out a dove. When the dove did not return to the ark, Noah recognized that it would soon be time for all those aboard to leave. What was the first thing Noah did when he left the ark? Genesis 8:20 says: "Then Noah built an altar to the LORD . . . and offered *holocausts* on the altar." Noah offered a burnt sacrifice to thank God for saving him and his family from the terrible destruction of the flood. God was so pleased with Noah's offering that He promised to continue to show His goodness and merciful love. "As long as the earth lasts, seedtime and harvest, cold and heat, summer and winter, and day and night shall not cease" (Gen 8:22). People may choose to sin, but God's goodness and mercy will be seen forever in the changing seasons.

1. How long did the flood last?

2. Even though Noah and his family were saved from the destruction of the flood, they still experienced some of the consequences of the people's sins. What were some of these consequences?

3. How is the ark a symbol of the Church?

4. How should we be like Noah?

5. What is grace?

6. How can we receive grace?

7. What was the first thing Noah did when he left the ark?

8. What is a holocaust?

*9. What was the covenant that God made with Noah?

Read Part III: God's Covenant with Noah (Gen 9:1–17).

A Discussion of the Covenant

In the last part of this story, God makes a new bond of love, a *covenant*, with Noah. In order for the definition of covenant to be complete, it should include the following three parts: (1) A covenant is an act of merciful love between God and people. (2) A covenant includes a promise to continue that love. (3) A covenant is expressed in words and deeds. God fulfilled all three conditions of the covenant when He said, "I will establish my covenant with you, that never again shall all bodily creatures be destroyed by the waters of a flood; there shall not be another flood to devastate the earth" (Gen 9:11). Because God drew the good of a covenant from the evil of the flood, God showed His merciful love to Noah and his descendants. This act of merciful love fulfills the first condition of a covenant. When God promised that the waters will "never again" flood the earth, He fulfilled the second condition of the covenant, to continue His merciful love. The words that God spoke to Noah and the rainbow that He sent as a sign of His promise completed the third condition of the covenant.

When this covenant was accepted by Noah, all his descendants, including us, inherited the covenant. God said to Noah, "Be fertile and multiply and fill the earth" (Gen 9:1). God renewed the special invitation He first offered to Adam and Eve. He invited Noah and his descendants to participate in the creation of new life, to "fill the earth" again with families. God also emphasized our responsibility to respect this new life by reminding Noah, and us, that "in the image of God has man been made" (Gen 9:6).

God's Merciful Love

The story of Noah is more than a story about a great flood. It is a story that tells us of God's merciful love. When sins are committed, they have certain effects or consequences. In the story of Noah, the destruction of the earth by a flood is the consequence of sinful behavior. God, however, in His goodness and mercy, did not allow the full effect of sin to be felt by His images. God saved Noah and his family from the flood.

God loves us mercifully, too. When God shows us His mercy, we, like Noah, are grateful and drawn closer to Him. This renewed love that we have for God is the good that can come from the evil of sin. We have read about God's merciful love in the stories of Adam and Eve, Cain, and now Noah. We can experience God's merciful love whenever we are sorry for our sins. Then we too can be united with God in a new bond of love and can choose to think and to act as images of God.

1. Describe the three parts of a covenant.
2. Are we included in the covenant God made with Noah?
*3. How is the story of Noah an example of God's merciful love?

Concepts of Faith

1. How is the story of Noah an example of God's merciful love?
God showed His merciful love when He spared Noah and his family from the flood and established a new covenant with him. This new bond of love was the good that God drew from the evil of sin.

2. When God made a covenant with Noah, what promise did God make?
God promised that the earth would never again be covered by a flood.

Vocabulary

deluge: A flood.

grace: God's life.

holocaust: A burnt sacrifice.

covenant: (1) An act of merciful love between God and people; (2) a promise to continue that love; (3) expressed in words and deeds.

Living the Lesson

1. Noah is an example of someone who chooses to do what is right when everyone around him chooses to do something that is wrong. Noah loved God and trusted in Him. Otherwise, Noah would not have chosen to listen to God when God asked him to build the ark. Noah must have looked pretty silly to all those around him. People must have laughed at him and ridiculed him for building such a huge boat in the middle of the desert! Yet Noah and his family worked together and continued to follow God's invitation.

Have you ever been in a situation in which you felt as if you were the only one doing what is right? It can be a very lonely position. It is not easy to do one thing when everyone else around you is doing something else. Share with your classmates and family an example of this type of difficulty.

2. In the story of Noah, God saved not only Noah from the flood, but his family too. They, like Noah, must have chosen to love God and to listen to Him. Together they worked to build the ark. They helped each other and supported each other throughout the terrible flood. People who love and care about each other can help each other to make the right choices.

Discuss these questions with your family and friends:

How can your family and friends help you to make the right choices?

If a friend encourages you to do something that is wrong, is that person really a friend?

How does the Church help us to choose what is right?

Prayers

Because Noah and his family are examples of faith and trust in God, traditional and scriptural prayers that emphasize these virtues are suggested.

The "Act of Faith".
The "Act of Hope".
Psalm 33. (A hymn of praise in which the just are invited to sing of the glories of God, Who is faithful to His promises.)

Map Activity: Refer to the map on Worksheet 1, page 61, and locate Mount Ararat. Three large lakes—Van, Sevan, and Urmia—encircle the mountain:
   —*Lake Sevan* is located northeast of Mount Ararat.
   —*Lake Urmia* is to the southeast.
   —*Lake Van* is to the southwest.
Write the names of these three lakes on the map.

Four other bodies of water form a larger circle around Mount Ararat:
   —The *Caspian Sea* is located east of Mount Ararat.
   —The *Black Sea* is to the north.
   —The *Mediterranean Sea* is to the west.
   —The Euphrates River flows into the *Persian Gulf*, which is to the south.
Write the names of these four bodies of water on the map.

It is easy to understand how these bodies of water could have contributed to the historical evidence behind the story of the flood. Some scholars think that a long time ago the waters from the Persian Gulf flooded a large coastland area. Underwater earthquakes, eruptions, and heavy rains also may have caused a sudden rise in the sea level.

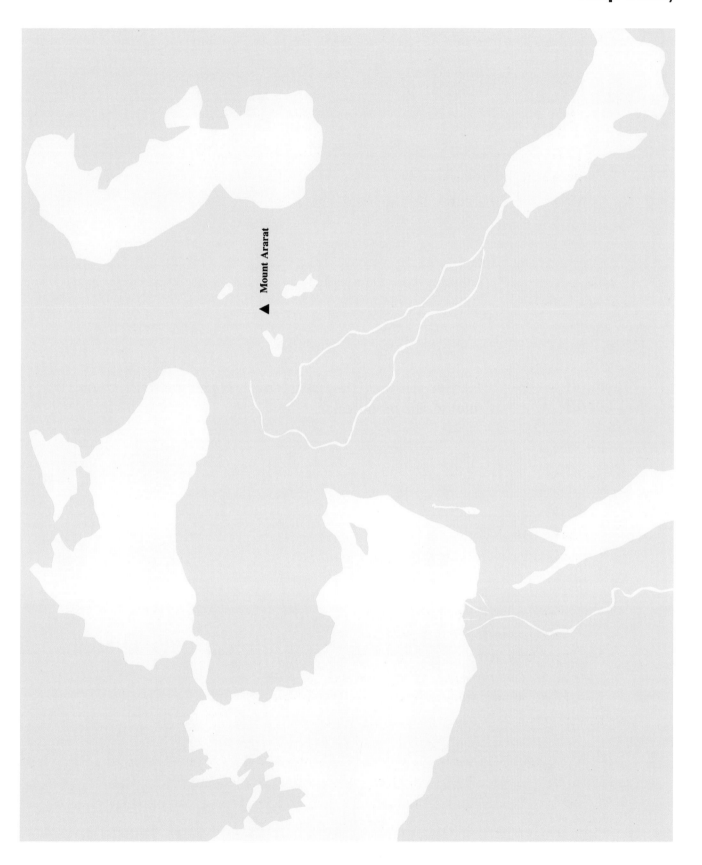

Mount Ararat

Complete the crossword puzzle by finding the answers in the Bible.

ACROSS

2. Gen 6:8   But Noah found _____ with the Lord.

4. Gen 6:19   Of all other living creatures you shall bring _____ into the ark.

6. Gen 6:14   Make yourself an ark of _____.

7. Gen 7:13   One of Noah's sons.

11. Gen 7:13   Another of Noah's sons.

12. Gen 8:4   The ark came to rest on Mount _____.

14. Gen 9:1   God blessed Noah and his sons and said to them: "Be fertile and _____ and fill the earth."

15. Gen 6:14   God told Noah to build an _____.

16. Gen 8:8   Noah sent out a _____ to see if the waters had lessened.

DOWN

1. Gen 9:13   God sent a rain_____ as a sign of His covenant with Noah.

2. Gen 6:17   A _____ destroyed everything on the earth.

3. Gen 9:11   God made a _____ with Noah that the earth would never again be destroyed by a flood.

5. Gen 6:9   _____ was a good man and blameless in that age.

8. Gen 7:12   It rained for _____ days and nights.

9. Gen 8:20   Noah built an _____ and offered sacrifice to God.

10. Gen 6:10   One of Noah's sons.

13. Gen 8:1   God made a _____ sweep over the earth.

Lesson 4: Noah, the Great Flood, and God's Merciful Love   **63**

The Tower of Babel

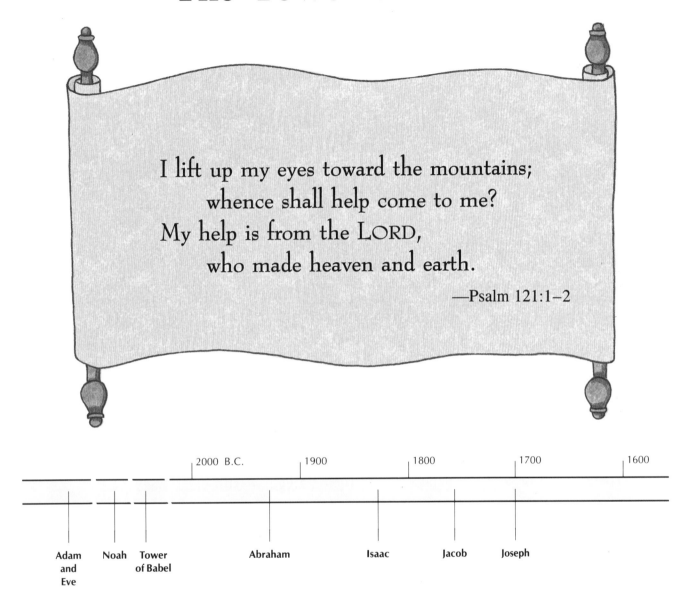

I lift up my eyes toward the mountains;
whence shall help come to me?
My help is from the LORD,
who made heaven and earth.

—Psalm 121:1–2

2000 B.C. 1900 1800 1700 1600

Adam and Eve · Noah · Tower of Babel · Abraham · Isaac · Jacob · Joseph

If you were to look up the word *babble* in the dictionary, one of the definitions would read: "to utter meaningless sounds". When people babble, it is difficult to understand what they are saying. This lack of understanding can lead to confusion. Confusion is how the city and tower of Babel received its name. The city of Babel was a real place in ancient times. Its name comes from two Hebrew words: *balal*, which means "to mix or confuse", and *babhel*, which means "the gate of God". When spoken, the words sound alike. The writer chose to use the story of the tower of Babel to remind us that without God, we can become as confused as those who tried to reach heaven, the "gate of God", by building a great tower.

Read Genesis 11:1-9 for the scriptural account of the tower of Babel. A paraphrase of the story follows.

The Tower of Babel

In the Land of Shinar the people said, "Come, let us build ourselves a city and a tower with its top in the sky; and so make a name for ourselves." They worked together, molding bricks and using them to build their lofty tower.

God saw the city and the tower that the people built. God knew why they chose to build such a tower. God knew that pride had caused the people to forget Him.

So God decided to remind the people of His love. He stopped their work on the tower by confusing their language. They could no longer understand each other. They were unable to finish building the tower. So the people left the city and scattered all over the earth.

A Discussion of the Tower of Babel

Look at the map of the land of Shinar. The city of Babel is located on the Euphrates River, northeast of the city of Ur. The cities that were built around 3000 B.C. generally had a temple where the people would worship their false gods. Next to the temple stood a high tower called a *ziggurat*. These ziggurats were very tall, sometimes rising two hundred feet or more. They had stairways leading from one level to the next. They were, in a sense, the first skyscrapers. The remains of several partially reconstructed ziggurats still exist today.

In the previous lesson on Noah, you learned that after the flood, Noah and his descendants were invited to people the earth again. Many of Noah's descendants, however, chose to sin. The story of the tower of Babel begins with an ambitious project. The people wanted to "build a city and a tower with its top in the sky". They even cooperated with each other in order to accomplish this difficult task. Why did they choose to build a temple-tower that would reach up to heaven? Was it a sign of their love for God? Was it to praise God or to thank Him for His blessings? No, it was not. The Scriptures say, "Come, let us build ourselves a city and a tower with its top in the sky; and so make a name for ourselves" (Gen 11:4). The people wanted to glorify themselves. They thought that they could do great things without God. They were proud and independent. They thought that they no longer needed God. They thought that they could do everything themselves. They thought that they could reach heaven by climbing the stairs on the tower. They forgot God. They forgot that they could not reach heaven without the help of God.

Land of Shinar

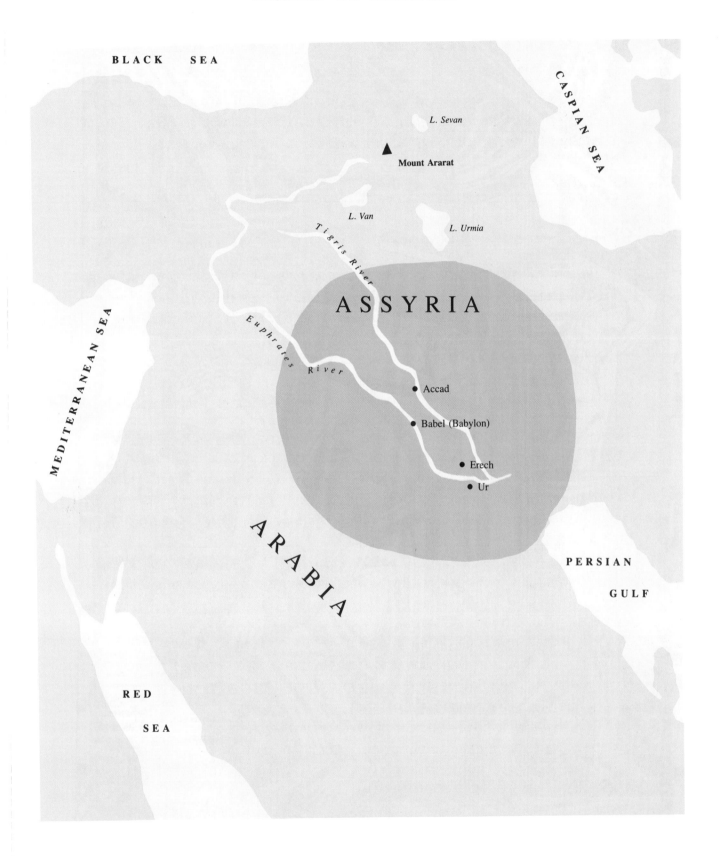

BLACK SEA

CASPIAN SEA

L. Sevan

▲
Mount Ararat

L. Van

L. Urmia

Tigris River

ASSYRIA

MEDITERRANEAN SEA

Euphrates River

Accad

Babel (Babylon)

Erech

Ur

ARABIA

PERSIAN GULF

RED SEA

Without God, the people no longer knew how to act as His images. Not knowing how to act, they became confused and unable to understand one another. When they could not understand one another, it became impossible for them to work together. When the people could no longer work together, there was no reason for them to live together. So the people left the city and were scattered all over the earth.

God's Merciful Love

God helped the people recognize that He loved them by showing them His love and mercy. He could have destroyed the tower that they were building to glorify themselves. But instead, God reminded them that He should be the most important Person in their lives. What is more, God's merciful love continued after the people were scattered. In the next chapter, you will see how God formed a new nation from among those people who were scattered. God saved some of the people from the full effects of their sin. You will learn how the new people, under the leadership of Abraham, were drawn closer to God through a new covenant of love.

REVIEW QUESTIONS

1. Why did the people of the land of Shinar want to build a tower "with its top in the sky"?
*2. What sin did the people commit in building the tower of Babel?
*3. What was the effect of their sin?
4. How did God show His merciful love to them?

Concepts of Faith

1. **What sin did the people commit in building the tower of Babel?**
   Pride led the people to think that they could do great things without God. They forgot God.
2. **What was the effect of their sin?**
   Their language became confused, and the people were scattered all over the earth.

Vocabulary

ziggurat: High temple-tower.

Living the Lesson

Have you ever traveled to a different country where a foreign language is spoken? Imagine that you are traveling in Italy. You are in Rome visiting all the sights. You have just spent the morning visiting the Vatican, and now it is lunch time. So you stop at an outside restaurant. You don't speak Italian, but you recognize "pepperoni pizza" printed on the menu. So you order a "pepperoni pizza".

A few minutes later the waiter brings you a pizza with peppers on it. You try to explain to the waiter that he has brought you the wrong pizza. You ordered "pepperoni pizza", not pizza with peppers. "Si," says the waiter, "pepperoni pizza!" And he keeps pointing to the pizza and saying, "Pepperoni pizza!" You hate peppers, so you keep shaking your head and saying, "No, this not a pepperoni pizza!" Soon, you and the waiter are almost shouting at each other. Another customer overhears the argument and comes to your table. She speaks both Italian and English, and you explain to her the mix-up in the order. She informs you that, in Italian, "pepperoni pizza" means pizza with peppers. You should have ordered "pizza con carne", which means pizza with meat. The waiter was correct, and you were wrong. You are embarrassed and ask that she explain to the waiter that you misunderstood the menu and that you offer him your apologies. The waiter laughs, accepts your apology, and brings you a pizza with meat.

Misunderstandings can easily lead to arguments. People can offend one another without meaning to. Think about how differences in language and cultures can

- —cause prejudice between people of different races.
- —affect relations between different governments.
- —increase tensions between countries.
- —cause wars.
- —affect progress toward world peace.

Discuss some of these topics with your friends and family. Can you think of ways in which we can come to understand each other in spite of our differences?

Prayers

Prayer to the Guardian Angel
Selected Psalms

The Land of Shinar

On page 67, look at the map titled "Land of Shinar". This geographical area
was also known as Mesopotamia and later became known as Babylonia. It lay
in the southern section of the valley of the Tigris and Euphrates Rivers. It
included several important cities: Ur, Babel (later known as Babylon), Erech,
and Accad.

The land of Shinar is mentioned numerous times in the Bible. Over the years it
came under the leadership of different kings, who, naturally, named their
kingdoms after themselves. If you look on a modern map, the land of Shinar is
now the country of Iraq.

Find the following scriptural references in the Bible. On the blank beside the
reference, write the name of the kingdom or of the event that took place in the
land of Shinar.

1. Gen 10:9-10 _____

2. Gen 11:1–9 _____

3. Gen 14:2, 9 _____

4. Jos 7:20–21 _____

5. Dan 1:1–2 _____

'Helpful' and 'Artful' Psalms

The story of the tower of Babel reminds us that we need God's help in everything that we do. Many of the Psalms express a need for God's help. Find the following Psalm verses in the Bible. Write the words of the verse beside the scriptural reference. Then choose one Psalm verse to decorate artistically. Your teacher can help you with ideas and materials.

Ps 3:5   _____

_____

Ps 5:3   _____

_____

Ps 25:4   _____

_____

Ps 46:2   _____

_____

Ps 54:6   _____

_____

Ps 61:2   _____

_____

Ps 62:6 _____

_____

Ps 70:2 _____

_____

Ps 79:9 _____

_____

Ps 88:3 _____

_____

Lesson 5: The Tower of Babel

Abraham, Our "Father in Faith"

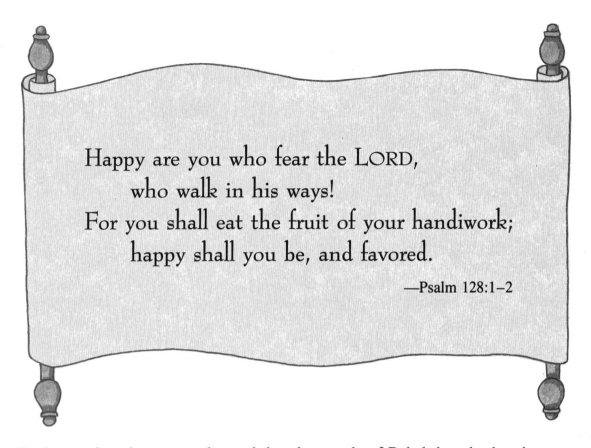

> Happy are you who fear the LORD,
> who walk in his ways!
> For you shall eat the fruit of your handiwork;
> happy shall you be, and favored.
>
> —Psalm 128:1–2

In the previous lesson, we learned that the people of Babel thought that they could do great things without God. They forgot that God should be the most important Person in their lives. Without God, the people of Babel no longer knew how to act as His images. They became confused and unable to understand one another. Eventually, the people left the city and were scattered all over the earth.

But God loved His people mercifully. In Genesis 12, the Bible focuses on one man, Abram, who later becomes known as Abraham. It is through Abraham that God drew good from the scattering of people from Babel. Through Abraham and the new nation that he formed, God continued His message of merciful love.

Abraham is known as our "father in faith". In fact, there are three world religions that call Abraham their "father in faith". Islam, Judaism, and Christianity share the belief that Abraham was called by God to play a special role in the formation of their faiths. In this chapter we will learn how Abraham answered this special call.

1. How did God show His merciful love after the people of Babel were scattered?

2. What three religions call Abraham their "father in faith"?

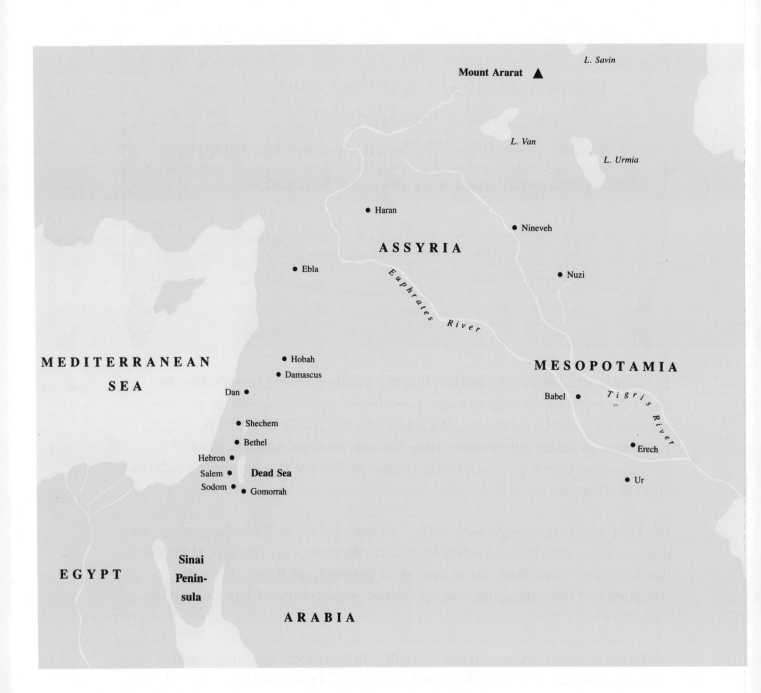

Abraham's World

Abraham lived nearly four thousand years ago, as you can see by the time-line. Abraham lived approximately one thousand years before Moses and two thousand years before Christ. Although this time period is now studied as ancient history, the culture of the people was quite advanced. Abraham lived in a world of many languages. His world had made much progress in the fields of science, astronomy, law, the arts, trade, and commerce.

| 2000 B.C. | | 1000 | 0 | 2000 |

Adam and Eve | Pyramids of Egypt | 1850 Abraham | 1700 Joseph | 1300 Moses | Christ is born

Trade routes had been long established, both by land and sea. Though travel was much slower then than it is today, neighboring countries shared their knowledge and goods. Metal products, including gold; jewelry; pottery; clothing; food, including grain; exotic fruits; spices—these were all exchanged between countries. Cities were established along trade routes, and many cities expanded to the size of some modern-day cities.

Look at the map on page 78. There are many cities labeled on this map. Throughout the reading of this chapter, the map will help us follow Abraham's journey of faith.

Locate these three cities: Ur, at the southern end of the Euphrates River; Nuzi, on a tributary of the Tigris River; and Ebla, located east of the island of Cyprus. Discoveries in these three cities have told us much about the world in which Abraham lived. Archaeologists have discovered thousands of clay tablets in Ebla and Nuzi. On these tablets were recorded many things about the world of Abraham. Laws, customs, trade agreements, and population counts help us to know more about these early times.

The city of Ur was prosperous. Located on the Euphrates River, it was a major center for commerce and trade. Archaeologists have discovered that Ur was a city with wide streets and large houses. And, as in the cities of Ebla and Nuzi, careful records of commerce, trade, and other business transactions were written down on clay tablets. Abraham was born in Ur. The Bible tells us that Abraham had many possessions and that he was "very rich in livestock, silver, and gold" (Gen 13:2).

Abraham's world was one that worshiped many gods. The people had forgotten the one true God. Knowledge of the one true God would come to the world again through Abraham.

REVIEW QUESTIONS

1. Approximately how long ago did Abraham live?
2. How have we come to know about Abraham's world?
3. In what city was Abraham born?
4. Did the people in Abraham's world know the one true God?

God Calls Abraham

The story of Abraham begins in Genesis 11:31. At first, Abraham was called Abram. "Abram" means "father". Later on, God changed Abram's name to "Abraham", which means "father of many nations". The name of Abraham's father was Terah. The family established their home and wealth in the city of Ur (refer to the map on page 78). But after the death of Abraham's brother, Terah decided to move his family and possessions to the land of Canaan. When Terah and his family arrived at the city of Haran, they settled there. Then Terah died, and Abraham became the head of the family.

The call of Abraham and his journey to the land of Canaan begin when Abraham hears the voice of God.

Read Genesis 12:1–3.

In this passage, God calls Abraham to leave his home. God promises to bless Abraham, to make his name great, and to form a new nation through him.

The Bible immediately continues, in Genesis 12:4, with Abraham's response to God's call. "Abram went as the LORD directed him." Now this was an amazing act of faith. Let us think about Abraham's situation. Abraham was well-established in Haran. He was prosperous and wealthy. He had many possessions. Everyone he knew worshiped many gods. Now one God, Whom no one else knew, asked him to leave everyone and everything he had for an unknown land. God did not even specify where the land was. He simply said, "I will show you." What was amazing is that Abraham did not even hesitate. He asked no questions. He simply went. This was the first time Abraham showed his tremendous faith in God.

The remaining verses in Genesis 12, 13, and 14 speak of Abraham's journey. The following paragraphs briefly summarize Abraham's journey and some of the events that took place along the way. Use the map on Worksheet 1 for this lesson, and trace the route with a marker.

Summary of the Journey of Abraham

1. Terah, his son Abram, and his family leave **Ur** for the country of **Canaan**. They settle in **Haran** (Gen 11:31).

2. Abraham hears God's call to leave **Haran**. He takes his wife, Sarah, his nephew, Lot, and his possessions and starts the journey to the land of **Canaan** (Gen 12:1–5).

3. Abraham stops at **Shechem**. The Lord appeared to Abram and said, "To your descendants I will give this land" (Gen 12:7).

4. At **Bethel**, Abraham builds an altar to the Lord and continues to journey through the desert (Gen 12:8).

5. A famine forces Abraham to travel to the country of **Egypt**. Here Abraham feeds his family and pastures his flocks until the famine is over (Gen 12:10).

6. After the famine, Abraham returns to **Bethel** (Gen 13:1–4).

7. The flocks and herds of both Lot and Abraham become too large to share the same pasture lands. So Lot and Abraham separate. Abraham offers Lot the first choice of land. Lot chooses the area east of the land of Canaan in the Jordan Plain and settles near the city of **Sodom** (Gen 13:5–12).

8. *Read aloud Genesis 13:14–18.* This beautiful passage renews God's first promise to Abraham. After God speaks to Abraham, he settles near the city of **Hebron** and builds an altar to the Lord. A mountain cave near Hebron later became the burial place of Abraham and Sarah.

9. From **Dan** to **Hobah**: A war takes place among the tribal kings of the cities located around the **Salt Sea** (now known as the **Dead Sea**). The victors of the battle capture the cities of **Sodom** and **Gomorrah** and take Abraham's nephew, Lot, and all his possessions to the city of **Dan**. Abraham comes to Lot's rescue. He defeats the enemy at Dan and chases them as far north as **Hobah**, which is near **Damascus** (Gen 14:1–16).

10. After the victory, Abraham and Lot travel back to their homes. On their way, they are met by the king of **Salem**, Melchizedek (Gen 14:18–20). Melchizedek is a priest-king. A *priest* is one who offers sacrifices to God to show love for God and others. The Church has always considered Melchizedek a "type of Christ", for at his meeting with Abraham, Melchizedek offers up bread and wine (an event recalled in Eucharistic Prayer I of the Mass). Then Melchizedek blesses Abraham.

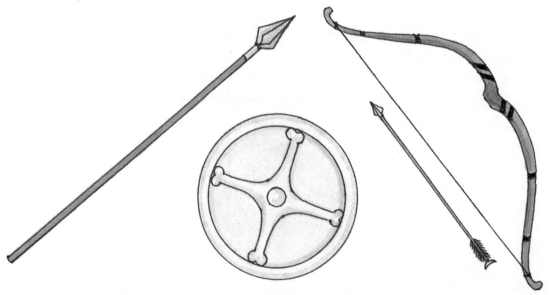

REVIEW QUESTIONS

1. By what name was Abraham first called, and what is its meaning?
2. What does the name Abraham mean?
3. How did Abraham respond to God's call?
4. Identify these persons: Terah, Sarah, Lot, Melchizedek.
5. What duties did the priest perform in Abraham's time?
6. Why is Melchizedek considered a "type of Christ"?

God's Promises to Abraham

You have already read Genesis 12:1–3, where God first made His promise to Abraham. God said, "I will make of you a great nation . . . and I will make your name great" (Gen 12:2). Much time passed before Abraham heard the voice of God again. Although Abraham still had faith in God, he wondered how God would be able to fulfill His promise. Abraham and Sarah did not have any children yet, and they were already quite old.

Read Genesis 15:1–6.

In these verses God renewed His promise that Abraham would have many descendants. "Look up at the sky and count the stars, if you can. Just so . . . shall your descendants be" (Gen 15:5). Again, "Abraham put his faith in the LORD" (Gen 15:6). God recognized that Abraham had the right attitude of faith. (In the New Testament, Saint Paul used Abraham as an example of faith for all Christians.) After this, Abraham made a sacrificial offering to God. During the offering, God made a covenant with Abraham, renewing His promise of land (Gen 15:18–21).

Time passed, and still Abraham and Sarah did not have any children. We know, from ancient records discovered by archaeologists, that there was a custom, under the ancient law, that suggested a way in which a childless couple could have a child. Sarah, past the age of having children, knew of this law. Chapter 16 of Genesis relates the story of how Sarah suggested to Abraham that he try to have a son by her slave girl, Hagar. Abraham agreed, and he and Hagar had a son, whom they named Ishmael.

This arrangement seems strange and shocking to us. *Polygamy*, having more than one wife at the same time, is not only against God's law, but it is also illegal. Yet in ancient times, polygamy was practiced often. There were many customs that would change as God's new nation of people came to know and understand Him. Later in the story, God made it clear to Abraham that his descendants would not come from Ishmael, but from his marriage to Sarah.

Genesis 17 tells about the third time that God renewed His covenant with Abraham. Again God promised that Abraham would have many descendants who would inherit the land of Canaan. It is also in this chapter that God changed Abram's name to Abraham.

Read Genesis 17:3–8.

This time, however, God asked Abraham and his descendants to make a visible sign of their faith in Him. For their part of the covenant, Abraham and his male descendants had to be circumcised, as a permanent and very personal sign of the covenant. Each new child would be a fulfillment of the promise, born from a father with the mark of the covenant in that part of a man's flesh from which the child came. The sign of circumcision would be a constant reminder to the people of their covenant with God. He would be their God, and they would be His people. Later, Jesus Christ, a descendant of Abraham, would give us a new sign of membership in God's family, the sacrament of Baptism.

Then God told Abraham that he and Sarah would have a son and that they should name him Isaac. The thought of his fathering a son at age one hundred with Sarah, who was ninety, made Abraham double over with laughter. In fact, he suggested to God that perhaps Ishmael might be a more realistic choice. God, however, reassured Abraham that He would care for Ishmael, but it was through Isaac, whose name in Hebrew means "laughter", that God would continue His covenant.

Read Genesis 17:15–22 for the biblical account of the promise of Isaac.

The fourth reminder of God's covenant with Abraham involves three visitors. The story is recorded in Genesis 10:1–15. These verses describe the renewal of the promise of a son, Isaac, to be born of Abraham and Sarah. They also describe in detail the hospitality that Abraham showed to the three strangers who happened to pass by his tent. To be hospitable means to "open your home" to guests; to welcome them with food, drink, and shelter. Hospitality was, and still is, an important custom, especially for those traveling in the desert, where water, food, and shelter from the sun are matters of survival. Abraham, however, did more than simply provide the necessities for his unexpected guests. He literally prepared a banquet for them. After the visitors finished their meal, one of them said, "I will surely return to you about this time next year, and Sarah will then have a son" (Gen 18:10). Sarah laughed when she heard this and said, "Shall I really bear a child, old as I am?" (Gen 18:13). The words "Is anything too marvelous for the LORD to do?" (Gen 18:14) reveal one visitor's true identity. Abraham and Sarah understood that the Lord had come to visit them to renew His promise.

God Fulfills His Promise

Read Genesis 21:1–8.

Just as God had promised, a son was born to Abraham and Sarah. They named him Isaac, which means "laughter". Sarah then said, "God has given me cause to laugh, and all who hear of it will laugh with me" (Gen 21:6).

1. List the promises that God made at various times to Abraham.
2. What was the name of Sarah's slave-girl?
3. What was the name of Abraham and Hagar's son?
4. What is polygamy?
5. What was the name to be given to the son of Abraham and Sarah?
6. Why was the name Isaac an appropriate one for the son of Abraham and Sarah?
7. What visible sign of their faith did God ask of Abraham and his descendants?
8. What sign of membership in God's family did Jesus give us?
9. Describe how Abraham showed hospitality to the visitors.

The Destruction of Sodom and Gomorrah

On the map on page 87, locate the Dead Sea. The Dead Sea is an inland lake. It is 53 miles long and from 2 to 10 miles wide. The River Jordan flows into this lake. The lake is 1,292 feet below sea level. It is the lowest body of water on the earth.

The Bible refers to the Dead Sea by several other names. In Genesis 14:3, it is called the Salt Sea. Deuteronomy 3:17 names it the Salt Sea of the Arabah. It is also called the Eastern Sea in Ezra 47:18. The Dead Sea contains a large concentration of salt. No animal, fish, or plant life can live in water containing so much salt. Hence this body of water is now called the Dead Sea.

Archaeologists know that, around 2000 B.C., the time of Abraham, a catastrophe destroyed the cities around the Dead Sea. An earthquake and an explosion of gasses mixed with sulfur and asphalt were probably the cause of the destruction. The shallow waters at the southern end of the Dead Sea now cover the remains of these cities. The two cities of Sodom and Gomorrah were destroyed in this catastrophe.

In the days of Abraham, Sodom and Gomorrah had the reputation of being wicked and sinful cities. Perhaps the writer of chapters 18 and 19 of Genesis used this "common knowledge" as an opportunity for Abraham to call upon God's merciful love. Genesis 18:16–33 is a bargaining session between God and Abraham. Abraham begged God not to allow the good people in the cities to be destroyed along with the bad. "Will you sweep away the innocent with the guilty? Suppose there were fifty innocent people in the city; would you wipe out the place, rather than spare it for the sake of the fifty innocent people within it?" (Gen 18:23–24). God agreed to spare the city. Then Abraham boldly bargained for more. What if there were only forty-five? forty? thirty? twenty? ten? Each time, God agreed to spare the city. This account is given as an example of God's merciful love. God cares for His people and will listen to their prayers for mercy if they choose to ask for it.

The people of Sodom and Gomorrah, however, chose to reject God. They hurt their relationship with God and with others, and they suffered the consequences of their sins. They brought destruction upon themselves. Abraham was not able to find even ten innocent people. But God allowed him to save his nephew Lot, and Lot's family. Lot was the only one willing to receive God's merciful love. Lot's wife was not. "But Lot's wife looked back, and she was turned into a pillar of salt" (Gen 19:26). The Dead Sea is surrounded by salt rock formations created by the earthquake and the fallout of gasses and sulfur.

Perhaps the writer of these chapters is warning his readers not to hesitate when given the opportunity to turn away from evil. Perhaps he is suggesting that we keep our eyes turned toward that which is good and our hearts and minds open to God's merciful love.

The map at right shows the cities of Sodom and Gomorrah on the southern shoreline of the Dead Sea. After an earthquake in this area, around 2000 B.C., the area covered by the Dead Sea was enlarged, and these and other nearby cities were covered by its waters.

REVIEW QUESTIONS

1. How did the Dead Sea get its name?
2. What caused the physical destruction of Sodom and Gomorrah?
3. How did the people of Sodom and Gomorrah hurt their relationship with God and each other?
4. How did God show His merciful love in the story of the destruction of Sodom and Gomorrah?
5. What lesson can be learned from this story?

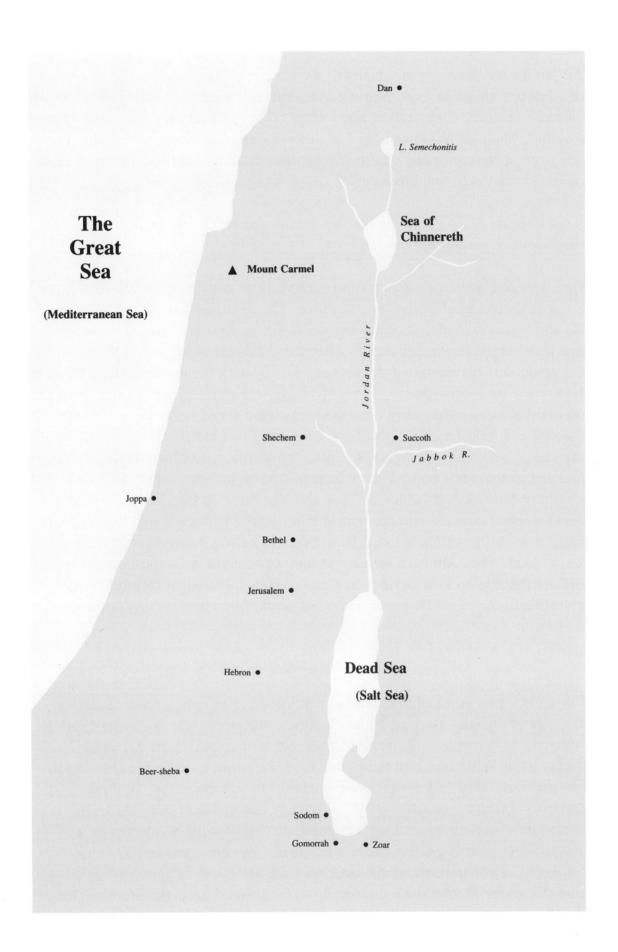

Dan •

L. Semechonitis

**The
Great
Sea**

**Sea of
Chinnereth**

(Mediterranean Sea)

▲ **Mount Carmel**

Jordan River

Shechem •   • Succoth

Jabbok R.

Joppa •

Bethel •

Jerusalem •

Dead Sea

(Salt Sea)

Hebron •

Beer-sheba •

Sodom •

Gomorrah •   • Zoar

Abraham Shows His Love for God

All throughout the story of Abraham, we have read many accounts that speak of Abraham's faith in God. Because Abraham responded to God's call, God blessed him many times and in many ways. One extraordinary and memorable way that Abraham responded to God's call is related in Genesis 22:1–19. In this story, Abraham was given the opportunity to show God that he loved Him more than he loved any other person, even Isaac, his own son.

Read Genesis 22:1–19 for the biblical account of this story; or you can read the following paraphrase instead.

One day God spoke to Abraham and asked him to take his only son, Isaac, to a mountain and to offer him as a sacrifice. The next morning, Abraham took his son, Isaac, a donkey to carry the wood for the fire, and two of his servants, and they set out for the mountain. After three days, they arrived at the foot of the mountain. Abraham told the servants to stay with the donkey, while he and Isaac went up the mountain to worship. Isaac carried the wood for the sacrifice on his shoulders. While they were walking, Isaac asked his father where the sheep was for the sacrifice. Abraham answered that God Himself would provide the sheep. When they arrived at the place of sacrifice, Abraham built an altar and placed the wood on it. Then Abraham tied up his son, Isaac, and put him on top of the wood. As Abraham was about to offer up Isaac as a sacrifice, an angel stopped him and told him not to harm Isaac. The angel told him that God knew how much Abraham loved Him, because he was ready to offer his only son to God. Then Abraham saw a ram that was caught in the bushes. So he offered the ram up as a sacrifice in place of Isaac. The angel then told Abraham that because he loved God so much, God would bless him and his descendants.

A Discussion of the Sacrifice of Isaac

During the time of Abraham, human sacrifice was a common practice among the pagan religions. To offer human sacrifice, therefore, was not as shocking to Abraham as it seems to us. Yet Abraham had turned away from his pagan background. When he heard the call of God, he chose to place his faith in the one true God. God had made certain promises to Abraham. One of these promises was that Abraham would have many descendants. It would seem logical for Abraham to ask God this question: "How will I be able to have many descendants if I kill my only son, Isaac, who does not yet have any children?" Yet Abraham did not question God. He chose to place his faith in God. He chose to trust in God. Somehow, God would keep His promise. He chose to love God more than anyone else. How difficult this must have been! Abraham had waited so long for a son, and he must have loved Isaac dearly.

Yet Abraham chose to do what God asked. What a wonderful example of faith and love Abraham is for us. God loved Abraham. For the fifth time, God renewed his covenant with Abraham. "I will bless you abundantly and make your descendants as countless as the stars of the sky and the sands of the seashore" (Gen 22:17).

We Share in Abraham's Blessings

We, too, are a part of this blessing, for the Bible continues, "and in your descendants all the nations of the earth shall find blessing" (Gen 22:18). Because Abraham chose to show his love for God in this extraordinary way, we, his descendants in faith, are able to share in his blessings.

Isaac is often referred to as a "type of Christ". That is, he was a person in the Old Testament who "foreshadowed" or "prefigured" Christ in the New Testament. In other words, Isaac reminds us of the Christ Who is to come.

Isaac was Abraham's only son. Jesus is God's only Son. Isaac carried the wood for the sacrifice on his shoulders. Jesus carried the cross on the way to Calvary. Isaac was to be sacrificed to God as a sign of Abraham's love for God. Jesus sacrificed Himself on the Cross as a sign of God's love for us.

As descendants of Abraham, our "father in faith", we are heirs of the covenant. Moreover, we are heirs of the new covenant of love that Jesus gave us. We show our love for God by acting as His images. We, like Abraham, can choose to live our lives as faithful believers in God's word.

1. What was the extraordinary way in which Abraham showed his faith in and love for God?
2. Why is Isaac called a "type of Christ"?
*3. Why is Abraham called our "father in faith"?
*4. How are we called to share in God's covenant of love?

Concepts of Faith

1. **Why is Abraham called our "father in faith"?**
   Abraham is called our "father in faith" because he responded to God's call by choosing to act as a faithful believer in God's word. We share in the covenant God made with Abraham.
2. **How are we called to share in God's covenant of love?**
   We are called to show our love for God by acting as His images.

Vocabulary

priest: One who offers sacrifices to God to show love for God and others.
"type of Christ": A person in the Old Testament who "foreshadowed" or "prefigured" Christ in the New Testament.
polygamy: Having more than one wife at the same time.

Living the Lesson

Vocations—a Personal Call from God

All of us are called by God to show our love for Him by acting as His images. Soon you will begin to think seriously about a vocation. The word *vocation* comes from the Latin word *vocare*, which means "to call". We might think of the word *occupation* as a synonym for *vocation*. However, *vocation* means more than just a job or occupation. A vocation is a call to a certain way of life. A vocation may be a call to serve God in the religious life, as a priest, sister, or brother. Or a vocation may be a call to either married life or single life.

Within each of these calls, there can be many occupations. For example, a person might choose to answer God's call to the religious life, but that person's occupation could be to be a teacher, nurse, or administrator. A person might choose to answer God's call to the married life or single life and hold a job as a doctor, lawyer, or construction worker. Choosing to answer God's call is a very important and possibly difficult decision. Like Abraham, we need to listen to God's call and place our faith in Him.

God's call will probably not come to us as a loud booming voice from the sky. But God's voice can be heard in many ways. Ask several people from different vocations to come to your class and discuss how they heard God's call and what you can do to be ready for it.

Prayers

Psalms 128 and 146. (These two Psalms speak of God's blessings on those who show their faith in Him.)

The "Act of Faith".

Hebron, Tomb of the Patriarchs.

The Journey of Abraham

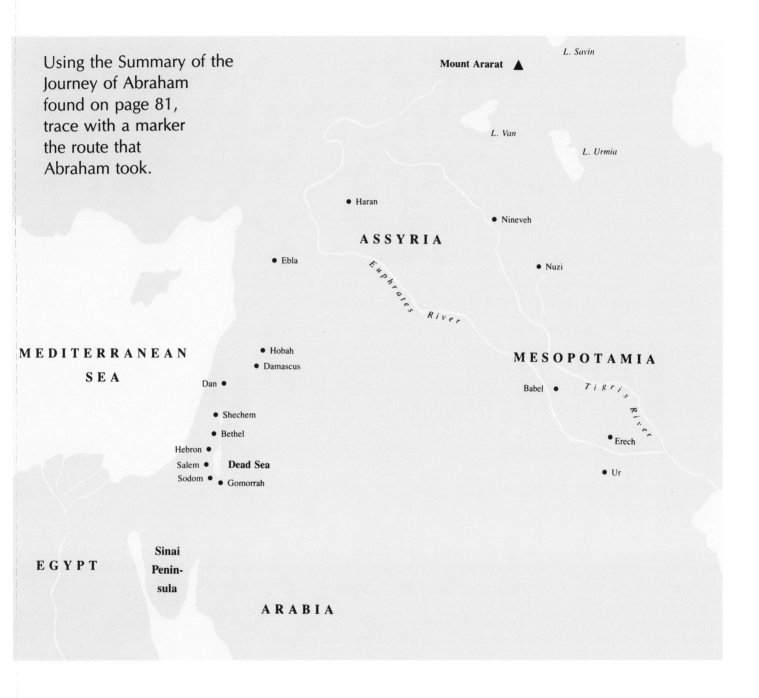

Using the Summary of the Journey of Abraham found on page 81, trace with a marker the route that Abraham took.

Lesson 6: Abraham, Our "Father in Faith"   **93**

God's Promises to Abraham

On several occasions throughout the story of Abraham, God made a covenant with Abraham and renewed His promises. Look up the biblical passages listed below and write a brief summary of each promise.

Gen 12:1–9 _____

_____

_____

Gen 15:1–6, 18 _____

_____

_____

Gen 17:1–27 _____

_____

_____

Gen 18:1–15 _____

_____

_____

Gen 21:1–8 _____

_____

_____

Gen 22:15–18 _____

_____

_____

Isaac and Jacob

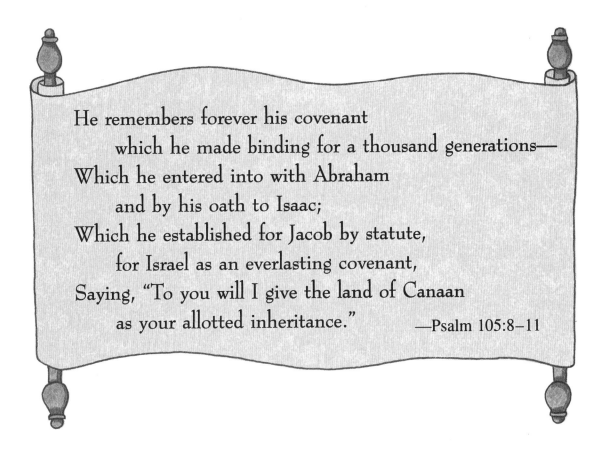

He remembers forever his covenant
   which he made binding for a thousand generations—
Which he entered into with Abraham
   and by his oath to Isaac;
Which he established for Jacob by statute,
   for Israel as an everlasting covenant,
Saying, "To you will I give the land of Canaan
   as your allotted inheritance."
                                        —Psalm 105:8–11

In the previous lesson we learned that God renewed His covenant with Abraham many times. This covenant included a promise of many descendants and the pledge that they would inherit the land of Canaan. In this lesson you will learn about Isaac, Abraham's son, and about Jacob and Esau, Isaac's sons. The covenant that God first made with Abraham is passed on to Isaac and Jacob.

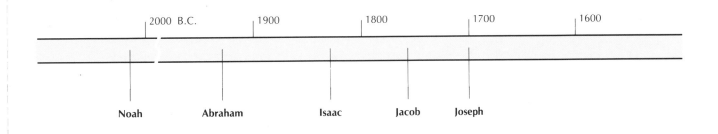

*1. What promises were included in the covenant that God made with Abraham?

2. What was the name of Abraham's son?

3. What were the names of Isaac's sons?

*4. Who inherited the covenant first made with Abraham?

Isaac and Rebekah

When it came time for Isaac to marry, Abraham wanted his son to marry a woman from his own tribe. So he sent his servant to his homeland in Haran to find a wife for his son (Isaac's wife was to be Rebekah). In those days it was the custom for the parents to find a suitable marriage partner for their children. In many instances, like this one, the couple never met until their wedding day! This custom seems quite strange to us today. But it was then the accepted custom, and Isaac would have looked forward to such an arrangement, as would have Rebekah. Knowing this, we can read about the marriage of Isaac and Rebekah as the romantic love story that it is.

Read Genesis 24:10–66 or the following retelling of the story.

The Marriage of Isaac and Rebekah

Abraham decided that it was time for Isaac to marry. So he sent his servant to find a wife for Isaac from among his family's tribe in his homeland. The servant took ten of his master's camels, bearing many gifts, and started for Haran, Abraham's homeland. While he journeyed he wondered how he would be able to choose the right wife for Isaac. He prayed to God for guidance. Then the servant thought of a plan. He knew that when he stopped at the town well, the women would be there to draw water. "If I say to a girl, 'Please lower your jug, that I may drink', and she answers, 'Take a drink, and let me give water to your camels, too', let her be the one whom you have decided upon for your servant Isaac" (Gen 24:14).

After his long journey, the servant arrived at the well. Soon Rebekah came to the well to draw water. Rebekah was very beautiful. The servant approached her and said, "Please give me a sip of water from your jug." "Take a drink, sir", she replied. "I will draw water for your camels, too, until they have drunk their fill" (Gen 24:17–19). When the servant heard these words, he knew that this was the girl the Lord had chosen for Isaac. Then the servant took out some of the gifts that he had brought with him. He gave her a gold ring and two gold bracelets. Then he asked her whose daughter she was and whether there was a place for him to sleep. She answered, "I am the daughter of Bethel the son of Micah, whom she bore to Nahor. There is plenty of straw and fodder at our place" (Gen 24:23–25). She also told him that there was room for him to sleep. The servant then thanked God for sending him to the house of Nahor, who was Abraham's brother.

When Rebekah arrived at her house, she told her family about the man at the well and showed them the beautiful gold jewelry he had given to her. After hearing Rebekah's story, her brother, Laban, rushed outside to greet the man and offered him the hospitality of his home. Then Abraham's servant explained who he was and why he had traveled so far from Canaan. He asked Rebekah's family if they would permit Rebekah to become Isaac's wife. They replied, "'Here is Rebekah, ready for you; take her with you, that she may become the wife of your master's son, as the LORD has said.' When Abraham's servant heard their answer . . . he brought out objects of silver and gold and articles of clothing and presented them to Rebekah; he also gave costly presents to her brother and mother" (Gen 24: 51–53).

The next morning, Abraham's servant wanted to return to Canaan. But Laban and Rebekah's mother wanted Rebekah to stay for a while. They asked Rebekah, "Do you wish to go with this man?" She answered, "I do" (Gen 24:58). At her answer, they blessed Rebekah and permitted her and her nurse to leave with Abraham's servant and his men.

"One day toward evening he [Isaac] went out in the field, and as he looked around, he noticed that camels were approaching. Rebekah, too, was looking about, and when she saw him, she alighted from her camel and asked the servant, 'Who is the man out there, walking through the fields toward us?' 'That is my master', replied the servant. Then she covered herself with her veil. The servant recounted to Isaac all the things he had done. Then Isaac took Rebekah into his tent; he married her, and thus she became his wife. In his love for her Isaac found solace after the death of his mother Sarah" (Gen 24:62–67).

A Discussion of the Marriage of Isaac and Rebekah

The story you have just read is one of the more beautiful love stories in the Old Testament. It is easy to imagine in your mind the scenes of the biblical story. Even though there is no detailed description of Rebekah, we can see her in our mind's eye. Her kindness and consideration to the stranger she meets at the well complement her beauty. We can imagine the joyful celebration of her engagement, the laughter of her family and guests, the receiving of gifts, the food, and the music.

We learn from the story that Rebekah is as anxious to leave as Abraham's servant is. She cannot wait to meet her new husband. She does not hesitate to leave her family and home to begin a new life with Isaac. At the end of the journey, when she sees Isaac at a distance, she veils herself, as was the custom. But the excitement of meeting her new husband cannot be hidden. Isaac, who is sad because of his mother's death, is comforted by his new wife. And so it is in love and tenderness that Rebekah and Isaac begin their married life together.

Throughout the Bible, the image of the bride and bridegroom is used to describe the love that God has for His people. In the Old Testament, the prophet Isaiah says, "As a bridegroom rejoices in his bride, so shall your God rejoice in you" (Is 62:5). In the New Testament, Saint Paul teaches us that Christ loves the Church as the bridegroom loves the bride (Eph 5:25). In fact, the Church uses Saint Paul's words as part of the marriage ceremony today. When we think of the love that Isaac and Rebekah shared, let it remind us of the love that Christ has for His Church.

REVIEW QUESTIONS

1. Why did Abraham send his servant to Haran to find a wife for Isaac?
2. How did the servant know Rebekah was the right choice for Isaac?
3. How did Rebekah show she was willing to marry Isaac?
4. Why did Rebekah need to comfort Isaac?
5. Rebekah and Isaac shared a beautiful married love. Of what does Saint Paul say married love should remind us?

Esau and Jacob

Many years passed, and Isaac and Rebekah did not have any children. Isaac prayed to the Lord and asked for His help. Rebekah became pregnant with twin boys. However, Rebekah's pregnancy was difficult. The children in her womb jostled each other so much that she exclaimed, "If this is to be so, what good will it do me!" (Gen 25:22). Rebekah was afraid that the babies in her womb might die. So she prayed to God, and He answered her: "Two nations are in your womb, two peoples are quarreling while still within you; But one shall surpass the other, and the older shall serve the younger" (Gen 25:2).

This answer reassured Rebekah that both her children would be born. But God's answer also included a statement that the firstborn child would serve the other. Moreover, this relationship would continue with their descendants. Rebekah must have wondered about this statement, because it was the custom in those times that the firstborn son was heir to the *birthright*. This meant that the older son would inherit most of Isaac's property, as well as God's promise, the covenant. This was his right, because he had been born first. When the twins were born, the firstborn was named Esau, and the second son was named Jacob.

As the boys grew up, Esau became a hunter. Jacob, however, did not like to hunt and preferred to stay at home. Isaac favored Esau because he liked the taste of wild game. Rebekah seemed to favor Jacob.

Once, when Jacob was cooking a stew, Esau came in from the open, famished. He said to Jacob, "Let me gulp down some of that red stuff; I'm starving." But Jacob replied, "First give me your birthright in exchange for it." "Look", said Esau, "I'm on the point of dying. What good will any birthright do me?" But Jacob insisted, "Swear to me first!" So Esau sold Jacob his birthright under oath. Jacob then gave him some bread and the lentil stew; and Esau ate, drank, got up, and went his way. Esau cared little for his birthright (Gen 25:29–34).

This incident can tell us much about the characters of Jacob and Esau. Jacob, who seemed to be quieter and enjoyed staying close to home, was, nevertheless, clever and shrewd. He took advantage of his brother's hunger by asking too great a price for a bowl of stew! Moreover, he didn't trust his brother. Jacob made Esau swear under oath that he had sold his birthright to him. On the other hand, Esau "cared little for his birthright" (Gen 25:34). He was more interested in satisfying his hunger than in remaining the heir to his father's property and, more important, to God's covenant.

Later on, when Isaac was old and blind, Rebekah helped Jacob trick his father into giving him a special blessing, one that should have been given to Esau, the firstborn. When Esau learned about Jacob's deception, he broke his oath to Jacob and tried to get back the birthright he had sold. When he saw that he had lost both his birthright and his father's blessing, Esau vowed to kill Jacob. Rebekah feared for Jacob's life, so she sent him to her brother, Laban, in Haran. Rebekah hoped that, in time, Esau would change his mind, so then she could send for Jacob to return home. But Rebekah never saw her favorite son again. Jacob fled to his uncle, Laban, who tricked him into serving him for many years.

It seems unfair that Esau should lose so much because of one wrong choice, and that Jacob should gain so much by cheating and lying. But if we look carefully at the story, we see that the entire family, not only Esau, suffered the consequences of their sins.

Esau lost his birthright and his father's blessing. His relationship with his brother, Jacob, would never be completely healed. When Jacob finally left home, he spent most of his life among people who were not from his family.

Yes, Jacob gained the birthright and his father's blessing. But he paid a higher price than the original bowl of stew. His brother hated him and wanted to kill him. Because of Esau's anger, Jacob had to leave his home and his mother, Rebekah. This must have been very difficult for Jacob, who preferred to stay close to home. You will learn in the next lesson that Jacob's life after he fled from Esau was very difficult. Jacob spent many years in Haran in the service of his uncle, Laban, who was as clever at deception as he was.

Rebekah never saw Jacob again. She also lost Esau, who knew of his mother's part in the deception, left home, and married into a family that did not meet the approval of his parents. In addition, the beautiful relationship between Isaac and Rebekah was strained at the end because of their sins.

What good can come out of this tragic story? Why did God allow Jacob to inherit His covenant, knowing that it was gained through deception? The answer to these questions can be found by following Jacob's journey to Haran, where he spent the next twenty years of his life with his uncle, Laban.

REVIEW QUESTIONS

1. What did God tell Rebekah when she was afraid that her unborn babies might die?
2. What was the importance of being the firstborn son?
3. What did it mean to inherit the birthright?
4. What price did Esau pay when he sold his birthright to Jacob?
5. How did Jacob receive his father's special blessing?
6. What consequences were suffered by Isaac's family because of their sinful behavior?

God's Merciful Love

So far we have learned from Jacob's actions that he really did not know the Lord. He did not act as an image of God. He tried to follow his own plans. Not once did Jacob pray to God for guidance. He took matters into his own hands and decided to gain the birthright for himself. He did not trust that God would keep His promise to Rebekah. The consequences of his behavior were suffered by his whole family.

Our first reaction to Jacob's behavior might be that God would take back the promises He had made. Jacob does not seem worthy to inherit the covenant. But God loves us mercifully. God did not forget Jacob or His promise of the covenant. Even though Jacob sinned, God was able to draw good out of this tragic story.

Jacob's Dream

One night, God made Himself known to Jacob in a dream. For the biblical account of Jacob's dream, read Genesis 28:10–22 or the following paraphrase.

One night, on his journey to Haran, Jacob stopped to rest at an old *shrine* at Bethel. A shrine is a sacred place. But Jacob did not remember that his grandfather, Abraham, had once built an altar to the one true God at that shrine. Jacob could think only of himself. He was tired and lonely. Already he missed home. He was also afraid and worried that his brother Esau might follow him and harm him. Jacob took one of the stones from the shrine to use as a pillow and lay down to sleep.

While he slept, Jacob had a dream. "A stairway rested on the ground, with its top reaching to the heavens; and God's messengers [angels] were going up and down on it" (Gen 28:12). There Jacob saw the Lord. God spoke to Jacob. He renewed the promises He had made to Abraham and to Isaac. God promised to give Jacob and his many descendants the land on which he was lying. God also promised to be with Jacob always, to protect him, and to bring him back to that land.

When Jacob woke up, he knew he had seen the Lord. "Truly, the LORD is in this spot, although I did not know it!" (Gen 28:16). Jacob's faith in the one true God was renewed. He promised to worship only the God of his fathers Abraham and Isaac and to give a tenth of everything he would ever own to the Lord.

A Discussion of Jacob's Dream

The importance of Jacob's dream can be found in his statement, "The LORD shall be my God" (Gen 28:21). With these words, Jacob renewed his faith in God. He promised to act as His image. God showed his merciful love to Jacob. God intended the covenant to be inherited through Abraham's descendants. When Jacob forgot God and sinned, he became unworthy of the covenant. Yet God did not abandon Jacob. God did not break His promise. God loved Jacob mercifully and drew good out of Jacob's sin. God gave Jacob the opportunity to choose to love Him again.

In Lesson 8, the story of Jacob is continued. Jacob spent many difficult years in Haran. But throughout all his difficulties, God protected him and continued to bring the promise of the covenant to fulfillment.

1. Describe how Jacob felt when he arrived at Bethel.
2. Describe the vision in Jacob's dream.
3. What promises did God make to Jacob in his dream?
4. After Jacob woke from his dream, what promises did he make to God?
*5. How did God show His merciful love to Jacob?

Concepts of Faith

1. How did God show His merciful love to Jacob?
God did not abandon Jacob because he sinned. Rather, God gave Jacob the opportunity to renew his love for Him.

2. What promises were included in the covenant that God made with Abraham?
God promised to give Abraham many descendants and to give his descendants the land of Canaan.

3. Who inherited the covenant first made with Abraham?
Isaac and Jacob.

Vocabulary

firstborn son: The son who usually inherits most of his father's property and the covenant promise.

shrine: A sacred place.

birthright: A right to which a person is entitled because of his birth or origin.

Living the Lesson

Think Before You Act!

Think before you act! How many of you have heard this expression? Moms, dads, and teachers are usually very fond of using it. In fact, you might be tired of hearing this saying by now. Nevertheless, remembering to *think before you act* can be very useful in everyday situations. Someone should have said this to Esau before he sold his birthright to Jacob for a bowl of stew! Esau was so hungry that he could not think of anything except his stomach. Esau had to have what he wanted immediately! He did not think about the consequences of his actions.

In the following situations, think of some consequences that might happen if you do not *think before you act*. Then discuss what possible actions could be taken to avoid those consequences.

1. You are at a party and your parents have told you to be home by 10:00 P.M.. You are having so much fun that you decide to stay past that hour.

Possible consequence:

_____

Way of avoiding the consequence:

_____

_____

2. It's 9:00 P.M. and you have not yet studied for the history test you have to take the next day. Your favorite TV show is on. You decide to watch it.

Possible consequence:

_____

Way of avoiding the consequence:

_____

_____

3. You are preparing french fries in cooking oil for a snack. The phone rings, and you spend 15 minutes talking to a friend.

Possible consequence:

_____

Way of avoiding the consequence:

_____

_____

Prayer

Psalm 105:1–11.

Bible Character Recognition

In the blank lines in the left column, write the letter of the description that correctly matches the name of the biblical character.

1. _____ Abraham   **A** Son of Abraham and Hagar.

2. _____ Sarah   **B** Twin brother of Jacob, who sold his birthright.

3. _____ Isaac   **C** The first to receive the covenant; our "father in faith".

4. _____ Ishmael   **D** Servant of Sarah and mother of Ishmael.

5. _____ Hagar   **E** Wife of Abraham and mother of Isaac.

6. _____ Rebekah   **F** Twin Brother of Esau and heir to the covenant.

7. _____ Jacob   **G** Inherited the covenant from his father, Abraham; husband of Rebekah.

8. _____ Esau   **H** Mother of Jacob and Esau; wife of Isaac.

Jacob and His Family

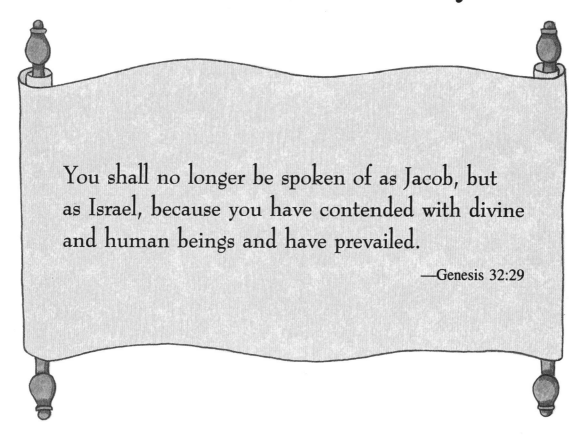

You shall no longer be spoken of as Jacob, but as Israel, because you have contended with divine and human beings and have prevailed.

—Genesis 32:29

The account of the arrival of Jacob in his family's homeland of Haran and his marriage to Rachel is found in Genesis, chapter 29. This Scripture reading is summarized in the following text.

Jacob Arrives in Haran

Throughout this lesson you will be asked to refer to the map on Worksheet 1. The map will help you follow Jacob's journey to Haran in Paddan-aram and his return to the land of Canaan.

In Lesson 7 we read that Jacob left his home in Beer-sheba to escape the anger of his brother Esau. While he rested at Bethel he had a vision or dream. In this dream God renewed the covenant that He had made first with Abraham and then with Jacob's father, Isaac. God also promised to protect Jacob throughout his journey. In return, Jacob promised to accept the God of his fathers as his own God.

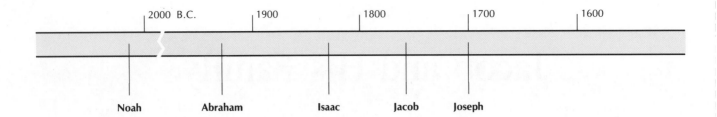

After Jacob left Bethel, he continued his journey to Haran, which is in the land of Paddan-aram, or Mesopotamia (refer to the map on Worksheet 1). After some time, Jacob arrived at a well. The mouth of the well was covered by a large stone. "Only when all the shepherds were assembled there could they roll the stone away from the mouth of the well and water the flocks" (Gen 29:3). Jacob spoke to the shepherds and asked them if they knew his uncle, Laban. They said they did know Laban and added, "And here comes his daughter Rachel with his flock" (Gen 29:6). Jacob was so excited to have found his family at last that he "kissed Rachel and burst into tears" (Gen 29:11). Jacob then told Rachel that he was the son of Laban's sister, Rebekah. Rachel ran to tell her father the news. Laban hurried out to meet his nephew, and he brought him to his house.

Jacob Marries Leah and Rachel

After Jacob had stayed with Laban for a month, he asked Laban for permission to marry his daughter Rachel. It was the custom in those days for a man to pay a *bridal price* to the parents of the bride. The parents of the bride also provided a *dowry* to be given to their daughter when she married. The bridal price and the dowry were usually gifts of money or property. Because Jacob had neither money nor property to pay a bridal price, he offered to work for Laban. "I will serve you seven years for your younger daughter Rachel" (Gen 29:18). Laban accepted the offer. "So Jacob served seven years for Rachel, yet they seemed to him but a few days because of his love for her" (Gen 29:20).

When the seven years of service were completed, Jacob asked to marry Rachel. Laban prepared a marriage feast and invited many guests to the celebration. However, when nightfall came, Laban tricked Jacob. Instead of bringing Rachel to Jacob's tent, Laban brought Leah, Rachel's older sister. Leah's face was veiled, and Jacob did not know that he had been deceived. In the morning Jacob was amazed: it was Leah! So he cried out to Laban: "How could you do this to me! Was it not for Rachel that I served you? Why did you dupe me?" "It is not the custom in our country", Laban replied, "to marry off a younger daughter before an older one. Finish the bridal week for this one, and then I will give you the other too, in return for another seven years of service with

me" (Gen 29:25–27). Because he loved Rachel, Jacob agreed to work another seven years for Laban. When the bridal week was over, Laban gave his daughter Rachel to Jacob in marriage.

REVIEW QUESTIONS

1. To what city and country was Jacob traveling?
2. What was the name of Jacob's uncle?
3. Whom did Jacob meet at the well?
4. Whom did Jacob love and wish to marry?
5. What is a dowry?
6. What is a bridal price?
7. What did Jacob offer to Laban in substitute for a bridal price?
8. How did Laban trick Jacob on his wedding night?
9. Why didn't Jacob recognize Leah?
10. Why did Laban trick Jacob?
11. What did Jacob agree to do in order to marry Rachel?

Jacob's Children

Now Jacob had two wives, Leah and Rachel. You may remember, from the lesson on Abraham, that polygamy was permitted in ancient times. *Polygamy* is the practice of having more than one wife at the same time. Both Leah and Rachel had maidservants. Rachel's maidservant was named Bilhah. The name of Leah's maidservant was Zilpah. They, too, became Jacob's wives. Jacob, then, had four wives. The custom of having up to four wives is still practiced in the Moslem religion today. Religions that follow the teachings of Jesus, however, do not practice polygamy. At this time, Jacob followed the custom of his land. He did not yet understand what God wanted marriage to be.

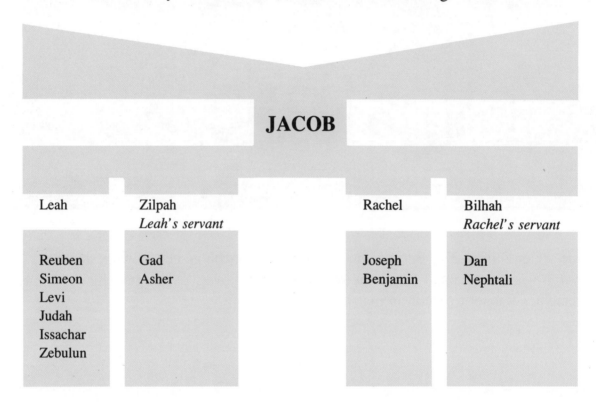

JACOB

Leah	Zilpah *Leah's servant*		Rachel	Bilhah *Rachel's servant*
Reuben Simeon Levi Judah Issachar Zebulun	Gad Asher		Joseph Benjamin	Dan Nephtali

The above chart shows Jacob's wives and the sons born to each. Later each of Jacob's sons would become the head of his own tribe, or family.

Jacob Leaves Haran

Jacob had to work another six years for Laban in order to build a herd of sheep large enough to support his family. After he completed this work, he made plans to return with his family and flocks to his own land in Canaan. The biblical account of Jacob's flight from Haran can be found in Genesis, chapter 31. Laban's pursuit of Jacob and their reconciliation are also narrated in this chapter of Genesis.

Read Genesis 31 or the summary below.

A Summary of Genesis 31

Jacob worked twenty years for Laban; seven years for Leah, seven years for Rachel, and another six to enlarge his flock of sheep. During those years, Laban deceived Jacob and changed his wages and the terms of Jacob's service several times. Therefore, Jacob did not trust Laban. When the time came for Jacob to leave, he feared that Laban would not allow him and his family to go and that Laban might cheat him out of his property. So Jacob decided to take his family and his flocks and leave without telling Laban. "Jacob proceeded to put his children and wives on camels, and he drove off with all his livestock and all the property he had acquired in Paddan-aram, to go to his father Isaac in the land of Canaan" (Gen 31:17–18).

Laban was angry when he found out that Jacob had fled with his family and property, so "he pursued him for seven days until he caught up with him in the hill country of Gilead" (Gen 31:23). (Refer to Worksheet 1.) That night God spoke to Laban in a dream and warned him not to harm Jacob.

The next day Laban and Jacob met in Mizpah, a town in the country of Gilead. (Refer to Worksheet 1.) They argued with each other. Finally Jacob said, "Of the twenty years that I have now spent in your household, I slaved fourteen years for your two daughters and six years for your flock, while you changed my wages time after time. If my ancestral God, the God of Abraham and the Awesome One of Isaac, had not been on my side, you would now have sent me away empty-handed. But God saw my plight and the fruits of my toil, and last night he gave judgment" (Gen 31:41–42).

After hearing this, Laban and Jacob reconciled with each other. To *reconcile* means to rebuild a friendship between persons. Laban said to Jacob, "Come, then, we will make a pact, you and I; the Lord shall be a witness between us" (Gen 31:44).

Then Jacob and Laban gathered some stones and made a mound. "This mound", said Laban, "shall be a witness from now on between you and me" (Gen 31:48). Then Laban asked God to watch over them. Both Laban and Jacob promised not to pass beyond the mound into one another's territories with any harmful intent. Jacob swore to keep this covenant of peace by the God of his father, Isaac. After their *reconciliation*, "Laban kissed his grandchildren and his daughters goodbye; then he set out on his journey back home, while Jacob continued on his own way" (Gen 32:1–2).

1. What is polygamy?
2. How many wives did Jacob have, and what were their names?
3. What religion allows the practice of having up to four wives?
4. Do religions that follow the teachings of Jesus practice polygamy?
5. How many sons did Jacob have?
6. How many years did Jacob work for Laban?
7. Why didn't Jacob tell Laban that he was leaving?
8. Why didn't Laban harm Jacob when he caught up with him in Gilead?
9. What does reconciliation mean?
10. How did Jacob and Laban reconcile with each other?

The Reconciliation of Jacob and Esau

After traveling for a while, Jacob arrived at another town in Gilead, called Mahanaim. (Refer to Worksheet 1.) Jacob knew that his brother Esau lived in the nearby country of Edom. Jacob also knew that Esau was a powerful man, with an army of four hundred men. Twenty years had passed since Jacob fled from Esau's anger. Yet Jacob was worried and feared that Esau might still be angry with him. Jacob prayed to God, asking for protection for himself and his family. Then Jacob sent messengers to Esau bearing many gifts. Jacob reasoned, "If I first appease him with gifts that precede me, then later, when I face him, perhaps he will forgive me." So the gifts went on ahead of him, while he stayed that night in the camp (Gen 32:21–22).

Jacob Struggles with the Angel

During the night, Jacob moved his family and all his possessions across the River Jabbok. (See Worksheet 1.) "Then some man [a messenger or angel of the Lord in human form] wrestled with him until the break of dawn. When the man saw that he could not prevail over him, he struck Jacob's hip at its socket, so that the hip socket was wrenched as they wrestled. The man then said, 'Let me go, for it is daybreak.' But Jacob said, 'I will not let you go until you bless me.' 'What is your name?' the man asked. He answered, 'Jacob.' Then the man said, 'You shall no longer be spoken of as Jacob, but as Israel, because you have contended with divine and human beings and have prevailed.' . . . Jacob named the place Peniel [Penuel], 'Because I have seen God face to face', he said, 'yet my life has been spared'" (Gen 32:25–31; refer to Worksheet 1).

A Discussion of Genesis 32:23–33

Jacob had struggled against God's will for most of his life. He chose to follow his own path and to make decisions without thinking about God. Jacob forgot that he needed God. He forgot that God loved him. In the story of Jacob's struggle with the angel, Jacob chose to remember God.

Jacob and Esau Meet

Jacob was worried about meeting his brother Esau. He was afraid that Esau would still be angry with him. The temptation to run away from Esau must have been very great. When we are afraid, it is always tempting to run away from our fears rather than confront them. Jacob, however, chose to meet Esau. He chose to reconcile with his brother. Jacob found the courage to do this because he remembered God. He remembered that God loved him and would always be with him.

We, like Jacob, often face temptations. It is not easy to avoid sin. We must struggle to make right choices. If we remember that God loves us and is always with us, we, like Jacob, will have the courage to struggle against the temptation to sin and to make the choice to act as images of God.

Read Genesis 33 for the biblical account of the meeting of Jacob and Esau. The following text is a brief summary.

When Jacob saw Esau coming, accompanied by four hundred men, he was afraid. He went ahead of his wives and children and bowed to the ground seven times until he reached his brother. "Esau ran to meet him, embraced him, and flinging himself on his neck, kissed him as he wept" (Gen 33:4). Then Esau asked to be introduced to Jacob's family. After greeting them, Esau asked Jacob why he had sent so many gifts to him. Jacob answered, "It was to gain my lord's favor" (Gen 33:8). Then the two brothers talked and made plans to meet again. After their reconciliation, Jacob continued his journey to Succoth, where he built his home. Then he went to the city of Shechem in the land of Canaan. (See Worksheet 1.) He set up a memorial stone there and invoked "El, the God of Israel" (Gen 33:20).

God's Merciful Love

Jacob's prayer at Shechem was the first time that he referred to himself by his new name, Israel. It was also the first time that Jacob prayed to God calling Him the "God of Israel". Before, Jacob had prayed to the God of his fathers, Abraham and Isaac. Now Jacob had a personal relationship with God. God had loved Jacob mercifully. He had promised to protect Jacob and to bring him back to the land of Canaan. God kept His promises, and, by doing so, He gave Jacob the opportunity to love Him. It took Jacob many years to return God's love. When Jacob prayed to God calling Him the "God of Israel", he showed God that he had finally accepted Him as his own. Jacob was now ready to renew the covenant between God and His people.

God Renews the Covenant with Israel

God said to Jacob: "Go up now to Bethel. Settle there and build an altar there to the God who appeared to you while you were fleeing from your brother Esau" (Gen 35:1). So Jacob took his family and revisited Bethel. (See Worksheet 1.) Jacob also instructed his family to rid themselves of all foreign gods. Some of Jacob's family had brought pagan idols of foreign gods with them from Paddan-aram. Jacob now took care to instruct his people about the one true God. "We are now to go up to Bethel, and I will build an altar there to the God who answered me in my hour of distress and who has been with me wherever I have gone" (Gen 35:3). Then God said to him: "You whose name is Jacob shall no longer be called Jacob, but Israel shall be your name." God also said to him, "I am God Almighty; be fruitful and multiply. A nation, indeed an assembly of nations, shall stem from you, and kings shall issue from your loins. The land I once gave to Abraham and Isaac I now give to you; And to your descendants after you will I give this land" (Gen 35:10–12). The name Israel, which was given to Jacob, shows how important he was to the history of God's chosen people. He was so important that God's people were called the Israelites.

The Death of Rachel and Isaac

At this time, Rachel was pregnant. After Jacob and his family left Bethel, "Rachel began to be in labor and to suffer great distress" (Gen 35:16). While she was giving birth, her midwife said to her, "Have no fear! This time, too, you have a son." With her last breath, for she was at the point of death, she called him Ben-oni; his father, however, named him Benjamin (Gen 35:17–18). Then Rachel died. She was buried near Bethlehem. (See Worksheet 1.) Benjamin was the second son born to Rachel and Jacob. The other son was Joseph, whose story will be read in Lesson 9. Jacob now had twelve sons. (Refer to the chart on page 112.)

After Rachel died, Jacob went home to his father, Isaac, at Mamre, in Kiriath-arba (that is, Hebron), where Abraham and Isaac had stayed. (Refer to Worksheet 1.) The lifetime of Isaac was one hundred and eighty years; then he breathed his last. After a full life, he died as an old man and was taken to his kinsmen. His sons Esau and Jacob buried him (Gen 35:27–29).

The ring, or circle, has always been a symbol of unity and eternity. Although gifts of jewelry were given to brides in the Old Testament, the use of the ring as a symbol for marriage dates from the time of the Roman Empire. Christianity accepted the ring as an appropriate symbol of eternal love. Three linked rings have come to represent the eternal love of God the Father, the Son, and the Holy Spirit, in the Holy Trinity.

1. What two things did Jacob do when he was worried that Esau might still be angry with him?
2. With whom did Jacob wrestle after he crossed the River Jabbok?
3. What new name was given to Jacob by the angel?
4. Why was Jacob given this name?
5. How did Esau greet Jacob when they met?
6. What did Jacob do after he arrived in the land of Canaan?
7. What did Jacob call God when he prayed to Him after arriving in the land of Canaan?
8. Why was it important that Jacob called God the "God of Israel"?
*9. How did God show His merciful love to Jacob?
*10. What promises did God make to Israel when He renewed the covenant with him?
11. What did God ask Israel to do in return?
12. How did Rachel die?
13. When did Esau and Jacob meet again?

Concepts of Faith

1. **How did God show His merciful love to Jacob?**
   God protected Jacob, brought him back to the land of Canaan, and gave Jacob the opportunity to love Him.
2. **What promises did God make to Israel (Jacob) when He renewed the covenant with him?**
   God promised that many nations and kings would descend from him; God gave Israel the land of Canaan and promised to give the land to his descendants.
3. **What is the sacrament of Reconciliation?**
   The sacrament of Reconciliation is the sacrament Jesus gave us for the forgiveness of our sins.
4. **How can we show God that we are sorry for our sins?**
   By receiving the sacrament of Reconciliation often.

Vocabulary

dowry: Gifts of money or property given to the bride by her parents.

bridal price: Gifts of money or property given to the parents of the bride by the groom.

polygamy: The practice of having more than one wife at the same time.

reconciliation: The act of rebuilding a friendship between persons.

sacrament: A physical sign given to us by Jesus through which Jesus meets us and gives us His grace.

penance: A loving act that the priest asks you to do after your sins have been forgiven.

absolution: The words spoken by the priest that take away our sins.

examination of conscience: Often using the Ten Commandments, we ask ourselves if we have been acting as images of God and how we are better able to act as images of God in the future.

sacrament of Reconciliation: The sacrament that Jesus gave us for the forgiveness of our sins.

Living the Lesson

1. Jacob and Reconciliation

In the story of Jacob there are two examples of reconciliation. To reconcile means to rebuild the friendship between persons. In Genesis 31:44–54, Jacob and his uncle Laban renewed their friendship. After many years of distrust, the two men reconciled with each other. They promised not to harm each other again. They made a "pact", or agreement, with the Lord as their witness. They set up a memorial stone as a physical sign of their reconciliation.

In Genesis 33, Jacob and his brother, Esau, renewed their friendship. Esau had been cheated out of his birthright by Jacob, and it had been twenty years since Jacob had fled from Esau's anger. And yet, when the two brothers met, "Esau ran to meet him, embraced him, and flinging himself on his neck, kissed him as he wept" (Gen 33:4). Jacob returned Esau's physical signs of reconciliation by giving his brother a gift.

Both Jacob and Esau were changed by their reconciliation. Esau's readiness to forgive Jacob for the terrible wrongs he had done against him showed that Esau had become a more loving and charitable person. Jacob's efforts to appease his brother with gifts showed that he was sorry for the sins he had committed against his brother.

2. The Sacrament of Reconciliation

The story of Jacob can teach us many things about reconciliation. Like Jacob, when we sin, we hurt God, ourselves, and others. Sin weakens the love

between God and us. We hurt God, because we do not return God's love. We hurt ourselves, because we do not act as images of God. We hurt others when we sin, because we do not treat them as images of God.

We show our love for God by admitting our sins. We should be sorry for our sins, and we should want to tell God that we are sorry. We should ask God for forgiveness.

Because we are human persons (persons with bodies) we need to experience God's forgiveness in a physical (bodily) way. When Jesus was on earth, many people experienced the physical, forgiving touch of Christ. When they were sorry for their sins, many times they were touched by Christ. Their sins were taken away, and their love for God was strengthened. God knows we need to experience this same "touch of Christ". We receive the forgiving "touch of Christ" in the sacrament of Reconciliation. A *sacrament* is a physical sign given to us by Jesus through which Jesus meets us and gives us grace.

In the sacrament of Reconciliation, we go to Jesus for help, and we experience His "touch". We tell our sins to the priest, who acts for Jesus. When the priest says the words of forgiveness, it is Jesus touching us with His words and forgiving us—healing us. Jesus gives us His grace, making it easier or at least possible for us to return God's love. In other words, our relationship with God is healed.

When we hurt our relationship with God through our sins, we hurt ourselves, because we are not acting the way we should as images of God. In the sacrament of Reconciliation, our sins are forgiven and we receive God's grace, which enables us to act as better images of God.

When Jacob sinned, the love between him and his family was weakened. Sin always weakens the love between us and other people. When Jacob expressed sorrow for his sin against Esau, he experienced Esau's forgiveness, and they were reconciled with each other. When we hurt the people we love, we should admit that we have hurt them and tell them that we are sorry. Loving people act as images of God and forgive us when we hurt them. Through the sacrament of Reconciliation the love between us and those we have hurt is strengthened, and the relationship is healed. In the sacrament of Reconciliaion, when we are reconciled with Christ, we are reconciled with the Church and with all the members of the Church.

3. A Review of How We Receive the Sacrament of Reconciliation
When we decide that we want to receive Jesus' forgiving and healing touch, we receive the sacrament of Reconciliation. The Church encourages us to receive this sacrament often, so that we may be better able to act as images of God.

Suggested Form for Receiving the Sacrament of Reconciliation

1. Make a good *examination of conscience*. Take time and ask yourselves if you have been acting as an image of God. Use the Ten Commandments as a guide to help you in your examination. Be ready to tell the priest your sins. Remember, when you tell the priest your sins, you are really telling Jesus.

2. Go into the confessional and kneel down, or go into the reconciliation room and sit or kneel down. Greet Father.

3. Make the Sign of the Cross and say, "Bless me, Father, for I have sinned." Then tell the priest how long it has been since your last confession.

4. Tell the priest your sins. When you are done, say, "I am very sorry for all my sins."

5. Father will talk with you and give you a *penance*. A penance is a loving act that the priest asks you to do after your sins have been forgiven.

6. Father will ask you to say an *Act of Contrition*. The Act of Contrition is a prayer telling God that you are sorry for your sins because you have hurt Him, yourself, and others and that with His help you will try not to sin again.

7. Father will give you *absolution*. The prayer of absolution is the words spoken by the priest that take away your sins. At the end of the prayer, make the Sign of the Cross and answer "Amen".

8. Father will tell you to "Go in peace." Thank Father, and leave the confessional or reconciliation room.

9. Do your penance immediately.

*1. What is the sacrament of Reconciliation?

2. Who acts for Jesus in the sacrament of Reconciliation?

*3. How can we show God that we are sorry for our sins?

4. What is an Act of Contrition?

5. What is an examination of conscience?

6. What is absolution?

7. What is a penance?

Prayers

Psalm 105:1–11.

The "Act of Contrition":

My God,
I am sorry for my sins with all my heart.
In choosing to do wrong
and failing to do good,
I have sinned against You,
Whom I should love above all things.
(I have hurt myself and others.)
I firmly intend, with Your help,
to do penance,
to sin no more,
and to avoid whatever leads me to sin.
Our Savior Jesus Christ
suffered and died for us.
In His name, my God, have mercy.

PADDAN-ARAM

SYRIA

Euphrates R.

Balikh R.

Follow Jacob's journey from Beer-sheba to Paddan-aram and back again to the land of Canaan.

WORSHEET 1

Jacob's Journey to Paddan-aram and His Return to the Land of Canaan

Draw a line connecting the following places.
1. Beer-sheba in the land of Canaan
2. Bethel
3. Haran in Paddan-aram
4. Mizpah
5. Mahanaim
6. Penuel
7. Succoth
8. Shechem
9. Bethel
10. Bethlehem
11. Mamre
12. Hebron

Place an asterisk (*) near the city of these important events.
1. Jacob's dream. (Bethel.)
2. Jacob's covenant with Laban. (Mizpah.)
3. Jacob's struggle with the angel and his reconciliation with Esau. (Peniel.)

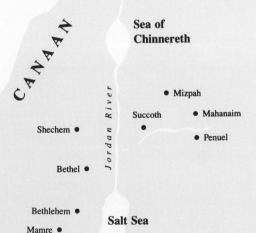

PHOENICIA

CANAAN

Sea of Chinnereth

Jordan River

• Mizpah

Succoth •   • Mahanaim

Shechem •

      • Penuel

Bethel •

Bethlehem •

Salt Sea

Mamre •

Hebron •

• Beer-sheba

Jacob's family heritage is drawn on the tree above. Jacob's grandparents were Abraham and Sarah, so their names are printed near the roots of the tree. Abraham and Sarah had a son, Isaac, who married Rebekah. Their names are printed on the main trunk of the tree. Isaac and Rebekah had twin sons, Esau and Jacob. Jacob's name was later changed to Israel. Jacob had four wives, Leah, Rachel, Zilpah, and Bilhah. Locate their names on the large branches that stem from Jacob's trunk. Jacob had 12 sons. These 12 sons later gave their names to the 12 tribes of Israel.

Write the names of Jacob's 12 sons in the clusters of leaves at the end of the small branches. Be sure that the name of each son connects with his own mother. Use the chart on page 112 to help you.

As you continue reading and studying the Scriptures, you will discover that the name "Israel" is used in different ways.

Here are the four early uses of "Israel" and their meanings.

1. Israel is the new name given to Jacob after he struggles with the angel. Israel is the name of one person.

2. Jacob's descendants are called Israelites, or the "children of Israel". Israel is the name of a group of people.

3. The land of Canaan, which God promised to Jacob and his descendants, is called Israel.

4. During the reigns of King David and King Solomon, the country they ruled was divided in two. One country, or nation, was named Israel; the other was named Judah.

Directions

Each of the four scriptural references given below mentions the name "Israel" in one of the four meanings just described. Write the number of the meaning on the line beside each reference.

Romans 9:4 _____

Genesis 35:10 _____

1 Kings 1:34 _____

Ezekiel 11:17 _____

Joseph

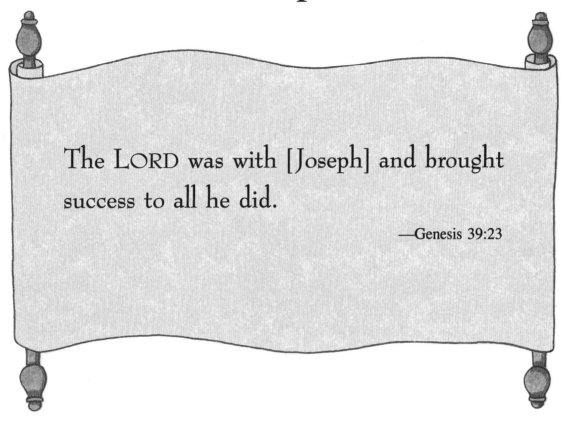

The LORD was with [Joseph] and brought success to all he did.

—Genesis 39:23

The story of Joseph and his beautiful coat of many colors is one that many of you have heard before. It is a favorite children's Bible story. In fact, this story is so popular that it was made into a musical called *Joseph and His Technicolor Coat*. If you tried to retell the story of Joseph now, what details could you remember?

Now it is time for you to read the story of Joseph as it appears in the Bible. You will discover as you read the Scriptures that there are more details and events in the story of Joseph than those you remembered. Stories are often simplified for young children. Later, these same stories can be reread with deeper appreciation and understanding.

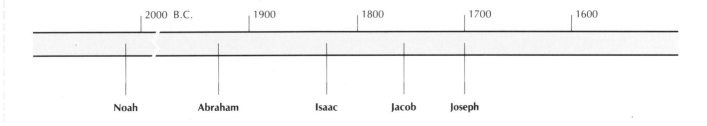

Before you begin to read the biblical version of the story of Joseph, look at the map on page 131. On this map there are two main regions: Canaan and Egypt. You are already familiar with the land of Canaan. This was the land promised to the Israelites in the covenant. It was the birthplace of Joseph. Egypt, however, became Joseph's new home and the home of his family and their descendants for four hundred years. What was Egypt like at Joseph's time?

The Land of Egypt

Life in ancient Egypt was closely tied to the Nile River. Look at the map on page 131. The Nile River is the longest river in the world. Its source is in southern Africa. Its waters flow northward in a winding course for over four thousand miles before reaching the Mediterranean Sea. The country of Egypt is located near the mouth of the Nile River. Egypt is divided into two sections: Lower Egypt and Upper Egypt. The Nile River played a very important role in the life of the Egyptians. If the river flooded the desert land along its banks, then there would be sufficient water for a plentiful harvest of crops. But if the river ran low, a drought would occur, and that would mean a poor harvest. If the river ran too high, flooding would cause widespread destruction. Today, the Nile River still plays a very important role in the lives of the Egyptians. But now the flood waters are controlled by the Aswan dam, located in Upper Egypt.

Most of the people of ancient Egypt lived near the banks of the Nile River. Therefore, most of Egypt's major cities were located near it. The river was not only a source of life because it watered the land, but it also was a major trade route. Spices, crops, precious metals and stones, and countless other products were transported from the nearby desert to the Nile and then by boat to various seaports. Trade routes by land were established also through the northeastern desert, to Canaan and beyond. (You will remember that the lessons on Abraham discussed the importance of trade routes.) Along this desert trade route, Joseph was sold to a caravan of traders heading for Egypt.

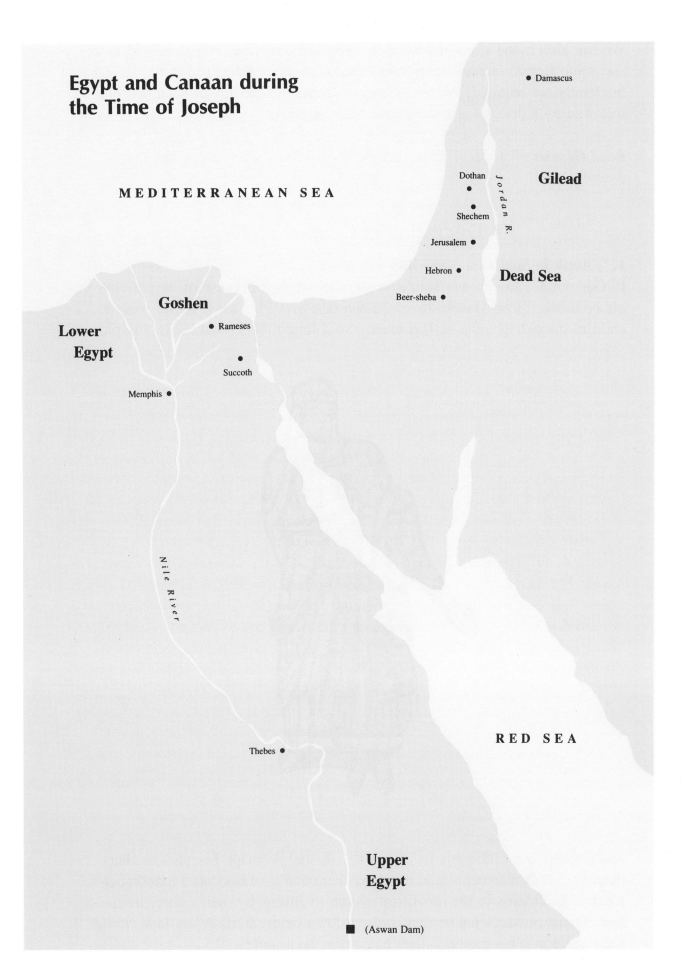

Egypt and Canaan during the Time of Joseph

MEDITERRANEAN SEA

• Damascus

Dothan
•

Gilead

Shechem
•

Jordan R.

Jerusalem •

Dead Sea

Hebron •

Beer-sheba •

Goshen

**Lower
Egypt**

• Rameses

• Succoth

Memphis •

Nile River

RED SEA

Thebes •

**Upper
Egypt**

■ (Aswan Dam)

We can look at the story of Joseph in three sections: first, Joseph is sold as a slave into Egypt; second, Joseph becomes a powerful ruler; and third, he and his family are reunited. We will read the scriptural accounts of each section, followed by a discussion and by review questions.

Read Genesis 37:1–36. This passage gives us the first section of the story of Joseph.

A Discussion of Genesis 37:1–36:

1. Joseph Is Sold as a Slave into Egypt

In Genesis 37, Joseph was sold as a slave into Egypt because of the jealousy of his brothers. "Israel [Jacob] loved Joseph best of all his sons, for he was the child of his old age; and he had made him a long tunic" (Gen 37:3). Joseph

was also the son of Jacob's favorite wife, Rachel. Perhaps Joseph's brothers thought that their father would overlook them and give his entire inheritance to Joseph. In addition to the favoritism shown to Joseph by their father, Joseph had dreams in which his brothers bowed down before him. When Joseph told these dreams to his brothers, they hated him even more.

One day, Joseph's brothers were tending the flocks in a pasture in Shechem, far from their home in Hebron. Joseph was sent by his father to see if his brothers and the flocks were safe. When Joseph reached Shechem he was told that his brothers had moved on to Dothan. (See the map on page 131.) The brothers saw Joseph approaching them and thought that this would be a perfect opportunity to get rid of him. At first they plotted to kill him: "Here comes that master dreamer! Come on, let us kill him and throw him into one of the cisterns here; we could say that a wild beast devoured him. We shall then see what comes of his dreams" (Gen 37:19–20). A *cistern* is an underground container usually used for storing rainwater.

Joseph, however, was not killed. He was taken to Egypt by a caravan of traders. The biblical text gives us two different accounts. In Genesis 37:21, 23–28, two of Joseph's brothers, Reuben and Judah, convinced their brothers to sell Joseph to a caravan of Ishmaelites. In Genesis 37:28–36, Joseph was rescued by Midianite traders, who pulled him out of the cistern and took him to Egypt. Reuben discovered that Joseph was missing. Then the brothers dipped Joseph's tunic in animal blood and deceived Jacob into thinking that Joseph was killed by a wild animal. "The Midianites, meanwhile, sold Joseph in Egypt to Potiphar, a courtier of Pharaoh and his chief steward" (Gen 37:36).

As with many of the Old Testament stories in Genesis, more than one author, or source, contributed to the writing of the text. And so there are two different stories about how Joseph was taken to Egypt. The end of this part of the story, however, remains the same. Joseph's life was spared, and he was taken to Egypt and sold as a slave. The inspired message is very clear, too. God loved Joseph and did not forget Joseph when he needed Him. God showed Joseph his merciful love. He protected him from harm. God did not allow Joseph to be killed. You will read in the next part of the story that God continued to show His merciful love throughout Joseph's stay in Egypt. God was able to draw good out of Joseph's new life as a slave.

REVIEW QUESTIONS

1. Why did Joseph's brothers hate him?
2. What did Joseph's brothers first plan to do to him?
3. What happened to Joseph?
4. How did Joseph's brothers deceive their father?
5. Who bought Joseph from the Midianite traders?
*6. How is God's merciful love shown in the story of Joseph?

2. Joseph Becomes a Powerful Ruler

From Genesis 37:36, we learned that Joseph was sold by the Midianite traders to a man named Potiphar, "a courtier of Pharaoh and his chief steward". The *Pharaoh* was the ruler or king of Egypt. A *courtier* was a person who attended the royal court. The *chief steward* was a person appointed by Pharaoh to supervise his business. Some of the chief steward's responsibilities were to supervise the servants and slaves, to collect and manage the money of various accounts, to manage the provision and distribution of food, and to attend to any other duties that the Pharaoh instructed him to do. He was the Pharaoh's "right-hand man". It was in Potiphar's household that Joseph began his new life as a slave.

Read Genesis 39.

Seth   Isis   Horus   Thoth   Amun-Re

A Discussion of Genesis 39

It must have been very difficult for Joseph to find himself as a slave in a foreign land. He was only seventeen years old when he was sold to Potiphar. He must have missed his father and his home very much. Yet Joseph knew that God was with him. He worked very hard to make the best of his situation. Joseph gained the trust of his master, Potiphar. Potiphar trusted him so much that he put Joseph in charge of his household. God continued to show Joseph that He loved him. "From the moment that he put him in charge of his household and all his possessions, the LORD blessed the Egyptian's house for Joseph's sake; in fact, the LORD's blessing was on everything he owned, both inside the house and out" (Gen 39:5).

Joseph, however, angered Potiphar's wife by refusing her attempts to get him to betray the trust that Potiphar had placed in him. She then lied to Potiphar and told him that Joseph mistreated her. Potiphar believed his wife and ordered Joseph thrown into jail.

"But even while he [Joseph] was in prison, the LORD remained with Joseph; he showed him kindness by making the chief jailer well-disposed toward him" (Gen 39:21). The chief jailer put Joseph in charge of all the prisoners. And in this way God showed Joseph His merciful love.

Again, God drew good out of this bad situation. Joseph spent many years in the prison. But "the LORD was with him and brought success to all he did" (Gen 39:23).

Min   *Anubis*   *Maat*   *Hathor*   *Osiris*

Joseph and Dreams

While Joseph was in jail, two of Pharaoh's courtiers, the royal cupbearer and the baker, angered Pharaoh. So Pharaoh put them in the same jail where Joseph was confined. One night they both had dreams that disturbed them. They could not understand what the dreams meant. Joseph said to them, "Surely, interpretations come from God. Please tell the dreams to me" (Gen 40:8). Then they both told Joseph their dreams. Joseph told the royal cupbearer that his dream meant that Pharaoh would restore his position to him within three days. The royal cupbearer was very pleased with Joseph's interpretation. Joseph asked the man to tell the Pharaoh that Joseph was innocent of any crime and to release him from prison. Unfortunately, the baker's dream did not have a happy meaning. Joseph told the baker that his dream meant that he would be executed in three days. Both dreams came true, just as Joseph had said.

Two years later, Pharaoh also had several dreams that disturbed him. "So he summoned all the magicians and sages of Egypt and recounted his dreams to them; but no one could interpret his dreams for him" (Gen 41:8). It was then that the cupbearer remembered Joseph and told Pharaoh of Joseph's ability to interpret dreams.

Dreams were taken very seriously in Egyptian culture. Archaeologists have discovered Egyptian dream-manuals. These manuals were kept by magicians and sages. A *sage* was a person considered to be very wise and capable of predicting the future. These "wise men" were paid by people to explain the meaning of their dreams. The interpreters would use their dream-manuals as reference books to help them interpret the meaning of dreams. Joseph, whose brothers had called him a "master dreamer" (Gen 37:19), had now become known as an interpreter of dreams. However, Joseph did not rely on a dream-manual to help him explain the meaning of dreams. Joseph relied only on God.

Read all of Genesis 41.

A Discussion of Genesis 41

In chapter 41, verses 1 to 32 describe Pharaoh's dreams and Joseph's interpretation of them. It is important to note that Joseph did not credit himself for his ability to tell the meaning of dreams. "It is not I", Joseph replied to Pharaoh, "but God who will give Pharaoh the right answer" (Gen 41:16). Joseph told Pharaoh that his dreams meant that there would be seven years of good harvests, followed by seven years of famine. Joseph then gave Pharaoh a plan of action to follow that would ensure that the land would not perish during the time of famine. "Therefore, let Pharaoh seek out a wise and discerning man and put him in charge of the land of Egypt" (Gen 41:33). Grain should be stored during the years of plenty so that there would be enough to give to the people during the years of famine. Pharaoh was pleased with Joseph's interpretation of his dreams. He took Joseph's advice and appointed a man to be in charge. "Herewith," Pharaoh told Joseph, "I place you in charge of the whole land of Egypt" (Gen 41:41).

Pharaoh bestowed many benefits upon Joseph and honored him with a wonderful ceremony to celebrate his new position of power. "Pharaoh took off his signet ring and put it on Joseph's finger" (Gen 41:42). This was no ordinary ring. It was the Pharaoh's *signet ring*, into which was set an engraved stamp or seal. The person wearing it would press the ring into hot wax and thus stamp or seal any official document with the sign, or signature, of the Pharaoh. Many rulers from different countries used a signet ring to stamp their seal of authority. This custom of stamping official documents with a seal has come down to us through the ages. Countries all over the world today have official state seals stamped on government documents. Even you can seal a letter with wax and such a stamp. The next time you are in a store that sells stationery, ask the clerk to show you some wax seals.

After Pharaoh gave Joseph his ring, "He had him dressed in robes of fine linen and put a gold chain about his neck" (Gen 41:42). There are many Egyptian paintings that show in detail the garments and jewelry worn by high officials of ancient Egypt. Chariots similar to the one on which Joseph rode are portrayed in paintings and sculptures from Egyptian tombs and coffins.

Pharaoh then gave Joseph a new, Egyptian name. Next, Pharaoh even arranged a marriage for Joseph! Joseph married the daughter of an Egyptian priest named Potiphera.

Joseph received all these honors when he was thirty years old. He had risen from slavery to a position of great power in only thirteen years.

Joseph worked very hard during the years of plenty to store grain. He "garnered grain in quantities like the sands of the sea" (Gen 41:49). During this time of plenty, Joseph and his wife, Asenath, had two sons. Joseph was grateful to God for His merciful love, and he remembered God when he named his sons. "He named his firstborn Manasseh, meaning, 'God has made me forget entirely the sufferings I endured at the hands of my family'; and the second he named Ephraim, meaning, 'God has made me fruitful in the land of my affliction'" (Gen 41:51–52).

When the famine came, "all the world came to Joseph to obtain rations of grain" (Gen 41:57). Joseph was now ready to meet his brothers again.

1. What was the ruler of Egypt called?
2. What did the chief steward do?
3. Why was Joseph put in charge of Potiphar's household?
4. After Joseph was put in charge of Potiphar's household, how did God remind Joseph that He loved him?
5. Why was Joseph thrown into jail?
6. How did God show his merciful love to Joseph while he was in jail?
7. What is an Egyptian dream-manual?
8. Who helped Joseph interpret dreams?
9. What was the meaning of Pharaoh's dreams?
10. Whom did Pharaoh put in charge of the whole land of Egypt?
11. What was so special about the ring that Pharaoh gave to Joseph?
12. Name some of the honors given to Joseph by Pharaoh.
13. How did Joseph thank God for His merciful love?

3. Joseph and His Family Are Reunited

Egypt was not the only country to experience the effects of seven years of famine. The surrounding countries, including the land of Canaan, also experienced the famine. Archaeologists have discovered writing tablets from Egypt and nearby countries that record the years of famine described in Genesis. "In fact, all the world came to Joseph to obtain rations of grain, for famine had gripped the whole world" (Gen 41:57).

And so it was that Joseph's brothers were sent to Egypt by Jacob to buy food. The story of what happened to them is quite dramatic and full of emotion.

Read chapters 42 to 45 of Genesis in their entirety.

A Summary of Genesis 42–45

When Jacob learned that grain rations were available in Egypt, he sent ten of his sons to buy food for their families. Benjamin remained at home with Jacob. When the brothers arrived in Egypt, they went to the man in charge of distributing the rations of grain. That man was Joseph. Joseph recognized his brothers as soon as he saw them. But the brothers did not recognize Joseph. Joseph was dressed in fine robes and was a man of great power. The brothers bowed down in respect to Joseph, and thus reminded him of the dreams he had had about them. Joseph did not tell his brothers who he was. He decided to give his brothers a "hard time". Joseph accused his brothers of spying on Egypt. The brothers protested with loud cries of denial and told Joseph, "We your servants . . . were twelve brothers, sons of a certain man in Canaan; but the youngest one is at present with our father, and the other one is gone" (Gen 42:13). Joseph told them to prove the truth of their story by bringing the youngest brother to him. As added insurance for their return, Joseph kept one of the brothers, Simeon, in jail until the rest returned with Benjamin. Joseph also confused his brothers by hiding, inside the bags of grain, the money they had paid for the food. When the brothers discovered the money, they were afraid. They did not know what to think!

When the brothers returned home, they told their story to Jacob. He was very upset. Jacob had already lost Joseph, and he was afraid to send Benjamin to Egypt. Judah finally convinced Jacob that there really was no other way to save Simeon. Besides, they would soon need to ask for more grain. Jacob finally agreed to let Benjamin go. But he told the brothers to take with them double the money they needed in case they were accused of not paying for the first ration of grain. The brothers also brought with them gifts of balm and honey, gum and resin, pistachios and almonds to give to the powerful governor, Joseph.

When the brothers met with Joseph a second time, Joseph was so overwhelmed to see his younger brother Benjamin that he had to leave the room so that his brothers would not see his tears. Joseph released Simeon from the prison and ordered the brothers to have lunch with him. During the dinner, Joseph had their sacks filled with grain and again hid their money in the sacks. In addition to this, he had a valuable silver goblet hidden in Benjamin's sack. The next day the brothers left for Canaan. Soon they were overtaken by Joseph's head steward, who accused them of stealing. The brothers were amazed and very much afraid when Joseph's silver goblet was found in Benjamin's sack.

When the brothers were brought before Joseph, he told them that, as punishment for their dishonesty, he was going to keep Benjamin as his slave. The brothers begged Joseph to have mercy on their father, Jacob, who would be heartbroken if he were to lose another son. Judah even volunteered to take Benjamin's place. Joseph then knew that his brothers loved their father and Benjamin. He said to them, "I am your brother Joseph, whom you once sold into Egypt" (Gen 45:4). Joseph's brothers could not believe it! Joseph told them not to be upset. "God, therefore, sent me on ahead of you to ensure for you a remnant on earth and to save your lives in an extraordinary deliverance. So it was not really you but God who had me come here" (Gen 45:7–8). "Joseph then kissed all his brothers, crying over each of them; and only then were his brothers able to talk with him" (Gen 45:15).

After this Joseph sent for his father and the families of his brothers. The entire family and all their flocks and belongings moved to Egypt. Joseph settled his family in the land called Goshen (see the map on page 145), so that they would be near him and he could care for their needs.

A Discussion of the Reunion of Joseph and His Family

In the final part of the story of Joseph, the brothers journeyed to Egypt for food rations. They did not recognize that the governor of Egypt was their brother Joseph. Joseph did not tell them until after he had put them through several "tests". Joseph discovered that his brothers loved their father and were willing to sacrifice themselves for his welfare. Then Joseph finally revealed his true identity and reunited his family.

Joseph's Character

We have already learned much about Joseph's character from the first two parts of the story. We know that Joseph tried to act as an image of God. He knew that God loved him and would care for him. Joseph was wise and prudent. He was modest and virtuous. Although he was talented in analyzing dreams, he did not take credit for himself. Joseph relied on God. Joseph was a handsome and likable fellow, well-spoken, and hard-working. He always made the best out of even the worst situations. Joseph was successful in all that he did. He was, in fact, a noble Egyptian. That is, he was an Egyptian in his way of life and in his work. But Joseph did not forget that he was an Israelite. He was faithful and loyal to the God of his people.

In the third and final part of the story, we learn that Joseph was also a loving and forgiving person. Even after the hateful treatment given to him by his brothers, Joseph still loved them. Who would have blamed Joseph if, instead of forgiving his brothers, he had thrown them all into jail or sold them as slaves? He was in a position to take revenge. Instead, he chose to act as an image of God. He forgave his brothers. Joseph, however, was not above giving them a hard time. He did not make it easy for his brothers. He tricked them several times, and as a result they were worried and concerned for their very lives. But throughout the story, we know that Joseph always loved them. What is more, Joseph discovered that his brothers loved each other and their father. It was then that Joseph revealed himself to his brothers and reunited his family by bringing them to Egypt.

Joseph Is a "Type of Christ"

Joseph can remind us of Jesus Christ in several ways. You may remember, from previous chapters, that a "type of Christ" was a person in the Old

Testament who "foreshadowed" or "prefigured" Christ in the New Testament. Joseph was rejected by his brothers. They hated him so much that they wanted to kill him. But instead, Joseph was brought to Egypt. He was sent there by God for an important reason. If Joseph had not been sold into slavery, he would not have been in a position to feed his family and save them from starvation. Joseph showed his love for his family by forgiving his brothers. He not only forgave them, but continued to show his love for them by moving them to Egypt. As Joseph continued to care for his family, so Christ continues to care for us. Jesus, too, was rejected by His people. Judas, one of His beloved Apostles, betrayed Jesus. And God the Father had a reason for sending His only Son to us. God the Father sent Christ to us to save us from our sins and to show us how to live as images of God. One day, when Jesus was teaching, He said to the people, "I am the living bread that came down from heaven; whoever eats this bread will live forever; and the bread that I will give is my flesh for the life of the world" (Jn 6:51). Jesus feeds us whenever we receive Holy Communion. Jesus loves us so much that He forgives us when we are sorry for the wrong choices we make. Jesus continues to show us His love and forgiveness in the sacrament of Reconciliation. It is in these ways that Joseph was a "type" of the Christ Who was to come.

God's Merciful Love

Why did God show Joseph His merciful love? God had made a covenant with Abraham, Isaac, and Jacob. But the covenant was not to be passed on to Joseph. You will discover, in later lessons, that it was Judah, Joseph's brother, who will receive the blessing of the covenant from their father, Jacob. How then does the story of Joseph fit in with the development of God's chosen people, the Israelites?

God wanted to save His chosen people from the famine that covered the entire land. You have already learned how Joseph cooperated with God to protect them. "God, therefore, sent me on ahead of you to ensure for you a remnant on earth and to save your lives in an extraordinary deliverance" (Gen 45:7). In this way, God showed His merciful love. God drew good out of Joseph's tragic situation. By saving Joseph and giving him the opportunity to prosper in Egypt, God saved His chosen people.

God continued to show His merciful love to the Israelites in their new home. Joseph's family lived in Goshen for four hundred years. During this time they grew from a family of seventy to more than three million men, women, and children. They lived under the protection of the Pharaoh. They were safe. During these years, there were many destructive wars in the land of Canaan. Had the Israelites stayed in Canaan, they surely would have experienced the effects of war. Instead, they prospered and multiplied in Egypt. Even after Joseph died and Egypt was ruled by pharaohs who made slaves of the Israelites, they were safe. God was making them ready to become a nation—a nation that would be led out of slavery and back to the Promised Land by a new leader, Moses.

REVIEW QUESTIONS

1. Why did Jacob send his sons to Egypt?
2. Why didn't Joseph's brothers recognize him?
3. Of what crime did Joseph accuse his brothers on their first journey?
4. What did Joseph's brothers have to do in order to prove the truth of their story?
5. Besides Benjamin, what else did Joseph's brothers bring with them on their second journey to Egypt?
6. Why did Joseph cry when he saw his brothers the second time?
7. What did Joseph have hidden in Benjamin's sack?
8. When did Joseph recognize that his brothers loved their father and each other?
9. Why did God send Joseph to Egypt?
10. How did Joseph show his brothers that he forgave them?
11. Describe Joseph's character.
12. In what ways is Joseph a "type of Christ"?
*13. How is God's merciful love shown in the story of Joseph?

Concepts of Faith

1. How is God's merciful love shown in the story of Joseph?
God drew good out of Joseph's situation. He saved Joseph from death and slavery. Through Joseph, God saved His chosen people from starvation and the effects of war.

Vocabulary

cistern: An underground container used for storing rainwater.

Pharaoh: The ruler or king of Egypt.

courtier: A person who attended the royal court.

chief steward: A person appointed by Pharaoh to supervise his business.

sage: A wise person who could predict the future and interpret dreams.

signet ring: A ring that held the stamp or seal of Pharaoh.

"type of Christ": A person in the Old Testament who foreshadowed, or prefigured, Christ in the New Testament.

Living the Lesson

Joseph is an important and memorable character of the Bible because he chose to act as an image of God. Even when he was treated unfairly, Joseph acted in a loving way.

Describe one situation in the story of Joseph that shows he acted as an image of God. Share your example with the class.

Think of a time when you or someone else was treated unfairly. How did this person react to the situation? Did this person act as an image of God? If not, how should this person have acted?

Prayers

Psalms 3 and 4. (Prayers of trust and confidence in God.)
"Act of Contrition".
Ten Commandments.
Sacrament of Reconciliation.

Map Activity (Worksheet 1)
Using the map on page 144, follow the journey of Joseph and his family to the land of Egypt.

1. *Draw a **solid line** connecting the cities mentioned in the following summary of Joseph's journeys:* Joseph was sent by Jacob to find his brothers. He left Hebron, traveled north as far as Dothan, met his brothers, and was sold into slavery. Joseph was taken by the Midianites along a trade route that stretched south along the Mediterranean Sea to Lower Egypt. Succoth and Memphis are two cities where Joseph might have been sold to Potiphar.

2. *Draw a **dashed line** connecting the following route:* Joseph's brothers made several trips to Egypt. They probably left their home in Hebron and traveled along the established trade route to a city in Lower Egypt. The final move of Joseph's family took them to the land of Goshen in Lower Egypt.

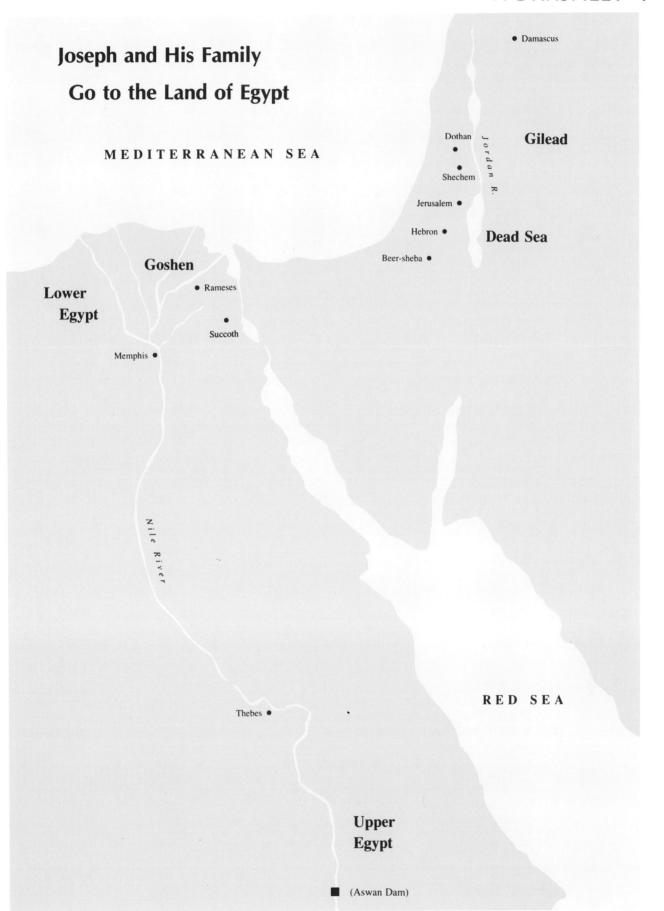

Joseph and His Family

Go to the Land of Egypt

MEDITERRANEAN SEA

Damascus

Dothan

Gilead

Jordan R.

Shechem

Jerusalem

Hebron

Dead Sea

Beer-sheba

Goshen

Lower Egypt

Rameses

Succoth

Memphis

Nile River

Thebes

RED SEA

Upper Egypt

(Aswan Dam)

Moses and the Flight to Freedom

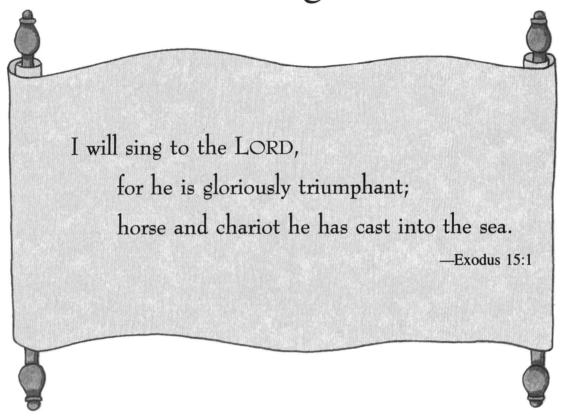

I will sing to the LORD,

for he is gloriously triumphant;

horse and chariot he has cast into the sea.

—Exodus 15:1

An Introduction to the Book of Exodus

Exodus is the second book of the *Pentateuch*. You will remember that the Pentateuch consists of the first five books of the Bible. These books are Genesis, Exodus, Leviticus, Numbers, and Deuteronomy. Lessons 10 and 11 will discuss the Book of Exodus. Its title comes from a Greek word meaning "going out" or "departure". The main character of Exodus is Moses. What do you remember about the life of Moses?

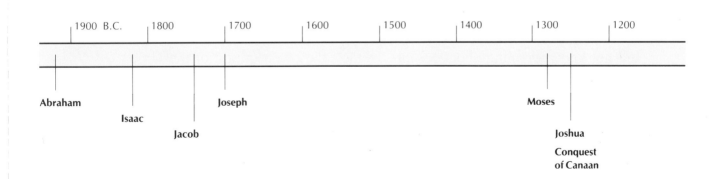

The stories that you might remember about Moses come from the Books of Exodus, Leviticus, Numbers, and Deuteronomy. Four out of the five books of the Pentateuch are devoted to telling the story of Moses. Who was Moses? Why is the story of Moses so important? Why did it take four books of the Bible to tell his story? How can a person who lived so long ago have anything to say to us now? What was God's message to the Israelites? What is God's message to us? The answers to these questions will be explored in Lessons 10, 11, and 12. Let's begin by finding out what happened to the Israelites after Joseph brought them to Egypt.

The Book of Exodus continues the history of God's chosen people, the Israelites. Genesis ended with the story of Joseph. Joseph reunited his family and moved all his relatives and their property to Egypt. There the Israelites lived under the protection of Joseph and the Hyksos pharaohs. The Hyksos pharaohs were not Egyptians. They were Asiatic people who had invaded and conquered Egypt. However, the Book of Exodus begins four hundred years after the time of Joseph! "Now Joseph and all his brothers and that whole generation died" (Ex 1:6). Egypt was no longer ruled by the Hyksos kings who had been friendly with the Israelites. The Hyksos rulers had been overthrown by the Egyptians. Look at the map on page 160.

The Egyptians were probably at the height of their military power. Upper and Lower Egypt had been united under a new dynasty of pharaohs. These pharaohs did not know anything about Joseph. In fact, they were afraid of the large number of Israelites living in Egypt: "Look how numerous and powerful the Israelite people are growing, more so than we ourselves!" (Ex 1:9). "The Egyptians, then, dreaded the Israelites and reduced them to cruel slavery, making life bitter for them with hard work in mortar and brick and all kinds of field work—the whole cruel fate of slaves" (Ex 1:12–14).

The Egyptians forced the Israelites to work as slaves on many building projects in the ruling cities of Thebes, Memphis, and Raamses. Great pyramids, palaces, and colossal statues were built to honor the powerful pharaohs and their many pagan gods. The Egyptians hoped that the Israelites would become weak under the hardships of such a life. But the Israelites continued to increase, just as God had promised in the covenant. Fearing that the Israelites would become too numerous to control, Pharaoh commanded, "Throw into the river every boy that is born to the Hebrews" (Ex 1:22). It was during this time that Moses was born.

REVIEW QUESTIONS

*1. Name the five books of the Pentateuch.
 2. What does the word *exodus* mean?
 3. Who is the main character of Exodus?
 4. What was the status of the Israelites at this time?
 5. Why did Pharaoh order every boy born to the Hebrews killed?

Read Exodus 2:1–10 or the following summary. Then continue with the next section, "Moses: An Egyptian or a Hebrew?"

A Summary of Exodus 2:1–10

A woman from the house of Levi gave birth to a healthy baby boy. She hid him for three months, because Pharaoh had commanded that all male Hebrew babies should be killed. When this baby's mother could not hide him any longer, she took a papyrus basket, made it watertight with bitumen and pitch, and laid the baby in it. Then she placed the basket among the reeds on the river bank. The baby's sister stood at a distance and watched over her brother.

The daughter of Pharaoh came down to the river to bathe. She saw the basket, opened it, and found the baby boy crying. She took pity on him and decided to keep him. The baby's sister stepped out from her hiding place and asked Pharaoh's daughter whether she should find a Hebrew woman to nurse the child. Pharaoh's daughter agreed, and so the sister brought her own mother to care for the baby. When the child was a little older, his mother brought him back to Pharaoh's daughter, who adopted him as her son. Because she had drawn him out of the water, Pharaoh's daughter named the baby Moses, which means "to draw out".

Moses: An Egyptian or a Hebrew?

God did not forget His promise to the chosen people. In the midst of their slavery God showed them His merciful love. How else could Moses have survived the terrible fate of the other Hebrew boys, if it had not been for God's merciful love? God drew good out of the evil of Pharaoh's command. God personally saved Moses. At first it seems strange that Moses should be adopted by the daughter of the Pharaoh—the same Pharaoh who had made the Israelites slaves. Now Moses, an Israelite by birth, would be raised as an Egyptian. But, as an Egyptian, Moses would learn many things that would help him to become a great leader. These events would serve a wonderful purpose in the life of Moses and God's chosen people. For Moses would lead the Israelites out of their slavery and into the Promised Land of the covenant.

What was it like for a Hebrew boy to be raised as an Egyptian? St. Luke wrote, in the Acts of the Apostles, "Moses was educated [in] all the wisdom of the Egyptians and was powerful in his words and deeds" (Acts 7:22). This means that Moses learned all those things that any Egyptian boy learned. He learned how to speak Egyptian and to read and write in hieroglyphics. He studied mathematics, the sciences, religion, music, art, and architecture. He probably practiced the many skills needed for sports, hunting, and warfare. He was given the best education possible. He was, after all, the adopted son of the royal princess. Moses grew up as an Egyptian.

One day, an occasion arose in which Moses had to choose between the Hebrews and the Egyptians. Moses was visiting one of the workplaces when he witnessed an Egyptian flogging a Hebrew. No one came to help the Hebrew slave. So Moses decided to defend the man. During the fight, the Egyptian was killed. By choosing to help the Hebrew slave, Moses renounced being an Egyptian. He knew that Pharaoh would seek to put him to death for killing an Egyptian. So Moses left Egypt and went to the land of Midian. (Refer to the map on page 160.)

Moses was befriended there by the family of Jethro, the priest of Midian. After living with the family for a time, Moses married Jethro's daughter, Zipporah. Zipporah and Moses had a son, whom he named Gershom. Gershom means "I am a stranger in a foreign land." While in the land of Midian, Moses lived the life of a semi-nomad, moving from place to place. Living in the desert was very different from living in Pharaoh's palace. But life in the desert prepared Moses to lead the long journey in the wilderness that would bring the Hebrew people to the Promised Land.

1. Tell about the birth and early life of Moses in your own words.
2. How is the early life of Moses an example of God's merciful love?
3. Why did Moses run away from Egypt to the land of Midian?
4. What happened to Moses in Midian?
5. How did life in the land of Midian prepare Moses to lead the Hebrew people?

The Call of Moses

Many years passed. A new Pharaoh reigned over the land of Egypt. The Israelites who lived there prayed that God would deliver them from the misery of their slavery. God heard their prayers and asked Moses to lead His chosen people out of the slavery of Egypt.

Read Exodus 3 for the scriptural account of the call of Moses, or read the following paragraph, which is a summary of this account.

A Summary of the Call of Moses (Ex 3)

One day Moses was tending the flock of his father-in-law, Jethro. He led his sheep across the desert to Mt. Horeb. While on the mountain Moses saw a burning bush and "was surprised to see that the bush, though on fire, was not consumed" (Ex 3:2). When Moses came over to get a closer look, God called out to him from the bush, "Moses! Moses!" He answered, "Here I am" (Ex 3:4). God told Moses to remove his sandals, because he was on holy ground. Then God said, "I am the God of your father, . . . the God of Abraham, the God of Isaac, the God of Jacob" (Ex 3:6). God told Moses that He had heard the cries from His people and knew that they were suffering. "Come now! I will send you to Pharaoh to lead my people, the Israelites, out of Egypt" (Ex 3:10).

But Moses was afraid. He did not think he could accomplish this tremendous task. God reassured Moses that He would be with him to help him and to guide him. God gave Moses a special staff, through which the people could see the power of God. Through it, God worked *miracles*. A miracle is an extraordinary event that shows the power of God. God told Moses that, at first, Pharaoh would choose not to let the Israelites go. God promised to help Moses convince Pharaoh and the Egyptians that He was all-powerful and that there were no other gods besides Him. When Moses still doubted that he could successfully speak to Pharaoh, God allowed Moses to ask his brother, Aaron, to help him accomplish this mission.

Moses said to God, "When I go to the Israelites and say to them, 'The God of your fathers has sent me to you', if they ask me, 'What is his name?' what am I to tell them?" God replied, "I am who am" (Ex 3:13–14). Then Moses went and did as the Lord had asked him.

A Discussion of the Call of Moses

It was on Mt. Horeb that Moses was called to lead the Israelites out of slavery. Another name for this mountain is Mt. Sinai. Ancient tradition identifies this mountain as Gebel Musa, which is located at the southern tip of the Sinai peninsula. (Refer to the map on page 160.) It was there that Moses saw the burning bush and heard the voice of God. You will read later in the Book of Exodus that this is also the mountain to which Moses brought the Israelites after their escape from Egypt and where Moses received the Ten Commandments. After his experiences on Mt. Horeb, Moses called it the "mountain of God".

Moses received his call from God in a very dramatic way. The burning bush and the special staff God gave to Moses would have convinced most of us that God was indeed powerful and not to be argued with. But Moses was most reluctant to become God's messenger. Moses tried more than once, five times in fact, to convince God that he was unworthy and not able to fulfill God's will. Each time Moses objected, God reassured him. God told Moses that He would always be with him.

God also gave Moses several visible signs to help him and the Israelites remember His presence. One sign of God's love, the fire first seen by Moses in the burning bush, remained with the Israelites in the form of a fiery cloud. You will read about the fiery cloud in later chapters of Exodus. The fire of God's love was visible to His people throughout their wanderings in the desert. It reminded them that God was ever-present.

That God is always present is what God meant when He told Moses that His name was "I am who am." There are many different names for God in the Old Testament. Yahweh is the Hebrew name for God that is often translated "I am who am". God chose this name to reveal Himself more clearly to the Hebrews. He is the Creator, the God Who always was, is now, and always will be, the God of their fathers, Abraham, Isaac, and Jacob, the God of the covenant, the God Who saves His people, the God Who is actively present at all times. He is the Lord.

In the next section, "Moses Confronts Pharaoh", you will read about more miracles. These miracles were extraordinary events that showed the power of God to both the Egyptians and to God's chosen people.

REVIEW QUESTIONS

1. What are several other names for the "mountain of God"?
2. In what spectacular way did God appear to Moses?
3. How did Moses respond when God asked him to be His messenger to Pharaoh?
4. How did God reassure Moses that he was indeed the right choice?
5. What visible sign did God use to show His presence?
*6. What does God's name, Yahweh, mean?
7. How did "I am Who am" describe God more clearly to the Hebrews?

Moses Confronts Pharaoh

Moses and his brother, Aaron, went to Pharaoh and said, "Thus says the LORD, the God of Israel: 'Let my people go' . . ." Pharaoh answered, "Who is the LORD, that I should heed his plea to let Israel go? I do not know the LORD: even if I did, I would not let Israel go" (Ex 5:1–2). Then Aaron threw Moses' staff on the ground, and it changed into a snake. Pharaoh ordered his magicians to do the same. Their staffs also turned into snakes. But Moses' staff swallowed their staffs. Yet Pharaoh remained stubborn and obstinate. He would not listen to them, just as God had foretold.

Ten times Moses and Aaron went to Pharaoh and asked that he let God's people go. Ten times Pharaoh stubbornly refused. After each refusal, the Egyptians were afflicted with a plague. A *plague* is a disaster, or calamity, that causes widespread disease and many deaths. The plagues came because Pharaoh rejected God and His loving care. When Pharaoh sinned, he hurt himself and his people. The list on page 155 summarizes the ten plagues.

A Discussion of the Plagues

Many people have attempted to explain the plagues as natural phenomena. It is true that nine of the ten plagues were events that natural causes could possibly have produced. Still, their timing and the way they occurred make a merely natural explanation very unlikely.

The Nile River often flooded in July and August. The excessive flood waters contained small organisms known as flagellates, which caused the water to turn red and also killed the fish. The dead fish floated ashore, and the frogs, which fed on the fish, followed. Then the frogs became infected. The gnats and flies breeded freely in the stagnant flood waters. The fifth plague was probably anthrax, which could have been carried by the dead frogs. The boils, or skin irritations, of the sixth plague could have been caused by gnat and fly bites. Hail and thunderstorms, the seventh plague, were common in February and could have destroyed the flax and barley. Again, in the eighth plague, the swarms of locusts are not uncommon at the time of year when the wheat is harvested. The desert windstorms called *khamsin* could have caused the darkening of the sky, the ninth plague.

God governs the universe and cares for all people. This takes a tremendous amount of power. When God's care was rejected by the Egyptians, they also rejected the power with which He governs all things. The Egyptians no longer wanted God's powerful protection. God honored their rejection and permitted the plagues to occur to show the Egyptians the seriousness of their sins. There are three considerations that support this reasoning. First, each of the plagues was announced ahead of time, and each ended when God, through Moses, said so. Second, the plagues went far beyond their usual intensity. They were disasters, total catastrophes. Third, and most dramatic, only the Egyptians were affected by the plagues. The land of Goshen was not infected with disease, flies, or gnats. Its water was not polluted. No Israelite suffered from skin irritations. The hail and locusts did not destroy their crops. The only light to be seen in Egypt during the three days of darkness was in the land of Goshen.

During the time of the plagues, God showed the Israelites His merciful love. Because they chose to love God, the Israelites were spared from all of the tragic effects of the plagues. The Egyptians, however, chose not to love God. By announcing the plagues ahead of time, God gave the Egyptians, through their leader, Pharaoh, an opportunity to know and to love Him. But each time, the Egyptians rejected God. They chose not to love Him. When the Egyptians chose not to love God, they sinned and rejected God's care. The plagues were the result of their sin. God, however, drew good out of the tragedy of the plagues. Pharaoh finally freed the Israelites from their slavery in Egypt and let the people go.

When Pharaoh first met with Moses, he said, "Who is the LORD . . .? I do not know the LORD" (Ex 5:2). The Egyptians did not know God. Furthermore, the Israelites did not know the Lord. They had lived under the influence of the pagan Egyptians for four hundred years. They had forgotten Who the God of the covenant was. God wanted to reveal Himself to them. He wanted to show them that the God of Israel was all-powerful. He was the only true God. The gods of the Egyptians were false gods. Not even Re, the sun-god of Egypt, could brighten the darkness of the ninth plague. None of their gods could save

The Ten Plagues

First Plague: Water Turned into Blood (Ex 7:14–24)
The Nile River was the source of life for Egypt. The pollution of its waters killed the fish and made the water undrinkable.

Second Plague: The Frogs (Ex 7:25–29; 8:1–11)
The river became so filled with frogs that the frogs left the riverbanks and came into the houses of the Egyptians.

Third Plague: The Gnats (Ex 8:12–15)
Fourth Plague: The Flies (Ex 8:16–28)
During the third and fourth plagues the land of Egypt was infested with thick swarms of gnats and flies.

Fifth Plague: The Pestilence (Ex 9:1–7)
During this plague, all the livestock of the Egyptians became diseased and died.

Sixth Plague: The Boils (Ex 9:8–12)
Moses took a handful of soot from a furnace and, in the presence of Pharaoh, scattered it toward the sky. It caused festering boils on all the Egyptians.

Seventh Plague: The Hail (Ex 9:13–35)
A fierce hailstorm fell upon the land of Egypt. "It struck down every man and beast that was in the open throughout the land of Egypt; it beat down every growing thing and splintered every tree in the fields" (Ex 9:25).

Eighth Plague: The Locusts (Ex 10:1–20)
Locusts entered the country of Egypt and ate any plants that had survived the hailstorm. The locusts were so numerous that they even entered the houses of the Egyptians.

Ninth Plague: The Darkness (Ex 10:21–29)
Total darkness descended upon the land of Egypt for three days.

Tenth Plague: The Death of the Firstborn (Ex 11)
The firstborn in every house of the Egyptians was slain, as well as the firstborn of all their animals.

the Egyptians. The Egyptians learned that the God of Israel was the only true God. The Israelites were reminded by the plagues that the God of the covenant was Yahweh. They were reminded of the loving power of God. They would forever remember that He was actively present among them. He was "I am Who am".

1. What is a plague?
2. How did Pharaoh respond each time Moses asked him to let the Israelites go?
3. Were the plagues caused by natural phenomena or were they the result of the Egyptians' rejection of God's care?
4. Why did the Egyptians, and not the Israelites, suffer the effects of the plagues?
5. How did God show His merciful love to the Israelites through the plagues?
6. How did the plagues demonstrate that God was Yahweh?

The First Passover

The tenth plague, the death of the firstborn, is first described in Exodus, chapter 11. In this chapter, Moses gave Pharaoh a final warning of what would happen if he did not agree to let the Israelites go. Pharaoh, however, refused to change his mind. After each plague, the Scripture text ends by describing Pharaoh's attitude as "obdurate" or "obstinate", and he "would not listen". Pharaoh chose to harden his heart. His own willful pride would not allow him to let the Israelites go. Pharaoh did not think of the people he ruled, nor of his own family. He chose to do only what he wanted. The tenth plague was the consequence of his choice.

The consequence of the tenth plague, as with the other nine plagues, did not affect the Israelites. God gave the Israelites specific instructions to follow during the tenth plague so that death would "pass over" them.

Read Exodus 12. The scriptural text includes the instructions for the Passover meal, the death of the firstborn, and Pharaoh's permission for the Israelites to go. The following text is only a summary of these events.

A Summary of the First Passover (Ex 12)

These were the instructions God gave to Moses and Aaron:

1. Passover would take place on the tenth day of "this month" (March or April).
2. Each family must obtain an unblemished year-old male lamb.
3. Four days later, "with the whole assembly of Israel present, it [the lamb] shall be slaughtered during the evening twilight."
4. "Take some of its blood and apply it to the two doorposts and the lintel of every house."
5. "That same night they shall eat its roasted flesh with unleavened bread and bitter herbs."
6. "Whatever is left over in the morning shall be burned up."
7. "This is how you are to eat it: with your loins girt, sandals on your feet and your staff in hand, you shall eat like those who are in flight."
8. "For seven days you must eat unleavened bread."
9. The first and seventh day shall be held sacred, without any work.
10. This feast day shall be observed for all generations.

Those Israelites who observed the Passover instructions, whose houses were marked with the blood of the sacrificial lamb, were spared from the tenth plague. But Pharaoh and all the Egyptians were not spared. During the night Pharaoh summoned Moses and Aaron and said, "Leave my people at once, you and the Israelites with you!" The Egyptians were so anxious to have the Israelites go that they gave them gold, silver, and clothing to hasten their departure.

A Discussion of the Feast of Passover and the Mass

The Passover was a new beginning for the Israelites. Their liberation from Egypt was to be remembered for all ages to come. The instructions given to the Israelites about this new feast reminded them of God's love for them. Israel was God's chosen people, His firstborn nation, represented by the lamb. The bitter herbs reminded them of the suffering they had endured as slaves of the Egyptians. The unleavened bread reminded them of the haste of their departure from the land of Egypt. Today, Passover is one of the more important celebrations in the Jewish religion. It is celebrated to honor God, Who saved their ancestors from slavery.

The Passover sacrifice of the Old Testament is a "type" of the Mass instituted by Jesus in the New Testament.

More than twelve hundred years after Moses and the Israelites ate the first Passover meal, Jewish people were still celebrating this historic event. When Jesus entered Jerusalem with His Apostles, they were there to celebrate the feast of Passover. On Holy Thursday, Jesus transformed the Passover meal into the first Mass. The unleavened bread that the Israelites ate was a "type" of the Holy Eucharist, the Body and Blood of Christ. The firstborn lamb, pure and unblemished, is Jesus, the Son of God. You may have heard Jesus called the "Paschal Lamb". *Pascha* is the Aramaic word for the lamb of the Passover. The Feast of Passover is remembered and fulfilled each time Mass is celebrated.

The Passover sacrifice of the Old Testament is also a "type" of the death of Jesus in the New Testament. In Exodus 12:46, God told Moses that in preparing the lamb, "You shall not break any of its bones." On Calvary, when the soldiers saw that Jesus was already dead, they did not break his legs. "For this happened so that the scripture passage might be fulfilled: 'Not a bone of it will be broken'" (Jn 19:36). The blood of the lamb that saved the Israelites from death is now the Blood of Christ. He is the Lamb of God, Who takes away the sins of the world. Christ saved us from slavery to sin and from eternal death by His loving sacrifice on the cross. This sacrifice is re-presented at each Mass.

REVIEW QUESTIONS

1. Why was the tenth plague a consequence of Pharaoh's pride?
2. What specific instruction was given to the Israelites so that death would "pass over" their house on the night of the tenth plague?
3. Lamb, bitter herbs, and unleavened bread were eaten during the Passover meal to remind the Israelites of specific things. What did each of these three foods represent?

4. Why is Passover an important celebration in the Jewish religion?

*5. Why was the Passover a "type of Christ"?

6. When did Jesus transform the Passover meal into the first Mass?

7. Whom does the lamb represent in the New Testament?

8. How did Jesus, the Lamb of God, save us from the slavery of sin and from eternal death?

9. What is the unleavened bread of the New Testament?

10. When is the Feast of Passover remembered and fulfilled?

The Exodus Begins

Refer to the map on page 160.

When the Israelites left Rameses (sometimes spelled Raamses), Moses did not lead them along the shortest trade route to Canaan. The Philistines occupied this territory, and the Israelites were not prepared to do battle against them. Instead, Moses was instructed by the Lord to head for Succoth. The Scripture text says that there were "about six hundred thousand men on foot, not counting the children. A crowd of mixed ancestry also went up with them, besides their livestock, very numerous flocks and herds" (Ex 12:37–38). Some biblical scholars have estimated that the number of people, including women and children, could have totaled two and a half million! Moses also took the bones of Joseph with him, as Joseph had requested before he died. From Succoth the people moved to Etham, near the edge of the desert. God gave the Israelites a visible sign of His presence that remained with them until the day they entered the land of Canaan. "The Lord preceded them, in the daytime by means of a column of cloud to show them the way, and at night by means of a column of fire to give them light" (Ex 13:21). Their next campsite was at Baalzephon, opposite the sea.

The Crossing of the Red Sea

Look at the map on page 160. The Red Sea is the long body of water separating Egypt from Arabia. Extending northward toward the Great Sea (the Mediterranean) are two narrower bodies of water which form a V. The Gulf of Suez borders the western Sinai peninsula, while the Gulf of Aqaba borders the eastern side. North of the Gulf of Suez are the Bitter Lakes. It is here, perhaps at Little Bitter Lake, that the crossing of the Red Sea took place. In this instance, the "Red Sea" is probably a mistranslation for "Sea of Reeds". The Sea of Reeds would most likely have been one of the Bitter Lakes.

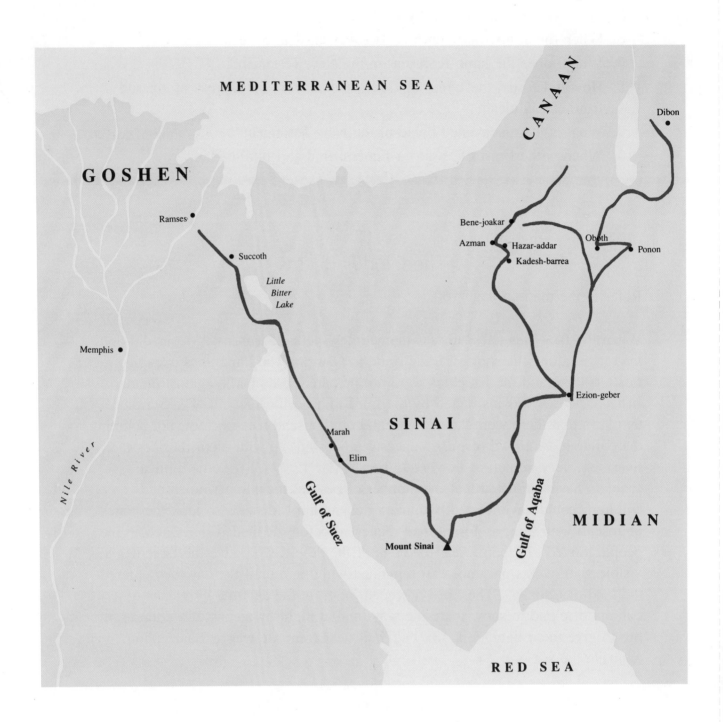

MEDITERRANEAN SEA

CANAAN

Dibon

GOSHEN

Ramses

Succoth

Little
Bitter
Lake

Bene-joakar

Azman

Hazar-addar

Oboth

Ponon

Kadesh-barrea

Memphis

SINAI

Ezion-geber

Marah

Elim

Nile River

Gulf of Suez

Gulf of Aqaba

MIDIAN

Mount Sinai

RED SEA

Read Exodus 14:5–31. The following is a summary of the biblical account.

A Summary of Exodus 14:5–31

After the Israelites left Egypt, Pharaoh regretted that he had let them go. He ordered his whole army, "six hundred first-class chariots and all the other chariots of Egypt, with warriors on them all", to bring them back. When the Israelites saw the Egyptians approaching, they cried out in fear to Moses. "Why did you bring us out of Egypt? . . . Far better for us to be the slaves of the Egyptians than to die in the desert" (Ex 14:12). Moses reassured the Israelites

that the Lord would fight for them. Then God told Moses to lift his staff over the sea. When Moses did as the Lord said, the sea split in two, and the people walked across on dry land to the other side. When the Egyptians followed them, the Lord said to Moses, "Stretch out your hand over the sea, that the water may flow back upon the Egyptians, upon their chariots and their charioteers" (Ex 14:26). When Israel "beheld the great power that the LORD had shown against the Egyptians, they feared the LORD and believed in Him and in His servant Moses" (Ex 14:31).

A Discussion of the Crossing of the Red Sea

Even after ten plagues, Pharaoh had not learned Who the God of Israel was! Pharaoh rejected God and His care for the Egyptians. Again he "hardened his heart". Pharaoh regretted that he had released such a large free labor force of slaves. He ordered his entire army to pursue the Israelites. The Israelites, also, had not learned about their God. Rather than trusting in God to defend them, they panicked and complained to Moses. "Why did you do this to us? . . . Far better for us to be the slaves of the Egyptians than to die in the desert" (Ex 14:11–12). Again Moses reassured them. "The LORD himself will fight for you; you have only to keep still" (Ex 14:14). And so God once again came to the rescue of His chosen people. As with the plagues, God used a natural event, "a strong east wind" (Ex 14: 21), with miraculous results, the parting of the waters. By impressing the Israelites with His overwhelming power, God showed them His merciful love. God drew good out of the suffering of the Israelites. The Egyptians would no longer be able to enslave God's people. God showed His people that He was Yahweh. He would always be with them, to defend them, to care for them. They, in turn, showed God that they were His chosen people: "They feared the LORD and believed in Him and in His servant Moses" (Ex 14:31).

The Israelites then praised God in song and dance. "The prophetess Miriam, Aaron's sister, took a tambourine in her hand, while all the women went out after her with tambourines, dancing, and she led them in the refrain:

> Sing to the LORD, for he is gloriously triumphant;
> horse and chariot he has cast into the sea.
> —Exodus 15:21

REVIEW QUESTIONS

1. What visible signs did God give the Israelites to show them His presence and lead them to the Promised Land?
2. Why did Pharaoh pursue the Israelites?
3. How did the Israelites react when they saw the Egyptians?
4. How did God show the Israelites His merciful love in the Exodus from Egypt?
5. How did the Israelites show God that they loved Him?

Concepts of Faith

1. **Name the five books of the Pentateuch.**
   Genesis, Exodus, Leviticus, Numbers, Deuteronomy.
2. **What does God's name, Yahweh, mean?**
   I am who am.
3. **Why was the Passover sacrifice a "type of Christ"?**
   The Passover sacrifice prefigured the death of Jesus, which is re-presented in the Mass.
4. **How did God show His merciful love to the Israelites?**
   God drew good out of the suffering of the Israelites. God freed the Israelites from slavery and showed them His love. They, in turn, believed in Him and were drawn closer to Him.

Vocabulary

Exodus: The second book of the Pentateuch; the title means "going out" or "departure".

Pentateuch: The first five books of the Bible: Genesis, Exodus, Leviticus, Numbers, and Deuteronomy.

plague: A disaster or calamity that causes widespread disease and many deaths.

miracle: An extraordinary event that shows the power of God.

Living the Lesson

"I have called you by name: you are mine" (Isaiah 43:1).

God is our Creator. He made us in His image. Each one of us is unique, that is, no one of us is exactly like another. Therefore, God's call to each one of us is personal and unique. Like His call to Moses, God calls each of us to act as His image. Like Moses, each of us is given the choice to respond to God's call. Like Moses, we are often reluctant to say "Yes" to God's call. Like Moses, we become better images of God when we finally do say "Yes" to God's call.

Sometimes it takes a while to figure out what "the call" is. In general, we know that God calls us to act as His images. But what does that mean specifically? How do we respond to God's call on a day-to-day basis? How do we answer God's call as a sixth grader? as a member of a family? as a friend? Is God's call to us something He wants us to *do*? Or is it something He wants us to *be*? Is there a difference between the two? Do we have to wait to choose a vocation before we answer God's call? Do only adults have a call from God? Why are we reluctant to say "Yes" to God's call?

Use these questions to help discuss the meaning of God's personal call to each of us.

Prayers

Exodus 15:1–18: The Song of Moses.

Psalm 103:1–10.

Psalms 105 and 106. (These Psalms recount the history of Israel from Abraham to Moses. Psalm 105 emphasizes God's goodness to Israel, while Psalm 106 emphasizes the rebellious spirit of the Israelites despite God's goodness to them.)

The "Our Father".

The word *reluctant* can be defined as: unwilling, hesitant, struggling against, opposing. These words certainly describe Moses' initial response to God's call to him to convince Pharaoh to free the Israelites. Five times Moses objected to God's call. Five times God responded to the objection and reassured Moses that he need not be reluctant to accept the call.

Listed below are five scriptural references. Read each passage in the Bible. Then write the objection Moses gave to God, and God's response to Moses.

1. Exodus 3:11   Moses' objection: _____

   _____

   God's response: _____

   _____

2. Exodus 3:13   Moses' objection: _____

   _____

   God's response: _____

   _____

3. Exodus 4:1   Moses' objection: _____

   _____

   God's response: _____

   _____

4. Exodus 4:10   Moses' objection: _____

   _____

   God's response: _____

   _____

5. Exodus 4:13   Moses' objection: _____

   _____

   God's response: _____

   _____

The authors who were inspired to write the Bible used many different names for God. Often, the names they used, originally written in Hebrew, were difficult to translate exactly into other languages. The different translations added to the many names of God. Some of the names of God, such as King, are titles. Some names, such as Creator and Judge, describe an action of God. Other names, such as God of the Hebrews, describe God's relationship to a group of people. Still others, such as God of Abraham, describe God's relationship with an individual. Many of the names describe God's attributes by comparing Him to something else. The following verses from Psalm 18 give an example.

> I love you, O LORD, my strength,
> O LORD, my rock, my fortress, my deliverer.
> My God, my rock of refuge, my shield,
> the horn of my salvation, my stronghold!   —Psalm 18:1–3

Listed below are twenty-five scriptural references. Find the biblical words in each passage that describe or name God. Write the name of God on the line for each scriptural reference.

Scriptural Reference   *Names of God*

1. **Exodus 3:14**   _____

2. **Genesis 2:4**   _____

3. **Genesis 14:18**   _____

4. **Genesis 21:33**   _____

5. **Genesis 33:20**   _____

6. **Isaiah 1:4**   _____

7. **Isaiah 40:28**   _____

8. **Genesis 18:25**   _____

9. **Jeremiah 10:7** _____

10. **Deuteronomy 32:4** _____

11. **Psalm 23:1** _____

12. **Psalm 18:2–3** _____

13. **Psalm 27:1** _____

14. **Psalm 37:39** _____

15. **Psalm 84:12** _____

16. **Psalm 89:27** _____

17. **Psalm 91:1** _____

18. **Psalm 115:9** _____

19. **Psalm 121:5** _____

20. **Isaiah 1** _____

21. **Isaiah 41:14** _____

22. **Isaiah 42:13** _____

23. **Isaiah 45:9** _____

24. **Jeremiah 2:13** _____

25. **Hosea 13:7–8** _____

The "Our Father" is one of the first prayers you learned. You might have memorized it when you were as young as four. Now that you are older, the prayers you have memorized can have a deeper meaning. As you study the story of Moses in Lessons 10, 11, and 12, the "Our Father" will be examined, with special emphasis on certain phrases appropriate to the lesson.

Read the words of the "Our Father", printed below. Pay particular attention to the phrases printed in *italics*. After each phrase, write a brief explanation of its importance in light of what you have learned in this lesson.

> Our Father Who art in heaven, *hallowed be Thy name*; Thy kingdom come; *Thy will be done* on earth as it is in heaven. Give us this day our daily bread; and forgive us our trespasses as we forgive those who trespass against us, and lead us not into temptation, *but deliver us from evil*. Amen.

hallowed be Thy name:

_____

_____

_____

Thy will be done:

_____

_____

_____

but deliver us from evil:

_____

_____

_____

The Israelites and God's Covenant of Love

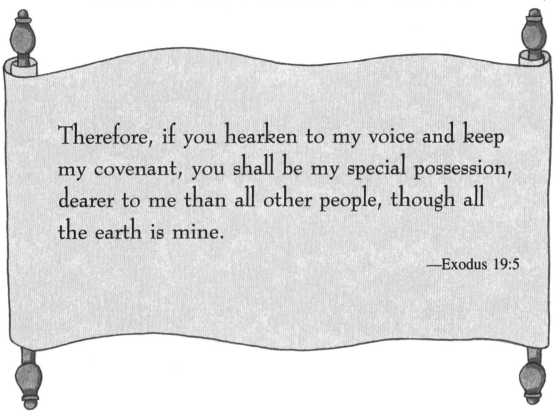

Therefore, if you hearken to my voice and keep my covenant, you shall be my special possession, dearer to me than all other people, though all the earth is mine.

—Exodus 19:5

God Cares for His Chosen People

After God saved the Israelites from the Egyptians at the Red Sea, Moses and the Israelites began their long journey to the promised land of Canaan. Look at the map on page 160. The Sinai peninsula is a continuation of the Arabian Desert. The land is dry and mountainous. It is a desert, a wilderness. It was through this wilderness that Moses led the Israelites. The Israelites were not used to such harsh conditions. Although they had been slaves in Egypt, at least they had food, water, and a roof over their heads. Here in the desert the Israelites found themselves without any of these necessities.

What is more, the Israelites forgot that God was with them. Their hunger and thirst soon made them forget that God had delivered them from slavery and had saved them from the Egyptians at the Red Sea. They forgot to trust in God's loving care. God, however, did not forget His chosen people. He constantly reminded them that He was with them. You have already read in the previous lesson that God gave them a visible sign of His presence in the form of a cloud by day and a pillar of fire by night. These signs remained with the Israelites throughout their long journey.

God also provided for the physical needs of His people. Exodus 15:22–27 and 17:1–7 are two accounts of how God miraculously provided water for His people. God also provided the Israelites with food. The miracle of the quail and manna is described in Exodus 16. The *manna* looked like small white wafers of bread. Because the manna was a gift from God, the Israelites called it "bread from heaven". "The Israelites ate this manna for forty years, . . . until they reached the borders of Canaan" (Ex 16:35). In the New Testament, Jesus referred to manna as a type of the Holy Eucharist. Just as the manna gave life to the Israelites in the desert, so Jesus, in the Holy Eucharist, gives eternal life to us. Jesus said, "I am the living bread that came down from heaven; whoever eats this bread will live forever; and the bread that I will give is my flesh for the life of the world" (Jn 6:51).

God showed the Israelites in many ways that He loved them. God took care of their physical needs. Moreover, God knew that the Israelites needed to learn how to act as His images. It was for this reason that God gave the Israelites the Ten Commandments.

The Covenant at Mount Sinai

Look at the map on page 160. Find Mount Sinai, located near the southern tip of the Sinai peninsula. It took the Israelites three months to travel from the Red Sea to Mount Sinai. When they arrived, Moses went up the mountain to meet God. God told Moses that He wanted to enter into a covenant with the Israelites. Do you remember what a covenant is? A covenant is (1) an act of merciful love between God and people, and (2) a promise to continue that love, (3) expressed in words and deed.

Read Exodus 19:5–9 for the scriptural account of God's promise to the Israelites and their response to Him.

God promised to make the Israelites His chosen people, "dearer to me than all other people, . . . a kingdom of priests, a holy nation" (Ex 19:5–6). In return, the Israelites promised to listen to God's voice and to follow the Ten Commandments. Moses explained God's message to the Israelites, and they agreed to everything God said. When Moses told God that the Israelites agreed to the covenant, God told Moses that He would show Himself to the Israelites in a dramatic way. "I am coming to you in a dense cloud, so that when the people hear me speaking with you, they may always have faith in you also" (Ex 19:9). Then God asked the Israelites to take three days to prepare themselves for His coming. On the third day, God showed Himself to the Israelites.

Read Exodus 19:16–19 for the scriptural description of God's dramatic coming.

God showed Himself to the Israelites in a dramatic way. Scripture describes God's appearance with thunder and lightning, trumpet blasts, and fire and smoke. When God shows Himself in such a spectacular way, it is called a *theophany*. This word means "a showing forth of God". God wanted to impress the Israelites with His wonderful power so that they would remember their promise of the covenant. After God showed Himself to the Israelites, Moses again went up the mountain to meet God.

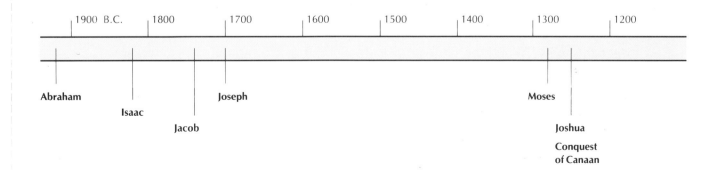

Then God gave to Moses His new covenant of love, the Ten Commandments.

Read Exodus 20:1–17.

The Ten Commandments

1. I, the LORD, am your God, you will not have other gods besides me.
2. You will not take the name of the LORD your God in vain.
3. Remember to keep holy the sabbath day.
4. Honor your father and your mother.
5. You will not kill.
6. You will not commit adultery.
7. You will not steal.
8. You will not bear false witness against your neighbor.
9. You will not covet your neighbor's wife.
10. You will not covet anything that belongs to your neighbor.

A Discussion of the Ten Commandments

The Ten Commandments are also called the *Decalogue*, which literally means "ten words". The Ten Commandments are directions God gives us so that we can act as Christ acted. Because we are made in God's image, we should want to act this way. When we choose to follow the Ten Commandments, we are really choosing to show God our love. God wants us to love Him, but God does not force us to love Him. He asks us to make a choice. When we follow the Ten Commandments we make the right choice. We act as images of God. When we choose not to follow the Ten Commandments we sin. We hurt God, ourselves, and others.

Common Laws

In addition to the Ten Commandments, God gave Moses the authority to establish laws for the Israelites. These laws showed the Israelites how to put the Ten Commandments into practice. Many of these laws were similar in form to the ancient laws of Mesopotamia, in particular, the laws contained in the famous Code of Hammurabi. Hammurabi was a king of Babylon who lived during the time of Moses. Biblical scholars think that Moses simply incorporated into Hebrew law many of the common laws of his time. These were laws dealing with personal injury and property damage, social laws (such as care for the poor and suffering), and religious laws of worship.

When Moses came down from Mount Sinai, he relayed God's word to the Israelites. All the people agreed to follow God's word. As a sign of their acceptance of the covenant, the Israelites built an altar and offered sacrifices to God. They also built around the altar twelve pillars, which represented the twelve tribes of Israel. Then Moses wrote down all the words of God in the Book of the Covenant. When God saw that the Israelites had agreed to follow the covenant, He asked Moses to come up the mountain again. "Come up to me on the mountain and, while you are there, I will give you the stone tablets on which I have written the commandments intended for their instruction" (Ex 24:12). Moses ascended Mount Sinai and stayed there forty days and nights.

REVIEW QUESTIONS

1. Describe the mood of the Israelites as they wandered throughout the desert.
2. How did God respond to the needs of His chosen people?
3. What is manna, and how is it a "type" of the Eucharist?
*4. What are the Ten Commandments?
*5. List the Ten Commandments.
*6. Why should we choose to follow the Ten Commandments?
7. What is a covenant?
8. Why are the Ten Commandments a covenant?
9. What is another word for the Ten Commandments?
10. Why did God give Moses the authority to establish common laws?
11. What are some examples of common laws?
12. What signs did the Israelites give God to show their acceptance of the covenant?

The Covenant Is Broken

The Israelites soon became impatient. Moses had been gone from them for a long time. They feared that something might have happened to him on the mountain. They forgot to trust in God. So they complained to Aaron and said to him, "Come, make us a god who will be our leader; as for the man Moses who brought us out of the land of Egypt, we do not know what has happened to him" (Ex 32:1). So Aaron instructed the people to gather all their gold jewelry. He melted the gold and fashioned a golden calf out of it. "Early the next day the people offered holocausts and brought peace offerings. Then they sat down to eat and drink, and rose up to revel" (Ex 32:6).

The Israelites had broken the first of the Ten Commandments. They did not show their love for God in the right way. They had promised not to worship false gods. By worshiping the golden calf, the Israelites had degraded both God and themselves. When God saw that the Israelites had broken their relationship with Him, He was disappointed. The Israelites had rejected God's loving care. They had chosen to subject themselves to harm. Moses pleaded with God and begged Him to save the Israelites from the consequences of their sin. God agreed to give the Israelites another chance. God showed them His merciful love. Then Moses came down from the mountain. "As he drew near the camp, he saw the calf and the dancing. With that, Moses' wrath flared up, so that he threw the tablets down and broke them on the base of the mountain. Taking the calf they had made, he fused it in the fire and then ground it down to powder, which he scattered on the water and made the Israelites drink" (Ex 32:19–20).

The smashing of the tablets of the Ten Commandments symbolized the breaking of the covenant. The sin the Israelites committed was very serious. Yet God was merciful to His chosen people. Even though the Israelites had broken the covenant, God did not abandon them. God renewed His covenant with them. As a sign of the renewed covenant, God said to Moses, "Cut two stone tablets like the former, that I may write on them the commandments which were on the former tablets that you broke" (Ex 34:1). Moses again spent forty days and forty nights on Mount Sinai. When he came down from the mountain, his face was so radiant that the Israelites were in awe at the power and wonder of God.

The Tabernacle and Its Furnishings

God knew that the Israelites needed a place where they could come together to worship Him. He told them to build a place of worship, which was called the *Tabernacle*. The Tabernacle was also called by several other names: the Dwelling, the Sanctuary, and the Tent of Meeting refer to the same structure. You can think of the Tabernacle as a portable temple or church.

Within the Tabernacle was placed the *Ark of the Covenant*. The Ark of the Covenant was a chest in which were placed the stone tablets inscribed with the Ten Commandments. God gave Moses specific instructions about how to build both the Tabernacle and the Ark of the Covenant. Many other furnishings and religious articles that decorated the Tabernacle are described in the remaining chapters of Exodus.

Read Exodus 25:10–22 for a detailed description of the Ark of the Covenant.

After the Tabernacle was built and all the furnishings were completed, God made His presence known. "In the daytime the cloud of the LORD was seen over the Dwelling; whereas at night, fire was seen in the cloud by the whole house of Israel in all the stages of their journey" (Ex 40:38). In this way the Israelites were reminded that God was always with them.

The Importance of the Book of Exodus

The Book of Exodus is one of the more important books of the Old Testament. The Book of Genesis traces the beginnings, or origin, of the Israelites. The Book of Exodus continues the story and relates the events that formed the Israelites into God's chosen people. In the Book of Exodus, God fulfilled the covenant first made with Abraham and inherited by Isaac and Jacob. God promised to bless them with many descendants and to make of them a great nation, His holy nation. When these descendants agreed to follow the covenant made on Mount Sinai, they agreed to be God's special people. When they agreed to live by the Ten Commandments, they agreed to live as images of God.

I II III IV V VI VII VIII IX X

When we agree to follow this same covenant made on Mount Sinai so long ago, we agree to be God's special people, too. When we agree to live by the Ten Commandments, we agree to live as images of God. The Book of Exodus continues to play an important role in our daily lives, even though it was written thousands of years ago.

REVIEW QUESTIONS

1. How did the Israelites break their covenant with God?
2. What was the Tabernacle?
3. What was the Ark of the Covenant?
4. Why is the Book of Exodus important?
5. How can God's message found in the Book of Exodus continue to play an important role in our lives?

Concepts of Faith

1. What are the Ten Commandments?
The Ten Commandments are directions God gives us so that we can act as Christ acted.

2. List the Ten Commandments.

1. I, the LORD, am your God, you will not have other gods besides me.
2. You will not take the name of the LORD your God in vain.
3. Remember to keep holy the sabbath day.
4. Honor your father and your mother.
5. You will not kill.
6. You will not commit adultery.
7. You will not steal.
8. You will not bear false witness against your neighbor.
9. You will not covet your neighbor's wife.
10. You will not covet anything that belongs to your neighbor.

3. Why should we choose to follow the Ten Commandments?
We should choose to follow the Ten Commandments because by following them we become better images of God.

Vocabulary

manna: Bread from heaven; small white wafers of bread.

covenant: (1) an act of merciful love between God and people, and (2) a promise to continue that love, (3) expressed in words and deeds.

theophany: "A showing forth of God".

Decalogue: The Ten Commandments; literally, "ten words".

Ark of the Covenant: A chest built as a container for the stone tablets on which the Ten Commandments were written.

Tabernacle (Old Testament): A place of worship; also called the Tent of Meeting, the Sanctuary, or the Dwelling.

Living the Lesson

The First Commandment
I, the LORD, am your God, you will not have other gods besides me.
In the First Commandment we learn that there is only one God. God created us in His image because He loves us. We should love Him with all our hearts and try to become better images of Him.

When the First Commandment says, "You will not have other gods besides me", it means that God should be the most important Person in our lives. Our parents, friends, and relatives are important to us, and God wants us to love them. But God is even more important. He must come first in our lives. Sometimes people will "love" other things more than they should. Money, possessions, or drugs become the most important things in their lives. These things become "other gods". When we choose to "love" these "other gods", we sin against the First Commandment. We hurt God, ourselves, and others because we are not acting as God's images.

How can we live the First Commandment?

_____

_____

_____

The Second Commandment
You will not take the name of the LORD your God in vain.
Because God should be the most important Person in our lives, His name should always be used in a reverent way. God deserves our love and respect. When we pray to God or talk about God to others, we should use His name in a respectful way. The respect that we should have for God's name extends, of course, to His Son, Jesus Christ, and to the Holy Spirit. In addition, the names of the saints should be said respectfully, because they acted as God's images. Sacred or holy objects, such as a crucifix or the Bible, should also be treated respectfully. These things are reminders of God and His love for us. As images of God, we should show a reverence for God and for all His creations.

When we choose to use God's name with disrespect, that is, "in vain", we hurt God, ourselves, and others. For example, cursing and swearing are improper uses of God's name, intended to hurt other people. Using bad language is demeaning and degrading, because it is disrespectful to God, Who created all of us and all of creation to reflect His love and goodness.

How can we live the Second Commandment?

_____

_____

_____

The Third Commandment

Remember to keep holy the sabbath day.

God asks us in the Third Commandment to come together to worship Him at Mass on certain days. The "sabbath day" includes all Sundays and all Holy Days. The Holy Days in the United States are:

December 8	Immaculate Conception
December 25	Christmas
January 1	Mary, Mother of God
40 days after Easter	Ascension Thursday
August 15	Assumption of Mary
November 1	All Saints' Day

When we attend Mass, we are given the opportunity to show our love for God in a special way. We recall the very first sabbath celebrated by Moses and the Israelites. We remember the first Mass celebrated by Jesus and the Apostles on Holy Thursday. We participate in Christ's sacrifice on the Cross. We can show our love for God in this way only by attending Mass.

God also asks us to remember Him throughout the entire day, not just during the time spent at Mass. You may remember from studying the first chapters of the Book of Genesis that, on the seventh day, after God had finished His creations, He rested. We also should try to use the "sabbath day" as a day of rest, a day to reflect on God's goodness and to thank Him for His wonderful deeds.

How can we live the Third Commandment?

_____

_____

_____

The Fourth Commandment

Honor your father and your mother.

God asks us in the Fourth Commandment to love and respect our parents. Our parents are gifts from God. They were given to us out of love, and they should be loved in return. Obeying our parents is one way to show them that we love and respect them. God has given parents the authority to teach their children how to act as His images. When our parents ask us to do good things, we should obey their wishes.

Jesus is the best example for us to follow. You may remember the story of the boy Jesus in the Temple. After the celebration of Passover in Jerusalem, Mary and Joseph began their journey back to Nazareth, thinking that Jesus was among their relatives. Jesus, however, had stayed in Jerusalem. After three days, Mary and Joseph found Jesus teaching in the Temple. They were understandably upset and anxious about Him. Then Jesus "went down with them and came to Nazareth, and was obedient to them; and his mother kept all these things in her heart. And Jesus advanced [in] wisdom and age and favor before God and man" (Luke 2:51–52). Even Jesus, Who is God, practiced the virtue of obedience. In this way, He showed us how God acts and how we should act as His images.

In addition to obeying our parents, the Fourth Commandment asks us to respect and obey others in authority. Jesus established His Church and asked the Apostles to continue His teaching on earth. The Pope and the bishops are the successors of the Apostles and are responsible for teaching us how to be better images of God. God asks us to honor and obey His representatives on earth. God also asks us to respect and obey our teachers. Teachers are an extension of our parents. They are "in charge". Loving teachers and loving parents have our best interests at heart. They, too, are responsible for teaching us how to be better images of God. Finally, we should respect and obey civil authorities and the laws they enforce. These persons are appointed or elected to help protect us and maintain law and order, so that all of us can live in a safe and peaceful environment.

It is important to remember, however, that God would never want us to obey anyone in authority who asked us to do something sinful. Unfortunately, there are some adults who have chosen not to follow God's commandments. These persons may take advantage of their authority over children and ask them to do something wrong, such as stealing. In this situation, obedience to God should come first. If you should ever be confused or doubtful about the good intentions of someone in authority, ask an adult whom you trust to help you.

How can we live the Fourth Commandment?

_____

_____

_____

_____

_____

The Fifth Commandment
You will not kill.

All life is a gift from God. Next to grace, human life is the most precious gift that we will ever receive. The gift of life is very different from any gift that we could give to each other. When we give someone a gift, that person then owns the gift and can use it like any other possession. We would hope that the person who received the gift would take good care of the gift. But, many times, the gift is eventually forgotten, broken, thrown away, or outgrown. This is not true of the gift of life, because we are made in God's image. We are persons. God gives us the gift of life to give us the opportunity to grow in His image. God gives this gift of life to each person. God makes each person with a body and a soul. The body which God gives us is a physical expression of the person. It is a visible reflection of God. When God gives us the gift of life, this gift is not ours to own and to do with as we please.

Many people think that they have never sinned against the Fifth Commandment because they have never killed anyone. But this is too narrow an interpretation. The Fifth Commandment asks us to do much more. It tells us that we should care for ourselves physically. Moreover, the Fifth Commandment asks us not to harm another person. There are many ways that we can harm ourselves and others. Children often get into fights. Uncontrolled anger, hitting, pushing, bullying, name-calling, hurting someone's feelings, and doing dangerous dares or tricks are some ways that children can sin against the Fifth Commandment.

As you grow older, the harm that you might do to your own body or to another person can be more serious. People who choose to use drugs or who drive when they have had too much to drink do harm to their own bodies and also endanger the lives of others. This is a sin against the Fifth Commandment. Abortion is wrong. When a person knows that abortion is wrong and then chooses to do it anyway, that person commits a mortal sin. The Fifth Commandment teaches us that human persons should not decide when a life should end. All life should be respected from its conception through all of its stages because all life is a gift from God. We should not take our own lives or the lives of others.

How can we live the Fifth Commandment?

_____

_____

_____

_____

The Sixth Commandment
You will not commit adultery.

When a man and a woman marry, they make a solemn promise before God to be faithful to each other "until death do us part". This means that the physical love that they express for each other should be reserved only for the two of them. As married people, they should not love any other man or woman in this way. When a married person breaks this promise, that person commits the sin of adultery.

Having read the above paragraph, you may think that the Sixth Commandment is only for married adults. This is not so. The Sixth Commandment is for everyone, because it teaches us how we should physically express our love for each other as images of God.

God created us in His image to love Him and other persons. He gave us bodies to express our love for each other in a physical way. The physical expression of our love for other persons should always reflect everything that is good, because God created all things good. When we misuse our sexuality or another person's sexuality, we hurt God, ourselves, and others.

As sixth graders, you are on the verge of becoming teenagers, young adults. Your bodies are beginning to change, to mature. Your interest in each other will also change. These changes are good. They are part of creation. The way you choose to act as you become a young adult should always reflect this goodness.

How can we live the Sixth Commandment?

_____

_____

_____

The Seventh Commandment
You will not steal.

In the Seventh Commandment, God asks us not to take anything that does not belong to us. This is a simple and straightforward request. If something doesn't belong to you, don't take it. When we choose not to steal, we are showing respect for the property of others. Furthermore, if we respect someone's property enough not to steal it, we should respect it enough not to damage it. Property refers not only to an individual's things—personal belongings—but also to public property, such as library books and school desks. For example, writing "graffiti" on buses and walls is damaging the property of others. The Seventh Commandment asks us not to do these things.

How can we live the Seventh Commandment?

_____

_____

_____

The Eighth Commandment
You will not bear false witness against your neighbor.

"To bear false witness" means to lie. "Not to bear false witness" means to speak the truth. As images of God, we should always want to "bear witness" to the Truth. God is the Source of all Truth. In the Gospel of Saint John, Christ says, "I am the way and the truth and the life" (Jn 14:6). God does not lie. He always speaks the truth. We should want to act in the same way. We should speak truthfully about all things and about all persons.

It is not always easy to tell the truth, especially if, by telling a lie, we can escape punishment for something we did. Courage does not always come easily, but it is a virtue that an image of God should want to practice.

When we tell lies about other people, we "bear false witness against our neighbor". We harm their good name, their reputation. To gossip and to spread rumors about others is not the way God wants us to act. As images of God, we should act like God and should want to help others do the same.

Using another person's ideas or work and passing them off as your own is also against the Eighth Commandment. This is called cheating. It is a dishonest act. God asks us to use the gifts He has given us. He asks us to practice the virtue of honesty. When we practice the virtue of honesty, we choose to reflect God's image in our actions.

How can we live the Eighth Commandment?

_____

_____

_____

The Ninth Commandment

You will not covet your neighbor's wife.

The Ninth and Tenth Commandments are similar. Both use the word *covet*. This word means "to wish for, to desire" what belongs to another. The Tenth Commandment asks us not to want another person's things so much that we dislike the person. The Ninth Commandment asks us not to want another person's wife or husband.

You learned that the Sixth Commandment tells a married couple to remain faithful to each other. The Ninth Commandment is an extension of this idea. When a man and a woman marry, God asks them to be happy with the person they marry. God asks them not to want, or "covet", someone else's husband or wife as their own. This includes not only the way they act (which is covered by the Sixth Commandment), but also their thoughts (which the Ninth Commandment covers).

The Ninth Commandment, however, is not only for married people. As sixth graders, you, too, should be happy with the family God has given you. Sometimes we do not get along with our parents, brothers, or sisters. This happens in most families, and usually these problems are worked out. God wants us to love and be satisfied with our own families. He would not want us to "covet" a friend's mother or father. Sometimes we might think, "Gee, I wish my dad were more like Tom's dad. Tom's dad can really play baseball!" Thoughts like these are not covetous. They are not sinful. But when these thoughts lead us to become envious of someone else's parents to the point of harming our relationship with our own parents, then we are sinning against the Ninth Commandment. God does not act this way, and, as His images, we should not act this way.

How can we live the Ninth Commandment?

_____

_____

_____

The Tenth Commandment

You will not covet anything that belongs to your neighbor.

In the Tenth Commandment, God asks us to be happy and satisfied with the things we have. This does not imply that it is wrong for us to want new things. For example, sometimes the desire for a new bike will motivate us to earn and to save money toward its purchase. This desire is a good thing. But sometimes it is not possible to buy a new bike. This can be difficult to accept and understand, especially when a friend has a new one. You might begin to resent your friend because he has a new bike and you do not. You might become so envious of your friend's bike that you choose not to be friends anymore, or you might be tempted to steal the bike or damage it. These are examples of the temptations that the Tenth Commandment warns against. Coveting another person's things can lead to envy. Envy is destructive, because it is a wrong choice and often leads us to make other wrong choices. An image of God does not act in an envious way. An image of God should be happy for a friend's good fortune.

Christ taught us a very useful lesson when He chose to be born in a humble stable. Christ lived a simple life, choosing not to allow His wants to exceed His needs. Jesus taught us not to be overly concerned about material things. He said, "Seek first the kingdom [of God] and his righteousness, and all these things will be given you besides" (Mt 6:33). When Christ died, He was buried in a grave that belonged to another person. Following the Tenth Commandment can help us to live as Jesus lived, that is, to become better images of God.

How can we live the Tenth Commandment?

_____

_____

_____

_____

Prayer and Prefigurement

Many events in the Book of Exodus prefigure events in the life of Jesus and His Church. You have already learned in Lesson 10 that Moses was a "type of Christ". The Ark and the Tabernacle can also be seen as prefigurements of some of the events of the New Testament. God made His presence visibly known to the Israelites by dwelling in the Tabernacle. God's word, the covenant, written on the stone tablets, was housed within the Ark of the Covenant. This special presence of God prefigured the dwelling of God made visible in the Person of Jesus. When Mary was asked to become the Mother of God, her body became the living Ark. Within her dwelt the physical presence of Jesus, God's Word made flesh. Whenever we receive the Eucharist, Christ's physical presence dwells within us. We, too, then become like living Arks.

Prayer

Litany of the Blessed Virgin Mary. (A litany is a prayer that consists of a series of petitions asking Jesus' help and asking Mary or the other saints to pray for us. In this particular litany, Mary is addressed by various titles or descriptions. One of her titles is Ark of the Covenant.)

Litany of the Blessed Virgin Mary

Lord, have mercy. *Lord, have mercy.*
Christ, have mercy. *Christ, have mercy.*
Lord, have mercy. *Lord, have mercy.*
Christ, hear us. *Christ, graciously hear us.*
God, the Father of heaven: *Have mercy on us.*
God, the Son, Redeemer of the world: *Have mercy on us.*
God the Holy Spirit: *Have mercy on us.*
Holy Trinity, one God: *Have mercy on us.*
Holy Mary: *Pray for us.*
Holy Mother of God:
Holy Virgin of virgins:
Mother of Christ:
Mother of divine grace:
Mother most holy:
Mother most pure:
Mother inviolate:
Mother undefiled:
Mother most amiable:
Mother most admirable:
Mother of good counsel:
Mother of our Creator:
Mother of our Savior:
Virgin most prudent:
Virgin most venerable:
Virgin most renowned:
Virgin most powerful:
Virgin most merciful:
Virgin most faithful:
Mirror of Justice:
Seat of Wisdom:
Cause of our joy:

Spiritual Vessel:

Vessel of Honor:

Singular vessel of devotion:

Mystical Rose:

Tower of David:

Tower of Ivory:

House of Gold:

Ark of the Covenant:

Gate of Heaven:

Morning Star:

Health of the sick:

Refuge of sinners:

Comforter of the afflicted:

Help of Christians:

Queen of angels:

Queen of patriarchs:

Queen of prophets:

Queen of Apostles:

Queen of martyrs:

Queen of confessors:

Queen of virgins:

Queen of all saints:

Queen conceived without original sin:

Queen assumed into heaven:

Queen of the holy Rosary:

Queen of peace:

Lamb of God, Who take away the sins of the world: *Spare us, O Lord.*

Lamb of God, Who take away the sins of the world: *Graciously hear us, O Lord.*

Lamb of God, Who take away the sins of the world: *Have mercy on us.*

Pray for us, O holy Mother of God: *that we may be made worthy of the promises of Christ.*

Grant, we beseech you, O Lord God, that we, your servants, may enjoy lasting health of mind and body, and, by the intercession of the Blessed Virgin Mary, be delivered from present sorrow and enter into the joy of eternal happiness. We ask this through the merits of Jesus Christ, our Lord. Amen.

LESSON 12

The Journey to the Promised Land

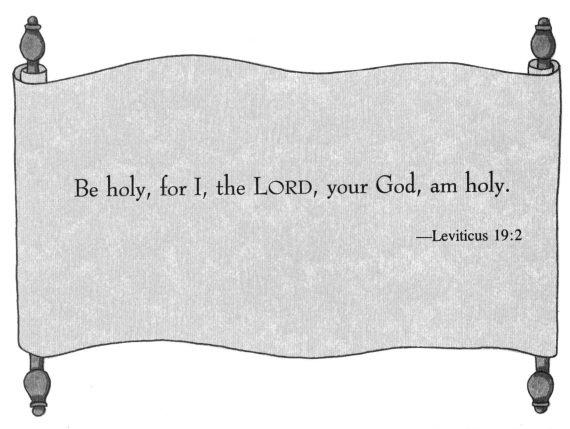

Be holy, for I, the LORD, your God, am holy.

—Leviticus 19:2

You have already studied several lessons taken from the Books of Genesis and Exodus. The next three books of the Bible are Leviticus, Numbers, and Deuteronomy. These five books make up the *Pentateuch*.

Genesis

The Book of Genesis traces the beginnings, or origins, of the Israelites. The lessons on creation, Adam and Eve, Cain and Abel, Noah, the tower of Babel, Abraham, Isaac, Jacob, and Joseph all come from the Book of Genesis. It is in this first book of the Bible that God makes a covenant with Adam and Eve, Noah, and Abraham and his descendants.

Exodus

The Book of Exodus continues the story of the Israelites and their leader, Moses. Through Moses, God delivered Israel from slavery in Egypt and led them to accept a covenant that stated that He would be their God, and they would be His people. In the Book of Exodus the Israelites become God's chosen people.

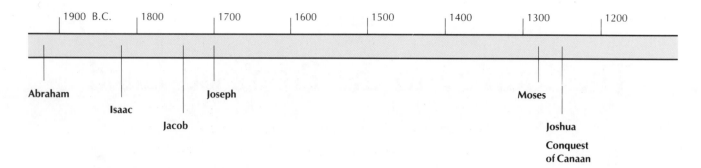

Leviticus

The next three books of the Pentateuch relate the Israelites' long journey to the Promised Land. During this forty-year journey, the Israelites learned how to live as God's chosen people. The Book of Leviticus is a collection of the laws, or rules, that helped govern the daily lives of the Israelites. There are rules for personal cleanliness, rules for eating certain foods, rules for living a holy life, and rules for celebrating special holidays. There are rules, or laws, for almost every situation. Many of these laws were commonly practiced by other Near Eastern peoples of this time. Their laws were recorded and written down on stone tablets. The Code of Hammurabi, the Code of Lipit-Ishtar, and the Code of Ur-Nammu (dating from 2050 to 1700 B.C.) are three of nine codes of law that have been discovered by archaeologists. The laws, or rules, given by God to Moses covered many of the same things that are listed on these tablets.

There are, however, certain differences that set the laws written in Leviticus apart from the laws practiced by other Near Eastern peoples. The most important difference is that the laws of the Israelites relate to the one true God. Their lives and the way they acted reflected their acceptance of only one God. Another distinctive characteristic of the Israelite laws is their concern for orphans, widows, women, slaves, and strangers. Many of the laws listed in Leviticus mention these concerns.

In addition to the rules that governed the people's daily lives, there were also rules for worship, which were carefully followed by the priests. The Book of Leviticus receives its name from Levi. Levi was one of the sons of Jacob, or Israel. Levi's tribe was chosen by God to serve as priests for the Israelites. These priests were responsible for offering sacrifices to God, teaching God's law to the Israelites, and serving as judges in difficult cases.

All the laws recorded in Leviticus were given by God to the newly-formed nation to show the people how to conduct themselves. Remember that the Israelites were just beginning to know God and to understand how to love Him. God, through His merciful love, showed the Israelites how to love Him by teaching them to act as He acts. God, the Holy One, wanted the Israelites to be a holy people. "Be holy, for I, the LORD your God, am holy" (Lv 19:2).

Numbers

The Book of Numbers follows the desert wanderings of the Israelites throughout the Sinai peninsula. (See the map on page 160.) Its name is taken from the two censuses of the Hebrew people described in chapters 1 and 26 of the Book of Numbers. A *census* is a count of the number of people in a given area. The first census of the Israelites was taken near the beginning of their journey, while they were encamped at the foot of Mount Sinai. The second census was taken when they arrived at the border of the Promised Land, 38 years later. An account of all twelve tribes is listed in this book. You may remember that Jacob, or Israel, had twelve sons (refer to Worksheet 2 in Lesson 8). The twelve tribes of Israel descended from these sons. Each tribe was then divided into clans, and each clan was divided into ancestral houses. In those days, people were not known by their family name, as we are. Rather, a person's first name was followed by mentioning the name of the "house" from which he was descended. For example, Jesus was from the "house of David". The "house of David" can be traced back to the tribe of Judah. After the Israelites entered and conquered the land of Canaan, each of the twelve tribes was given a portion of the land.

Throughout their long journey in the desert, the Israelites were given many opportunities to show God their love. Many times they chose to act as God wanted them to act. When the Israelites conducted themselves as images of God, they became better reflections of Him. But sometimes the Israelites made wrong choices. They rebelled against God's wishes, against the rules that were given to them to help them live as His chosen people. Then they suffered the consequences of their actions. They continued to wander for forty years in the desert until they were ready to accept Him as their God. When the Israelites were ready to accept God as their own, then they entered the Promised Land. The Book of Numbers ends with the Israelites' finally crossing the Jordan River and entering the Land of Canaan.

Deuteronomy

The Book of Deuteronomy is the fifth and last book of the Pentateuch. Its name means "second law". It contains, actually, a repetition and explanation of the law of the covenant given on Mount Sinai. It also includes a reminder of the important events and lessons learned during the wanderings of the Israelites in the desert. Moses is again the central figure. By this time, Moses was very old. He used the final days of his life to remind the Israelites of their promises given to God in the covenant. In the "Song of Moses", Deuteronomy 32, Moses pleads with the Israelites to remain loyal to God by choosing to obey His commandments. Before Moses died, he appointed Joshua to lead the Israelites into Canaan. This last book of the Pentateuch ends with the death and burial of Moses. "Since then no prophet has arisen in Israel like Moses, whom the LORD knew face to face" (Dt 34:10).

REVIEW QUESTIONS

*1. Name the five books contained in the Pentateuch.

2. With whom did God make a covenant in the Book of Genesis?

*3. What does the Book of Genesis trace?

*4. What is included in the Book of Exodus?

*5. What is contained in the Book of Leviticus?

6. What was the purpose of these laws?

7. What were some differences between the laws of the Israelites and the code of laws practiced by other peoples of the Near East?

*8. From whom does the Book of Leviticus receive its name?

9. For what duties were the priests responsible?

*10. The Book of Numbers tells us about what events?

*11. From what did the Book of Numbers receive its name?

12. What is a census?

13. Into how many tribes were the Israelites divided?

14. What happened to the Israelites when they rebelled against God's laws?

15. When did the Israelites enter the Promised Land?

*16. What does "Deuteronomy" mean?

*17. What is contained in the Book of Deuteronomy?

18. Who succeeded Moses as leader of the Israelites?

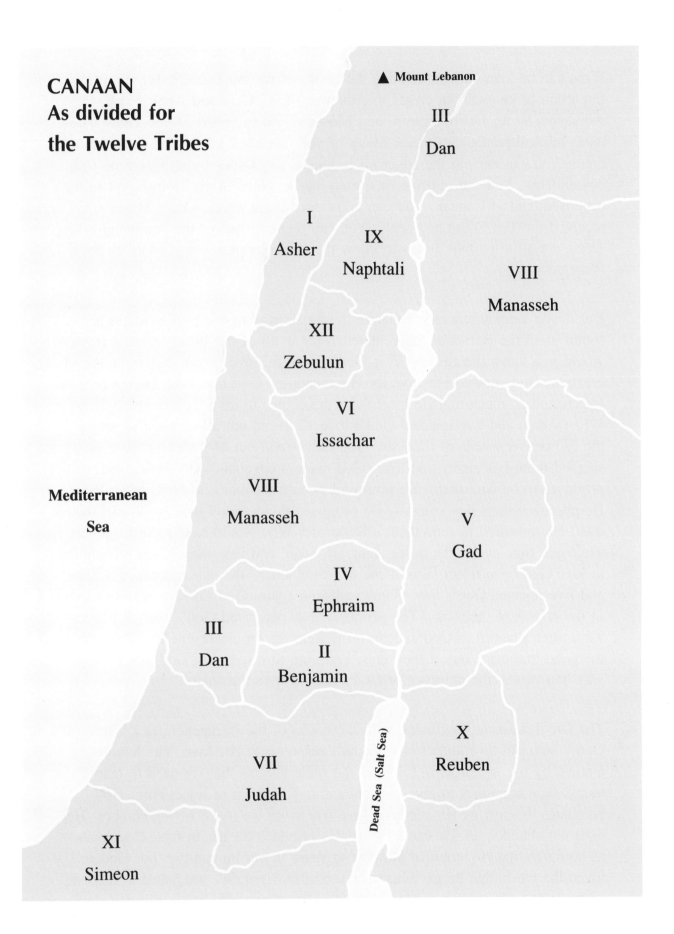

CANAAN
As divided for
the Twelve Tribes

▲ Mount Lebanon

III
Dan

I
Asher

IX
Naphtali

VIII
Manasseh

XII
Zebulun

VI
Issachar

Mediterranean

Sea

VIII
Manasseh

V
Gad

IV
Ephraim

III
Dan

II
Benjamin

X
Reuben

Dead Sea (Salt Sea)

VII
Judah

XI
Simeon

The Message of the Pentateuch

What can be learned from reading the books of the Pentateuch? Why is it important to know about creation, Adam and Eve, Cain and Abel, Noah, Abraham, Isaac, Jacob, Joseph, and Moses? By now, most of you know who these biblical personages were. Many of you can retell the stories surrounding them. You can explain the covenant promised to Abraham and passed on to his descendants. You can indicate on a map the Israelites' flight from Egypt to the promised land of Canaan. You can point out Mount Sinai, where Moses received the Ten Commandments. You can recite all ten of the commandments. These are all important things to know from the Scriptures that make up the Pentateuch.

But if you were asked to summarize in one short phrase the chief message found in all the stories of the Pentateuch (or in all of the Bible, for that matter), would you know the answer? It is God's merciful love. From the beginning of creation, God showed His love for His creatures. God loved the human persons He created so much that He gave them the choice to love Him or reject Him. When Adam and Eve rejected God's love, God did not allow them to suffer the full consequences of their sin. God drew good out of the evil of sin. God showed them His mercy and love. God made a covenant with them. God promised to be with them. He promised to care for them, to provide for them. He promised them descendants. He promised them a land they could call their own. He promised to send them a Redeemer Who would save them from sin. Time and time again, the descendants of Adam and Eve were given this choice: to love God or to reject Him. Time and time again, the descendants of Adam and Eve rejected God's love. Time and time again, God saved them from some of the effects of their sins. The people who experienced God's merciful love were often grateful to God and, in turn, were drawn closer to Him. This was the good that came out of their sins. Learning to respond to God in a loving way was one of the purposes of God's acts of merciful love.

The Old Testament, beginning with the books of the Pentateuch, is a history of God's merciful love and of His people's response to His love. The lessons learned by our ancestors in faith are the same lessons that we need to learn today. God continues to give us a choice: to love Him or reject Him. God continues to show us His merciful love whenever we make wrong choices. He does not abandon us. He cares for us. He provides for us. In fact, God loves us so much that He humbled Himself to share in our humanity. "For God so loved the world that he gave his only son" (Jn 3:16). We are asked to respond to this great gift of merciful love by acting as images of God, by loving mercifully.

1. What is the chief message of the Pentateuch?
*2. How did God show His merciful love?
3. What was one of the purposes of God's acts of merciful love?
4. Does God continue to show us His merciful love?
5. How are we asked to respond to God's merciful love?

Concepts of Faith

1. **Name the five books contained in the Pentateuch.**
   Genesis, Exodus, Leviticus, Numbers, and Deuteronomy.

2. **What does the Book of Genesis trace?**
   The beginnings, or origins, of the Israelites.

3. **What is included in the Book of Exodus?**
   The stories surrounding Moses and the deliverance of the Israelites from slavery in Egypt; the acceptance of a new covenant: the Ten Commandments.

4. **What is contained in the Book of Leviticus?**
   A collection of laws.

5. **From whom does the Book of Leviticus receive its name?**
   Levi, one of the sons of Jacob.

6. **The Book of Numbers tells us about what events?**
   The wanderings of the Israelites in the desert.

7. **From what does the Book of Numbers receive its name?**
   From the census taken of the Israelite people.

8. **What does "Deuteronomy" mean?**
   Second law.

9. **What is contained in the Book of Deuteronomy?**
   A repetition and explanation of the law of the covenant (the Ten Commandments); a reminder of the important events and lessons learned during the wanderings in the desert; and instructions by Moses to remain faithful and obedient to God's laws.

10. **What is the chief message of the Old Testament?**
    God's merciful love.

11. **How did God show His merciful love?**
    Whenever God's people chose to sin, God did not allow them to suffer the full consequences of their sins. God drew good out of their sins. The people were often grateful and, in turn, were drawn closer to God.

Vocabulary

Pentateuch: The first five books of the Bible.

census: A count of the number of people in a given area or territory.

Living the Lesson

> "Be holy, for I, the LORD, your God, am holy".
> —Leviticus 19:2

How many of you have ever asked, or thought, the following questions in some form or another? "Aw, Mom, why do I have to do this?" "This is a stupid rule!" "No one will know if I break this rule." "Gee, Dad, I'm too old to have to obey all these silly rules." "I can decide for myself what is best." "I absolutely refuse to do this!"

All of us have said, or thought, these complaints. In this, we are no different from the Israelites. They, too, did not always want to obey the rules. They, too, sometimes rebelled against the law. And they, like us when we choose not to follow the rules, suffered the consequences of their wrong choices.

Perhaps if we take some time to think about *why* we should follow certain rules or laws, it may be easier for us to make the right choices about them without complaining. How many of you have ever asked a parent or teacher this question, "Why do I have to do this?" And the answer was, "Because I said so!" That is not a very satisfying answer, is it? It would have been better to have received a detailed explanation. But then adults don't always have to give you an explanation, even though you think they should. Part of the challenge of being a young person is to listen and to obey those who are in authority. Parents expect you to trust them (and their rules) because they love you. That is why you will often receive as a reply to your questions of "Why?", "Because I know what is best!" This is probably true in most cases, even though you might not want to admit it.

When God gave the Israelites the laws recorded in Leviticus, they complained and asked "Why?". More often than not, God replied by saying, "For I am the LORD your God". In other words, "I know what is best." But several times God replied with an explanation that was short, simple, and understandable. "Be holy, for I, the LORD God, am holy" (Lv 19:2). God was telling the Israelites to become more like Him. How could they do that? By following His laws.

God extends the same invitation to us. He wants us to become more like Him. He wants us to become better images of Him. How can we do this? God has given us the answer in many ways. We can find the answer in the Old Testament. We can find the answer in the teachings of Jesus. We can find the answer in the teachings of the Church. Our parents and teachers know some of the answers, too.

Take the time to ask your parents, teachers, and friends to help you find the answer to the question that each faithful Israelite probably asked thousands of years ago.

"How can I be holy?" "What should I do to become a better image of God?"

Prayer

Psalm 16. (In Psalm 16 God is praised because He is the Supreme Good. God has wonderfully made us, makes us holy, and shows us the path to eternal life.)

Jesus and the Book of Deuteronomy

Jesus often quoted from the Old Testament. Read the story of the temptation of Jesus found in Luke 4:1–12. Jesus responded to the temptations put to Him by the devil by quoting from the Book of Deuteronomy. After you have read the story, look up the specific passages that are quoted from Deuteronomy. Compare the Old Testament passage to the quotation given in Luke. Then write the responses Jesus gave to the devil's three temptations.

1. Deuteronomy 8:3.

When the devil asked Jesus to turn the stones into bread, Jesus said:

_____

_____

2. Deuteronomy 6:13.

When the devil tempted Jesus with power and glory if He would bow down and worship him, Jesus said to him:

_____

_____

3. Deuteronomy 6:16.

When the devil asked Jesus to test His Father by throwing Himself off the roof of the Temple, so that His angels would save Him, Jesus said:

_____

_____

Find the following passages in the Bible. Then answer the questions.

1. Numbers 1:5–15.
What were the names of the twelve tribes of Israel?

_____

_____

2. Numbers 9:16.
How did God make His presence visible to the Israelites?

_____

_____

3. Deuteronomy 6:5.
What great commandment did God give to His people?

_____

_____

4. Deuteronomy 7:12–15.
List some of the blessings God promised to the Israelites as a reward for their obedience.

_____

_____

_____

5. Deuteronomy 14:7–8.
What animals were the Israelites forbidden to eat?

_____

_____

6. Deuteronomy 15:8.

How should you treat a poor person?

_____

_____

7. Deuteronomy 22:1.

How should you care for a lost animal?

_____

_____

8. Deuteronomy 32:49.

What was the name of the mountain from which Moses was able to see the land of Canaan?

_____

9. Deuteronomy 34:7.

How old was Moses when he died?

_____

10. Deuteronomy 34:9.

Who became the new leader of the Israelites?

_____

Joshua

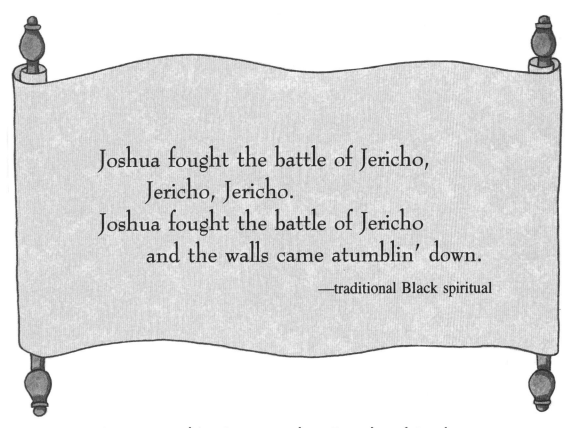

Joshua fought the battle of Jericho,
Jericho, Jericho.
Joshua fought the battle of Jericho
and the walls came atumblin' down.

—traditional Black spiritual

An Introduction to the Book of Joshua

In Lesson 1, "Learning about the Bible", you learned that the books of the Bible were written in many literary forms. Literary forms are different types of writing. The literary forms of the Old Testament include history, law, prophecy, prayer, and wisdom. So far, you have studied two of these forms, history and law. Genesis is a history book. Leviticus, Numbers, and Deuteronomy are law books. Exodus is both a history and a law book. In this lesson, you will study the Book of Joshua. This book of the Bible is a history book.

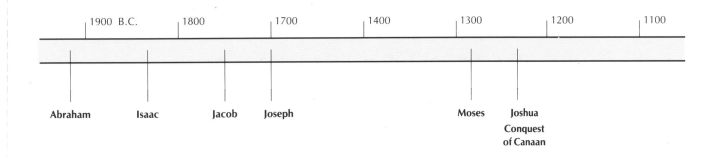

It is important to remember that the writers of Joshua were writing this book not to teach a history lesson, but to teach a religious truth. Yes, the story the writers tell is historical and based on real events. It is an account of the conquest of the land of Canaan under the leadership of Moses' successor, Joshua. According to archaeological evidence, the conquest of Canaan took place around 1240 B.C. Biblical scholars estimate that the Book of Joshua was written approximately 200 years later, in 1045 B.C. The purpose of the book, however, is to demonstrate God's faithfulness in fulfilling the covenant first made to Adam and then inherited by Noah, Abraham, Isaac, Jacob, and Moses. Canaan is the land God promised to give the Israelites for an inheritance. The writers intended to demonstrate God's faithfulness when they were inspired to retell the historical events of the conquest of Canaan.

REVIEW QUESTIONS

1. What are the different types of literary form used in the Old Testament?
2. What type of literary form is the Book of Joshua?
3. What historical event is retold in the Book of Joshua?
4. What was the authors' purpose in writing the Book of Joshua?

Who Was Joshua?

Joshua was born in Egypt. He left Egypt along with the other Israelites under the leadership of Moses and was part of the forty-year exodus to the Promised Land. He is mentioned several times in the Books of Exodus, Numbers, and Deuteronomy. He was a military commander and led the Israelites in several battles against their enemies. Joshua was with Moses when he went up the mountain to receive the Ten Commandments. He was one of the twelve spies Moses sent ahead to scout the land of Canaan. Upon their return, only two of the spies, Joshua and Caleb, had the courage to recommend to Moses that the Israelites advance into Canaan. Moses trusted Joshua, and he became the obvious choice as Moses' successor. "Now Joshua, son of Nun, was filled with the spirit of wisdom, since Moses had laid his hands upon him; and so the Israelites gave him their obedience, thus carrying out the LORD's command to Moses" (Dt 34:9).

God Promises to Be with the Israelites

Look at the map on the next page. This is the land God promised to give the Israelites. "Your domain is to be all the land of the Hittites, from the desert and from Lebanon east to the great river Euphrates and west to the Great Sea"

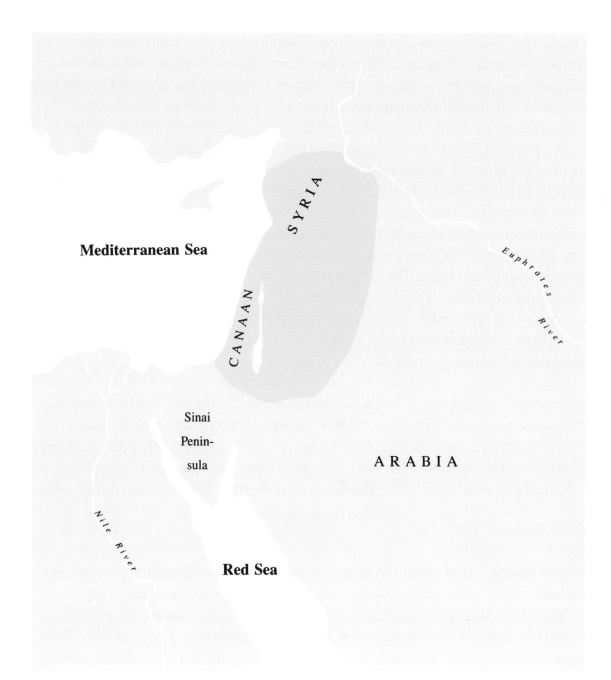

Mediterranean Sea

SYRIA

CANAAN

Euphrates River

Sinai
Penin-
sula

ARABIA

Nile River

Red Sea

(Jos 1:4). Canaan, however, was already occupied by many different tribes. Hittites, Amorites, Canaanites, Perizzites, Girgashites, Hivites, and Jebusites were among the fierce tribes who had already conquered the land of Canaan for themselves. These civilizations were quite advanced. Their cities were well-planned and well-built. They had fortified many of them with fifty-foot-high walls. Many of the streets were paved. They had built drainage systems to remove waste. They were known for their fine pottery and metalwork. They used their knowledge of metalwork to design a chariot wheel that had sharp, blade-like spokes. The land was rich in produce. They had developed a prosperous foreign trade with neighboring countries. These were a civilized and powerful people. They were not about to surrender their territory to the Israelites without a fight. The Israelites knew that they were about to undertake a dangerous and seemingly impossible mission. They had been wandering in the desert for forty years. They did not even have one chariot! Were they ready to make war on such a powerful nation? It was no wonder that they needed to be reminded of God's presence.

In the very first chapter of Joshua, God reassured Joshua and the Israelites that He would always be with them. "I will be with you as I was with Moses: I will not leave you nor forsake you" (Jos 1:5). God also reminded the Israelites to be "firm and steadfast". In fact, God says these words to them three times: "Be firm and steadfast." What did God mean by this? God explained it to them.

Read Joshua 1:7–9.

In this passage, God asked the Israelites to be "firm and steadfast", to "observe the entire law". The word *steadfast* means not changing or moving. God reminded the Israelites that they should not change their promise to remain faithful to Him. God reminded them that the covenant was a partnership. The Israelites were to act as images of God. They could do this by showing their love for God when they faithfully followed His laws. "Then you will successfully attain your goal" (Jos 1:8).

REVIEW QUESTIONS

1. Why was Joshua the obvious choice as Moses' successor?
2. Describe the Canaanite civilization.
3. What did God say to the Israelites in the first chapter of Joshua?
4. What did God mean when He told the Israelites, "Be firm and steadfast"?

Joshua Prepares for Battle

Joshua was an experienced military leader. He had a plan for conquering the land of Canaan. Look at the map on page 213. The Israelites were encamped on the east side of the River Jordan. Joshua's master plan was to drive a wedge between the cities of the north and those of the south. The city of Jericho lay directly in his path. The Israelites had to conquer Jericho decisively. This would be their first battle. Victory was essential to their success. Joshua was a wise leader. He decided to send two spies to "reconnoiter the land and Jericho" (Jos 2:1). The two spies would have been discovered and captured in Jericho if a woman named Rahab had not helped them.

Read Joshua 2 for the scriptural account of the spies' mission. The following paragraph is a retelling of this event.

Spies Saved by Rahab

When the spies entered Jericho, they found lodging in the house of Rahab. Rahab's house was a good place to gather information, and they thought that they would go unnoticed there. But they were mistaken. The king heard of their mission and sent soldiers to Rahab's house. Rahab, however, hid the two spies under the flax that was drying on her roof. Flax is a long, slender plant whose fibers were used for weaving. When the soldiers came, Rahab told them that two men had been there, but she did not know they were spies. They had already left during night. She told the soldiers that they would have to pursue them immediately to overtake them. After the soldiers left, Rahab asked the spies to repay her for saving them. She told them that she and all of Canaan had heard of the power of the God of Israel. Everyone feared the Israelites. Rahab convinced the spies that she believed in their God. She asked them to spare her family from death when they conquered the city. The spies agreed not to harm her family. They told her to tie a red cord in the window of her house, so that the Israelites would know not to harm anyone in her house. Then she helped the spies escape by dropping a rope out of her window and over the city wall.

A Discussion of Rahab

It is important to understand that Rahab's motivation for helping the two spies came not from fear, but from her faith and belief in the God of Israel, the one true God. Rahab told the spies: "Everyone is discouraged because of you, since the Lord, your God, is God in heaven above and on earth below" (Jos 2:11). With this statement, Rahab denounced all the pagan gods of her people and took the God of Israel as her own. This was a tremendous leap of faith. The New Testament mentions the faith of Rahab in a letter of instruction to the

Hebrews (Heb 11:31). Rahab's faith was rewarded. The Israelites kept their promise to her. When Jericho was conquered, Rahab and her family were spared from death. She and her family were taken in by the Israelites. Later, Rahab married a man named Salmon, and, through their son Boaz, she became the great-great-grandmother of David, and thus an ancestor of Jesus.

REVIEW QUESTIONS

1. Why did Joshua send two men to Jericho?
2. Where did the two spies stay in Jericho?
3. Where did Rahab hide the spies?
4. Why did Rahab help the spies?
5. What payment did Rahab ask for helping the spies?
6. How did the spies escape?
7. How was Rahab's faith in God rewarded?

The Miracle at the Crossing of the River Jordan

Joshua was now ready to cross the River Jordan and do battle at Jericho.

Read Joshua 3:7–17, or read the summary below.

God wanted to show the Israelites and the people of the land of Canaan that He was the one true God. He told the Israelites to choose twelve priests, one from each tribe, to carry the Ark of the Covenant ahead of the people into the Jordan River. God predicted that "When the soles of the feet of the priests carrying the ark of the LORD, the LORD of the whole earth, touch the water of the Jordan, it will cease to flow; for the water flowing down from upstream will halt in a solid bank" (Jos 3:13). The priests did as the Lord directed. When the priests waded into the water, the waters flowing from upstream halted, causing the river bed to dry up. "While all Israel crossed over on dry ground, the priests carrying the ark of the covenant of the LORD remained motionless on dry ground in the bed of the Jordan until the whole nation had completed the passage" (Jos 3:17).

A Discussion of Joshua 3

It had been forty years since God had parted the waters of the Red Sea. Now, at the end of their long journey, God again showed the Israelites how powerful His love was for them. God knew that the Israelites needed to know that He was actively present among them. God also wanted the people of Canaan to know that He was the one true God. The Israelites, too, needed reassurance of Joshua's leadership. Moses had led them for forty years, and God had repeatedly performed miracles through him to remind the Israelites of His presence. Now, God again showed the Israelites His love, but this time through their new leader, Joshua.

Again we are faced with the question, could this event really have happened? Did God really perform a miracle? Is there a scientific explanation for the drying up of the river? The answer is "Yes" to all of these questions! In A.D. 1927, there was a minor earthquake that caused the collapse of the high river banks at the same spot as described in the Scriptures. The Jordan River was dammed up for more than 21 hours. The Scripture account says that, as the priests stepped into the river, God made a blockage at Adam, a site sixteen miles up the river, which dammed the stream, leaving twenty to thirty miles of riverbed dry. Perhaps God used this "natural" occurrence, a landslide, to perform His miracle. Was it "natural" for the stream to dry up at just the precise moment when the priests touched the water? No, this was miraculous. This was a visible show of God's power. How did Joshua know that the river would dry up? God predicted the miracle in Joshua 3:13. This event was miraculous, whether or not God used natural forces to accomplish His will.

After the crossing, Joshua directed the people to build a memorial to praise and thank God for His merciful love. Joshua chose twelve men, one from each tribe, to build two piles of twelve stones each. They placed one pile where the priests stood, on the east edge of the river, and one at Gilgal, near their camp on the west bank of the river. This memorial would serve as a symbol for all generations to come of God's merciful love and of this miraculous event. It was here, at this same stretch of water, where John the Baptist carried out his ministry and where the baptism of Jesus took place.

The Israelites also wanted to show God in a more personal way that they were willing to keep His covenant of love. One of the signs of the acceptance of the covenant was circumcision. You may remember that Moses and the Israelite men who had left Egypt were circumcised as a sign of their part of the covenant. All of this generation had died in the forty-year wanderings of the exodus. Their children were now willing to offer this personal sacrifice as a sign of their love and acceptance of the covenant. After this, the Israelites celebrated the Passover. "On that same day after the Passover on which they ate of the produce of the land, the manna ceased. No longer was there manna for the Israelites, who that year ate of the yield of the land of Canaan" (Jos 5:12).

1. Describe the miracle that occurred at the River Jordan.
2. Why did God perform a miracle at the River Jordan?
3. Even though the damming of the river can be explained by "natural" forces, why was this event providential?
4. How did the Israelites praise and thank God after the crossing of the river?
5. How did the Israelites renew their covenant with God?

The Battle of Jericho

The Israelites were now ready to follow Joshua. They knew, and Joshua knew, that God was really the head of their army. What is more, their enemies knew it, too, and they feared the Israelites. The story of the fall of Jericho is one that you may have heard as a young child. You may have even sung the traditional song "Joshua Fought the Battle of Jericho". It is an exciting and miraculous story.

Read Joshua 6, or the summary below.

God instructed Joshua and the Israelites to march around the city once each day for six days. Seven priests, carrying ram's horns, led the march, carrying the Ark of the Covenant. On the seventh day they marched around the city seven times. Then they sounded their horns. Upon hearing this signal, all the Israelites gave a great shout. The walls of the city collapsed, and the Israelites entered the city from the front gates. They killed all the inhabitants except Rahab and her family. They were careful not to take any silver and gold or objects made from bronze or iron for themselves. These were given to the Lord's treasury. Then Joshua ordered the city burned and cursed the man who should attempt to rebuild it.

The city of Jericho lay in ruins for almost four hundred years. In 1 Kings 16:34, the Scriptures tell us that Hiel, a man from Bethel, rebuilt Jericho. "He lost his firstborn son, Abiram, when he laid the foundation, and his youngest son, Segub, when he set up the gates, as the Lord had foretold through Joshua, son of Nun". Jericho was eventually rebuilt, but archaeologists have not found ruins of the Jericho that was sacked by the Israelites around 1250 B.C. Jericho is mentioned several times in the New Testament. Jesus healed the blind man Bartimaeus and went to the house of Zachaeus while visiting the city of Jericho. Modern Jericho, built on top of the New Testament Jericho, lies west of the site where the Old Testament Jericho was built.

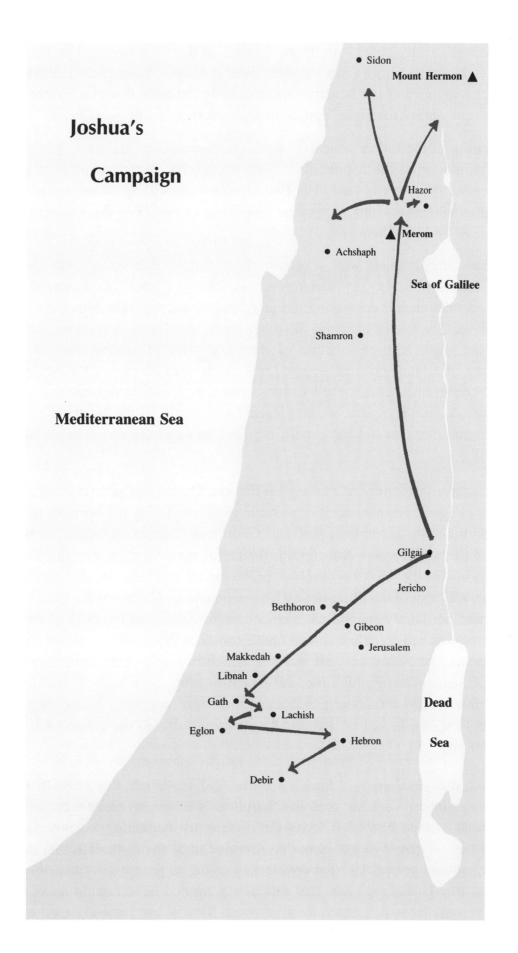

Joshua's

Campaign

Sidon

Mount Hermon ▲

Hazor

Merom

Achshaph

Sea of Galilee

Shamron

Mediterranean Sea

Gilgal

Jericho

Bethhoron

Gibeon

Jerusalem

Makkedah

Libnah

Gath

Lachish

Eglon

Dead

Hebron

Sea

Debir

A Discussion of the Fall of Jericho

Did the walls really come "atumblin' down", as the song says, when the Israelites blew their horns and shouted? Was it another earthquake? Perhaps. The fact remains that the Israelites miraculously defeated this city by obeying God's commands. It was the first of many victories for the Israelites.

The reading of the fall of Jericho is both exciting and entertaining. Yet, the total annihilation of the population is very disturbing. Jesus taught us to love our enemies. How could God, His Father, allow the killing of an entire city? To help us understand this, it may be helpful to know about the ancient history of this area and its inhabitants.

Joshua and the Israelites were a people of their time. War was a brutal and bloody business. It was not uncommon for victors to "sack" a conquered city— killing its inhabitants, destroying the city, and taking the valuables for themselves. The Canaanites and the other tribes that lived throughout the land of Canaan practiced these customs of war. The battle of Jericho was the beginning of a long series of sieges. Look at the map on page 213. According to the Scripture accounts, only two more cities were totally destroyed by the Israelites, Ai, south of Jericho, and Hazor, which was in the North. There are many more cities that did battle with the Israelites and did not suffer total destruction.

We know from the study of this region that the Canaanites practiced a pagan and evil religion. Human sacrifice to their gods, including the burning of their own children, was a common practice. God knew that the Israelites might be attracted to the Canaanite gods and to the sinful ways of these people. Total destruction was the way the Israelites protected themselves from the influence of pagan religions. However, not all of the people in Canaan were killed, as Rahab and her family remind us. They chose to believe in the God of Israel and were protected by Him. Others chose to reject God. They suffered the consequences of their choice. It took the Israelites many years to occupy all the land of Canaan. During this time, the Israelites often drew away from God and were influenced by the sinful practices of the pagan religions. When they chose to reject God, the Israelites, like the Canaanites, suffered the consequences of their actions.

There are many instances of brutality in the Old Testament that are difficult for us to understand. When we read the Scriptures we have to place these events in the context of their history. The Israelites were just beginning to know God. The fullness of His love would not be revealed until the birth of Jesus, more than a thousand years later. They were still trying to accept fully that there was only one true God! God knew that this newly formed nation could never master all the lessons He had to teach them at once. Slowly and patiently God taught the Israelites His ways. In other words, He gradually revealed Himself to them. In addition, the Israelites often neglected their covenant promise and sinned by worshiping false gods. In other words, they did not always follow what they did know about God. We should not be so quick to judge harshly the actions of the Israelites, such as the sacking of Jericho. We have been privileged to know the fullness of God's love through the redemption of His Son, Jesus. Yet, we, too, often forget the lessons of love that Jesus taught us. It is comforting to know that God is patient with us too.

REVIEW QUESTIONS

1. Describe the fall of Jericho.
2. What does it mean to "sack" a city?
3. Why did God allow the total destruction of Jericho?
*4. Did God reveal Himself all at once to the Israelites?

The Division of Land

After the fall of Jericho, Joshua continued his plan and conquered the major cities in the South. He then carried out his northern campaign. Chapters 7 through 12 of the Book of Joshua give the account of this long campaign. It took many years for the Israelites to take possession of the land of Canaan. There still remained many scattered areas that had not been conquered.

By this time, however, Joshua was "old and advanced in years" (Jos 13:1). The Lord advised Joshua to divide the land among the twelve tribes. Then each tribe would be responsible for conquering and inhabiting the remainder of its land. Joshua 13 through 21 is an account of the division of land. The map on page 195 is a sketch of this settlement. You will notice that two of the tribes, Dan and Manasseh, were given split portions of land. Also, you may notice that the tribe of Levi is not listed among the twelve tribes. The Levites served as priests to the Israelites. They were the leaders of the nation's faith and worship. They needed to live among all the tribes to carry out their work. Therefore, the tribe of Levi was not given a portion of land. Instead, the Levites were given 48 cities and pasture land by the other tribes. In this way, the Israelite nation ensured that the knowledge and practice of their faith would be passed on to each generation.

Joshua's Farewell

The last two chapters of the Book of Joshua tell of Joshua's final days as leader of the Israelites. Joshua reminded the Israelites of the faithfulness of their God. "So now acknowledge with your whole heart and soul that not one of all the promises the LORD, your God, made to you has remained unfulfilled. Every promise has been fulfilled for you, with not one single exception" (Jos 23:14). Joshua then continued to instruct his people by giving the Israelites a historical account of God's goodness, from Abraham to the conquering of the land of Canaan. Joshua pleaded with the Israelites to remember their promise of the covenant. He stirred the hearts of the Israelites, and they said, "We will serve the LORD, our God, and obey his voice" (Jos 24:24). Then Joshua and the Israelites renewed their covenant with God.

"After these events, Joshua, son of Nun, servant of the LORD, died at the age of a hundred and ten. Israel served the LORD during the entire lifetime of Joshua and that of the elders who outlived Joshua and knew all that the LORD had done for Israel" (Jos 24:29, 31).

Joshua—A "Type of Christ"

Joshua's name tells us that he was a "type of Christ". His name in Hebrew is a form of the name Jesus, which means "Yahweh is salvation". Like Jesus, Joshua was faithful and obedient to the will of God. Moses, his predecessor and another "type of Christ", also was faithful and obedient to God's will. Moses freed the Israelites from the slavery of Egypt and led them to the Promised Land. Joshua completed the journey. He fought the Israelites' enemies and led them victoriously into the Promised Land. Through both Moses and Joshua, God loved the Israelite people mercifully. He drew good (the Promised Land) out of evil (slavery) and thereby brought the Israelites closer to Himself. Christ is our leader. He leads us out of the bondage of sin. He leads the fight against our spiritual enemy, sin. He shows us the way into the promised land, heaven. Jesus loves us mercifully. He draws good (heaven) out of evil (sin) and thereby brings us closer to God. Just as Joshua pleaded with the Israelites to be "firm and steadfast", so Christ asks us to remain faithful to His teachings. Christ wants us to follow Him. He invites us to act as images of God and to love mercifully.

REVIEW QUESTIONS

1. How was the land divided?
2. Why didn't the tribe of Levi receive a portion of the land?
3. What portion did the Levites receive?
4. What did Joshua tell the Israelites before he died?
5. Why is Joshua a "type of Christ"?
*6. How did God love the Israelites mercifully?
*7. How does Jesus love us mercifully?
*8. What does Christ ask us to do?

Concepts of Faith

1. **Did God reveal Himself all at once to the Israelites?**
   No, God revealed Himself gradually.
2. **Through Whom was God's revelation completed?**
   Jesus Christ.
3. **How did God love the Israelites mercifully?**
   Through both Moses and Joshua, God drew good (the Promised Land) out of evil (slavery) and brought the Israelites closer to Himself.
4. **How does Jesus love us mercifully?**
   Jesus draws good (heaven) out of evil (sin) and brings us closer to God.
5. **What does Christ ask us to do?**
   To act as images of God and to love mercifully.

Vocabulary

steadfast: Not changing or moving.

Living the Lesson

War—Is It Any Different Today?

The killing of other human beings has existed since the murder of Abel by his brother, Cain. There are many descriptions relating the brutality of war recorded in the Old Testament and in other ancient historical writings. Jesus was born during the time when His country, Israel, was under the rule of the Roman Empire. At the height of its power, the Roman Empire had conquered most of the known world. Many who knew Jesus hoped that He would lead the Israelite nation to victory over the Romans. But, throughout His ministry, Jesus spoke of peace and love of one's neighbor. Loving one's neighbor included loving one's enemies. Many people would not accept this message. Christ's message of peace has now been taught for two thousand years. Many still do not accept Christ's message of peace and brotherly love. War still exists today.

Discuss with your classmates and family the questions below. Perhaps you can interview a person who has fought in a war.

1. Are there any differences between the wars of ancient times and modern times?

2. Are warring nations permitted to "sack" or totally destroy life and property?

3. How has the power of nuclear weapons affected the threat of war?

4. What progress has been made in trying to prevent wars?

5. What does the Catholic Church teach about war?

6. Jesus said, "Blessed are the peacemakers, for they will be called children of God" (Mt 5:9), and "This is how all will know that you are my disciples, if you have love for one another" (Jn 13:35). As sixth-graders, what can you do to contribute to the cause of world peace?

Song

Sing the Black spiritual "Joshua Fought the Battle of Jericho".

Prayer

Psalm 33. (This Psalm has 22 verses. It is a hymn of praise to God, Who is faithful to His promises, all-powerful, the wise and mighty Ruler of the world, and the source of our victory and salvation.)

The Battle of Jericho.

Bible Search

Read each of the following Scripture verses in your Bible. Then write a summary of the passage. If the passage is short, you may write the exact words. Then answer the three questions that conclude this worksheet.

1. Exodus 17:10

_____

2. Exodus 24:13

_____

3. Numbers 13:1–4, 8, 16

_____

4. Deuteronomy 34:9

_____

5. Joshua 1:6

_____

6. Joshua 1:7

_____

7. Joshua 1:9

_____

8. Joshua 1:18

_____

9. Joshua 24:21

_____

10. Joshua 24:24

_____

Questions 1, 2, 3, and 4 are descriptions of which Bible character?

_____

To whom are the words of questions 5, 6, and 7 being spoken?

_____

Who is renewing the promise of the covenant in questions 9 and 10?

_____

Fill in the names of the twelve tribes of Israel on the map below. You may refer to the map on page 195. Remember that Dan and Manasseh were given split portions of the land. Place a color code beside each of the names of the twelve tribes. Coordinate the map with your color codes.

Color Code

I Asher

II Benjamin

III Dan

IV Ephraim

V Gad

VI Issachar

VII Judah

VIII Manasseh

IX Naphtali

X Reuben

XI Simeon

XII Zebulun

Judges

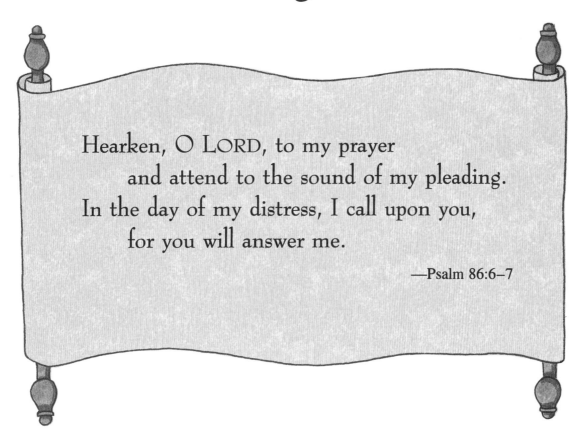

Hearken, O LORD, to my prayer
　　and attend to the sound of my pleading.
In the day of my distress, I call upon you,
　　for you will answer me.

—Psalm 86:6–7

In this lesson you will read about a period of history recorded in the Book of Judges. Look at the time-line on this page. Find the dates 1250–1050 B.C.. The events recorded in the Book of Judges took place approximately during these two hundred years. The Book of Judges begins with the death of Joshua and ends just before the time of Samuel. You will read about Samuel in a later lesson. The writers of this book probably lived during the early days of the kings. They are looking back on a period of Israel's history that was in *transition*. Its way of life was changing.

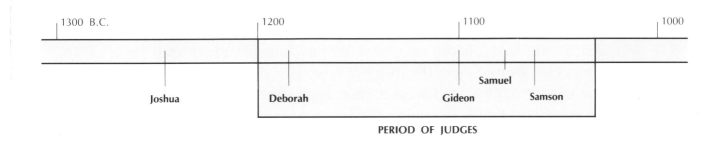

PERIOD OF JUDGES

Beginning a New Way of Life

The Israelites had completed numerous military campaigns under the leadership of Joshua. They had conquered some of the land of Canaan. Many Canaanites survived the invasion. It was left to the individual Israelite tribes to secure their own sections of the land. Although fighting did occur periodically, more often than not the Israelites learned to live peacefully with the remaining Canaanites.

The Israelites were also adjusting to a new way of life. For forty years they had led a nomadic life, wandering through the desert. Now they would have to settle down in one area. The Israelites were familiar with raising sheep, but not with grazing them in a limited area. So new agricultural skills had to be learned.

Joshua did not appoint a successor to lead all of Israel. After Joshua died, the Israelites did not have a leader, nor did they have any form of government. A *monarchy* was not established among the Israelites until two hundred years later. In a monarchy, a king or a queen rules over the people.

The Israelites Forget God

Read Judges 2:10–23.

When the twelve tribes took possession of the land, only two things united them—a common language and their faith in the one true God. However, without a leader and without a way to rule the scattered tribes, the Israelites soon became strongly influenced by the Canaanite way of life, including, unfortunately, their pagan religion. The Israelites repeatedly forgot the covenant they had made with God, and they chose to worship the false gods of the Canaanites.

When the Israelites chose to sin, God allowed them to suffer the consequences of their sin. The Canaanites and other enemies overpowered the Israelites. They suffered greatly at the hands of their enemies. After a while, however, the Israelites remembered the God of the covenant. They cried out to Him for help. God heard the cries of His chosen people. He answered their prayers by sending men who led the Israelites in victory against their enemies. These heroes then ruled Israel until their death. They became known as the *judges*. The Israelites repeatedly offended God by worshiping the pagan Canaanite gods. Each time, God allowed them to suffer the consequences of their sin. Each time, God showed them His merciful love. God drew good out of this evil. Out of their misery, the Israelites once again turned to God for help. God sent the judges to help the Israelites. The Israelites were then drawn closer to God and were able to renew their covenant of love with Him.

1. When does the Book of Judges begin and end?
2. Explain why this period was a time of transition for the Israelites.
3. What were some reasons why the Israelites forgot God?
4. What sin did the Israelites commit?
5. How did God show the Israelites His merciful love during the time of the judges?

Who Were the Judges?

If you were asked to define the word *judge*, you might say that a judge is a person, either appointed or elected, who rules in a court of law. A judge makes decisions or judgments according to the law. The judges discussed in this book of the Old Testament were not the same sort of judges that we know today. First of all, except for Deborah, they were all military leaders. They had won victories over various enemies of Israel. They ruled, not in a courtroom, but over a tribe, possibly several tribes. They never ruled over the entire nation of Israel. They were not appointed or elected in the way modern-day judges are. The Old Testament judges were chosen by God to save His people from the hands of their enemies. They won the favor of their particular tribe because they had been victorious in battle.

Second, the judges were ordinary people of their time. Several, in fact, led very sinful lives. None are described as virtuous, or as outstanding citizens. They all had faults. They all struggled with temptation, sometimes winning, sometimes choosing to sin. And yet God chose them to do His work. The Bible does not in any way approve of their sinful lives. It does, however, praise their faith and their courage. The author of the letter to the Hebrews spoke of their faith: "What more shall I say? I have not time to tell of Gideon, Barak, Samson, Jephthah, of David and Samuel and the prophets, who by faith conquered kingdoms, did what was righteous, obtained the promises; they closed the mouths of lions, put out raging fires, escaped the devouring sword; out of weakness they were made powerful, became strong in battle, and turned back foreign invaders" (Heb 11:32–34).

A Show of Faith

The judges were chosen because they accepted God's invitation to rise above their weaknesses, to act as men and women of faith, to act as images of God. The Book of Judges is important because it reminds us that our own weaknesses need not prevent us from acting as images of God. We can act as images of God in spite of our weaknesses. Time and time again the Israelites forgot their promise to love God. When they sinned, they suffered the consequences. When they called upon God to help them, God always responded to their cry. The Book of Judges is not just a history book. It reminds us that we, too, are like the Israelites. Time and time again we choose to forget our promise to love God. When we choose to sin, we suffer the consequences. But when we call upon God to help us, God is always there. He listens to our cries for help. He shows us His merciful love.

REVIEW QUESTIONS

*1. Who were the judges?
2. Even though the judges often led sinful lives, God chose them to do His work. How did the judges show their faith in God?
3. How can we show our faith in God?
4. How does God show us His merciful love?

The Twelve Judges

The author names twelve judges who ruled during this period of history. Look at the chart on page 227. This chart is a summary of the Book of Judges. It shows the names of the twelve judges, the biblical passage that describes each one's story, the names of the enemies they fought, the number of years that Israel suffered as a conquered nation, and the number of years each judge ruled. You will notice that there were six major judges and six minor judges. The major judges are described in some detail in the Bible. The minor judges are mentioned only briefly. You will notice that one woman, Deborah, is listed with Barak. Deborah was a prophetess. She advised Barak, who was the military leader who fought against the Canaanites and then became a judge. The story of Deborah is discussed in Lesson 15, "Women of Faith in the Old Testament".

Are Numbers Important?

You may have noticed that the total number of years mentioned in the biblical passages is much greater than the two hundred years that historians generally allow for this time period. There are several reasons. First, the dates given for this time period are only estimates. Historians and archaeologists must often use approximate dates when placing historical events. It is rare that an exact

The Major and Minor Judges

The Major Judges	Bible Passage	Enemy	Conquered Years	Years of Rule
Othniel	3:7–11	Aram Naharaim	8	40
Ehud	3:12–30	Moabites	18	80
Deborah and Barak	4–5	Canaanites	20	40
Gideon	6–8	Midianites	7	40
Jephthah	10:6–12:7	Ammonites	18	6
Samson	13–16	Philistines	40	20

The Minor Judges				
Shamgar	3:31	Philistines		
Tola	10:1–2			23
Jair	10:3–5			22
Ibzan	12:8–10			7
Elon	12:11–12			10
Abdon	12:13–15			8

date can be verified for historical events of ancient times. Second, the biblical text itself is a compilation of several authors who based their writings on tribal stories that were passed down from one generation to another. The number forty was a favorite among biblical writers. A generation was given the length of forty years in most Old Testament writings. Noah and the ark endured the rain for forty days and forty nights. Moses and the Israelites wandered in the desert for forty years. Many judges ruled for forty years. Jesus fasted in the desert for forty days and forty nights. Biblical writers used the number forty to stress the importance of the event, not its exact length.

We must take these factors into consideration, therefore, when all the dates and numbers don't match or add up to exact calculations. The most important reason for writing these stories was to teach a religious lesson, not a mathematical one. When we look at the chart printed above, we should be amazed at the number of times the Israelites forgot God and even more amazed at the number of times God showed them His merciful love. Those are numbers we can count on!

LEAD·US·NOT INTO TEMPTATION

1. How many judges ruled during this period?
2. Name at least two of the major judges.
3. What is the important thing to remember when reading the stories of the Old Testament?

Concepts of Faith

1. Who were the judges of the ancient Israelites?
The judges were heroes, or military leaders, whom God chose to lead the Israelites in victory over their enemies. They ruled over several tribes for a period of time and helped renew the faith of the Israelites.

Vocabulary

transition: A time of change.

monarchy: Rule by kings and queens.

biblical judges: Heroes or military leaders.

Living the Lesson

Bad Influences: The New False Gods

The Israelites offended God because they chose to worship the false gods of the Canaanites. They were influenced by the Canaanites and their way of life. They forgot that there is only one true God. They forgot that He should be the most important Person in their lives.

There are many kinds of false gods that can influence us. When someone or something becomes more important to us than God, then that person or thing is a false god.

Make a list of some of the false gods that people, including sixth graders, can have today. Share your ideas with the class. Then discuss the questions that follow.

1. Why do you think the Israelites fell into sin so often?

2. Why do you think people choose to sin today?

3. What can you do to avoid having false gods?

4. Does God love us when we sin?

Prayers

"Our Father". (Discuss the following words of the "Our Father" in light of this lesson: " . . . and forgive us our trespasses as we forgive those who trespass against us. And lead us not into temptation, but deliver from evil.")

Psalm 86. (The words of Psalm 86 are as appropriate today as they were during the days of the Israelites. Psalm 86 is divided into three sections. Sections I and III ask God to listen to our cries of help in time of distress. Section II is a short hymn of praise. It denies the reality of all false gods and praises the deeds of the one true God. Read the Psalm aloud and discuss its meaning.)

Samson (Judges 13–16)

When you were younger, many of you may have heard the story of Samson and his gift of strength. Now that you are older, you can learn more details about the story of this famous judge. Find the answers to the following questions about Samson by using your Bibles.

1. Why were the Israelites under the power of the Philistines (Jgs 13:1)?

   _____

2. Who announced to Samson's mother that she would have a son (Jgs 13:3)?

   _____

3. The angel told Samson's mother that he was to be consecrated to God. What special directions were given to the mother as a sign of this? Later, Samson was asked to observe the same signs of consecration (Jgs 13:4–5).

   _____

4. What happened to Samson on the way to Timnah (Jgs 14:5–6)?

   _____

5. The following Bible passages tell about the times that Samson used his strength to hurt the Philistines. Describe what happened in each passage.

   Judges 15:4–5: _____

   Judges 15:14–15: _____

   Judges 16:1–3: _____

6. For how many years did Samson judge Israel (Jgs 15:20)? _____

7. What was the name of the woman with whom Samson fell in love (Jgs 16:4)? _____

8. What did the Philistines ask Delilah to do, and what did they promise to give her in return (Jgs 16:5)?

_____

9. Samson tricked Delilah three times when she repeatedly asked him to tell her the secret of his strength. What were the three wrong answers he gave her?

Judges 16:7: _____

Judges 16:11: _____

Judges 16:13: _____

10. What was the secret of Samson's strength (Jgs 16:17)?

_____

11. What did the Philistines do to Samson after Delilah shaved his head (Jgs 16:21)?

_____

12. God forgave Samson for breaking his special vow. While Samson was in prison, God gave Samson a sign of His merciful love. What was the sign (Jgs 16:22)?

_____

13. Why was Samson brought to the celebration of the pagan god Dagon (Jgs 16:23)?

_____

14. How did Samson show God that he believed in Him (Jgs 16:28)?

_____

15. How did Samson die (Jgs 16:29)?

_____

Bonus question: Did Samson really get his strength from his hair? Explain.

Gideon was one of the judges who ruled in Israel before the monarchy. The Israelites had offended God by worshiping the false gods of Canaan. They forgot their covenant to love and to be faithful to the God of Israel. Because of their sin, God allowed the Israelites to be conquered by the Midianites. For seven years the Israelites suffered at the hands of the Midianites. The Midianites destroyed the produce of the land, and the Israelites lived in fear of them. "Thus was Israel reduced to misery by Midian, and so the Israelites cried out to the LORD" (Jgs 6:6).

The Lord heard the prayer of His people. He showed them His merciful love by calling Gideon to save the Israelites from the Midianites. Then the Israelites once again renewed their covenant with God. The story of Gideon is found in the Book of Judges. Find the answers to the following questions about Gideon by using your Bibles.

1. What was Gideon doing when the angel of the Lord appeared to him (Jgs 6:11)?

   _____

   _____

2. How did Gideon respond to God's call to save Israel from the Midianites (Jgs 6:15–18)?

   _____

   _____

3. Gideon brought an offering and presented it to the Lord. What sign did God give Gideon to assure Him that He was the Lord (Jgs 6:20–22)?

   _____

   _____

4. The Israelites, including Gideon's father, offended God by worshiping a pagan god named Baal. What did God ask Gideon to do to stop this false worship (Jgs 6:25–26)?

   _____

   _____

5. Gideon then gathered an army from the surrounding tribes. But again Gideon needed to be assured of God's help. So he asked God, not once, but twice, for a sign of His favor. Describe the signs that God gave to Gideon (Jgs 6:36–40).

_____

_____

6. God knew that Israel would defeat Midian. But He wanted the Israelites to know that it was His power, and not their own, that brought them victory. So God asked Gideon to reduce the number of soldiers in his army. How did Gideon accomplish this reduction (Jgs 7:3 and 7:5–7)?

_____

_____

7. Were the Israelites outnumbered (Jgs 7:12)?

_____

_____

8. How did Gideon, with only three hundred men, defeat the Midianites (Jgs 7:16–22)?

_____

_____

9. After the defeat of Midian, the Israelites asked Gideon to rule over them. What was his reply (Jgs 8:23)?

_____

_____

Bonus Question:

10. Gideon did act as judge in Israel for forty years. What did he mean, then, when he said, "I will not rule over you. The LORD must rule over you"?

_____

_____

_____

Women of Faith in the Old Testament

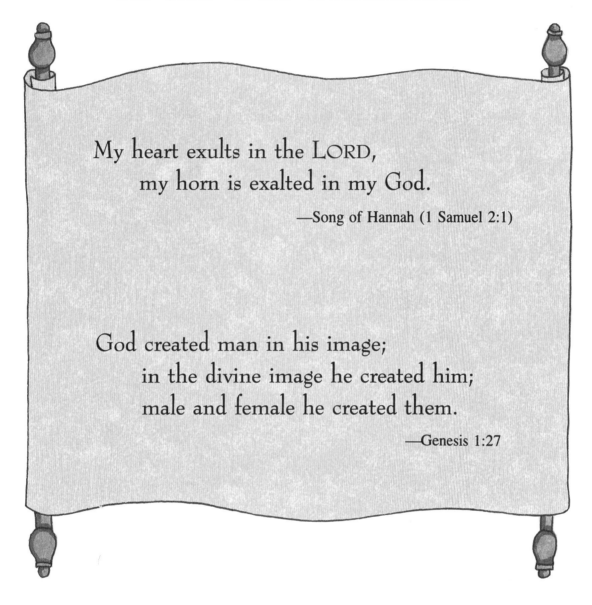

My heart exults in the LORD,
   my horn is exalted in my God.

—Song of Hannah (1 Samuel 2:1)

God created man in his image;
   in the divine image he created him;
   male and female he created them.

—Genesis 1:27

God created all men and women in His image so that they might come to know and love Him. Furthermore, He shares His divine life with us. Through this divine life, called *grace*, God gives us the power by which we come to know and believe in Him. This power that God gives us to help us believe in Him is called *faith*.

We might think of the Bible as a series of writings that tell us how men and women of faith came to know and love their Creator. The more they knew about God, the more they believed in Him. As their knowledge of God grew, so their love for Him grew. When we love someone, we want to show that person our love. These men and women expressed their love for God in the way they acted. These actions of love were recorded in the writings of the Bible.

When we read and study the Bible, our knowledge of God grows. The more we know God, the more we should believe in Him. The gift of faith gives us the power to know and believe the truths about God. What we know and believe about God should increase our love for God. When we love God, we should want to show our love for Him. We can show our love for God by acting as He would act, by acting as images of God.

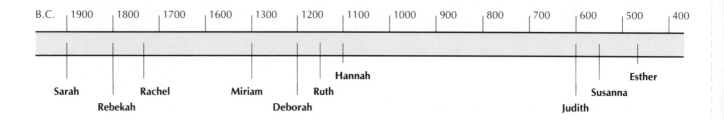

In this lesson, you will read about several women of the Old Testament who had a deep faith in God. These women lived during a time of history when men were the leaders of the government and of family life. The customs and laws of Israel limited a woman's education, legal rights, and choice of occupation. Yet the stories of these women reflect how their faith in God allowed them to rise above limitations. These women were not afraid to express their faith. They did so by acting as images of God. Because of their actions, these women were able to influence the history of their nation. When we learn about them, our own faith is strengthened. They are examples of how we should act. These women of faith can help us become better images of God.

REVIEW QUESTIONS

1. What is grace?
*2. What is faith?
3. How do we show our love for God?
4. What can we learn from the women of faith in the Old Testament?

Women of Faith in the Old Testament

Sarah, Woman of the Promise

The story of Sarah can be found in Genesis 11:29–23:17. Sarah is also mentioned in the New Testament, in Hebrews 11:11 and in 1 Peter 3:6.

A Summary of the Story of Sarah

Sarah is first mentioned in Genesis 11:29. She was the wife of Abram (later called Abraham). "Sarah was barren; she had no child." The story of Sarah centers on her desire to bear a son and God's promise to give her one. Sarah's story is told in conjunction with that of her husband, Abraham. God promised to make a great nation of Abraham. As Abraham's wife, Sarah knew that she would share in this promise. So, to follow God's call to settle in a new land, Canaan, with all her possessions, she willingly left her homeland of Haran.

To escape a famine that came upon the land, Sarah and Abraham traveled to Egypt. The Egyptians were powerful, and Abraham was afraid that they would kill him and take all his possessions. Sarah was a beautiful woman. Abraham hoped that her beauty would find favor with the Pharaoh. He asked Sarah to tell the Egyptians that she was his sister, not his wife. Sarah was willing to do this to spare her husband's life. "On her account it went well with Abram, and he received flocks and herds, male and female slaves, male and female asses, and camels" (Gen 12:16). God, however, helped Sarah when she was taken into the Pharaoh's house. Pharaoh and his household were afflicted with plagues. When Pharaoh saw that Sarah was spared these sufferings, he knew that he had been deceived, and he sent Sarah back to her husband. Sarah was instrumental in saving Abraham and their possessions from the Egyptians.

Ten years passed, and the promise of a son had not been fulfilled. Sarah, however, did not give up hope of bearing an heir for Abraham. Instead, she became more determined and decided to take matters into her own hands. The Israelite laws provided a "loophole" for such situations. If a man's wife could not bear him a son, then the wife could give her servant to her husband so that the wife could have a son through her servant. Sarah was willing to take advantage of the law. The child born to Sarah's servant would by law belong to Sarah. This law seems very strange and immoral to us, but to Sarah her actions were simply in accord with the customs of her people. Abraham did as Sarah asked. Hagar, Sarah's servant, became pregnant and had a son, whom she named Ishmael. Sarah, however, was not happy. Hagar "looked on her mistress with disdain" (Gen 16:4). Sarah became angry, and she was envious of Hagar. Sarah had accomplished her purpose—technically, the baby was her son. But Sarah was unhappy because her servant had been able to bear Abraham a son, while she herself could not. When Sarah complained to Abraham about Hagar's attitude, Abraham told Sarah, "Your maid is in your power. Do to her whatever you please" (Gen 16:6). The Bible tells us that Sarah mistreated Hagar so much that she ran away, taking her son with her. God took pity on Hagar and her son, Ishmael. He showed them His merciful love and cared for them. God also promised Hagar that Ishmael would have many descendants.

Then God repeated His promise to Abraham. This time, however, God made it clear that Abraham would have a son through Sarah. Sarah's son, not Hagar's son, would be the promised one, the one destined to lead a great nation. God also changed Sarah's name. Before this time, her name had been spelled Sarai. The new spelling, Sarah, means "princess". The spelling was changed to emphasize that Sarah would be the mother of a ruler of nations. Abraham was a hundred years old and found all this to be so incredible that he "prostrated himself and laughed". Doubled over with laughter, Abraham asked, "Can Sarah give birth at ninety?" (Gen 17:17). God reassured Abraham that Sarah would indeed have a son, and they were to name him Isaac. God promised to renew His covenant with Isaac and his descendants.

In Genesis 18 there is another version of this part of the story. In this version, three visitors announced to Abraham that Sarah will have a son within the year. Sarah, who was in the tent preparing a meal for them, overheard their conversation and laughed aloud at the thought of having a child at her age. The visitor, now addressed as the Lord, said, "Why did

Sarah laugh? . . . Is anything too marvelous for the LORD to do? At the appointed time, about this time next year, I will return to you, and Sarah will have a son" (Gen 18:14).

A year later, Sarah gave birth to a son. The parents named him Isaac, which means "laughter". Sarah then said, "God has given me cause to laugh, and all who hear of it will laugh with me" (Gen 21:6).

Sarah lived a long life. After she died, Abraham mourned for her and buried her in Hebron in the land of Canaan.

How Was Sarah a Woman of Faith?

Sarah was a woman of faith. She believed in the promise of the covenant. She willingly left her homeland to fulfill it. She was beautiful and courageous. Abraham must have looked on her with high esteem. He did not command her to help him when he was endangered by the Egyptians, even though it was his right to do so. Instead, he *pleaded* with her and *asked* her to protect him. Sarah came to her husband's aid, believing that God would not abandon her. Sarah was clever, too. She was not afraid to take matters into her own hands to help fulfill God's promise of a son. Sarah was not perfect, however. It is easy for us to understand (but we should not accept) her envy of Hagar after patiently waiting for a son of her own for so many years. Yet Sarah did not become embittered, even after she knew she was far beyond the age of bearing children. She was able to laugh at herself, because she had accepted God's will and was content with it. Her laughter was a mixture of disbelief, relief, and resurgent hope in the power of God.

Sarah chose to act as an image of God. Her faith remained strong throughout the long wait for her promised son. Her actions were a reflection of her faith and love in God. Sarah played a significant role in the development of the Chosen People. It was through Sarah that the promise of the covenant given to Abraham was fulfilled. The Chosen People would not have come to be without this woman of faith.

REVIEW QUESTIONS

1. Who was Sarah?
2. Why was Sarah unhappy?
3. What promise did God give to Abraham that included Sarah?
4. How did Sarah act as an image of God?

Rebekah, Mother of Two Nations

The story of Rebekah can be found in Genesis 24, 25, 27, and 28:1–10. Rebekah is also mentioned in Romans 9:10.

A Summary of the Story of Rebekah

Rebekah is first mentioned in Genesis 24:15. A servant had been sent by Abraham to find a suitable wife for his son, Isaac. The servant was anxious to make the right choice, for he wanted to please his master. He prayed to God for help in devising a plan. He thought: when I stop at the town well, the women will be there to draw water. "If I say to a girl, 'Please lower your jug that I may drink', and she answers, 'Take a drink, and let me give water to your camels, too', let her be the one whom you have decided upon for your servant Isaac" (Gen 24:14). As Rebekah approached the well, the servant noted that she was very beautiful. He asked her for a drink of water, and Rebekah answered him according to his plan. Then the servant knew that this must be the girl whom God had chosen to be Isaac's wife. He told Rebekah of his purpose, and she took him to her family's house. The servant gave Rebekah and her family gold and silver articles and many other gifts. He asked Rebekah's family if they would permit Rebekah to become Isaac's wife. They agreed and asked Rebekah, "Do you wish to go with this man?" She answered, "I do" (Gen 24:58).

Isaac and Rebekah first met on the journey to his father's house. When the servant told Isaac of Rebekah's willingness to become his wife, "Isaac took Rebekah into his tent; he married her, and thus she became his wife. In his love for her, Isaac found solace after the death of his mother Sarah" (Gen 24:67).

Like Sarah, her mother-in-law, Rebekah thought that she was not able to have children. Isaac prayed to the Lord and asked for His help. Finally, Rebekah became pregnant with twin boys. Her pregnancy was difficult, and Rebekah was afraid that the babies in her womb might die. So she prayed to God, and He answered her: "Two nations are in your womb, two peoples are quarreling while still within you; But one shall surpass the other, and the older shall serve the younger" (Gen 25:23). These words reassured Rebekah, but also troubled her. She felt relieved that both sons would live, but she was concerned that the younger son would gain authority over the firstborn, the heir to the birthright. Rebekah and Isaac named the firstborn Esau and the younger twin Jacob. As the boys grew, Rebekah favored the younger son, Jacob, whose character was quiet. Isaac tended to favor Esau, who was a hunter. Esau's manner was gruff and self-satisfying. One day Esau was so hungry that he sold his birthright to his brother Jacob for a bowl of stew! Jacob took advantage of his brother's weakness of character and offered this lowly price for the cherished birthright.

Rebekah became convinced that God intended Jacob to be the heir not only of Isaac's property, but also of the covenant. She devised a plan to deceive Isaac into giving his final blessing to Jacob, rather than to his firstborn, Esau. When Esau discovered the treachery, he vowed to kill Jacob. Rebekah sent Jacob away to her brother Laban. She hoped that, in time, Esau would forgive Jacob, and then she could send for him. Rebekah, however, never saw Jacob again. She also lost Esau, who knew of his mother's part in the deception. He left home, and married into a family that did not meet the approval of his parents. In addition, the beautiful relationship between Isaac and Rebekah was strained because of her actions.

How Was Rebekah a Woman of Faith?

The story of Rebekah is marked by emotional extremes. In the beginning, the reader feels the intense happiness that Rebekah must have felt as the events of the love story unfold. Her emotions changed from love and happiness to anxiety over her seeming inability to have children. And once she does conceive and is afraid because of her difficult pregnancy, God's words to Rebekah concerning her sons lead her down a path of favoritism and deception, which ends in sorrow and hatred. How, then, can Rebekah be considered a woman of faith? We must look to the motivation behind Rebekah's actions to find the answer.

Rebekah's character is first revealed to us at the meeting with Abraham's servant at the well (Gen 24:1 ff.). Rebekah's courtesy goes beyond that usually extended to a stranger. Her kindness and consideration to the stranger she meets at the well complement her beauty. Her behavior convinces the servant that his prayers to God for guidance have been answered. She is the one whom God has chosen for Isaac. We learn from the story that Rebekah cannot wait to meet her new husband. She does not hesitate to leave her family and home to begin a new life with a man she has never even met. Rebekah trusts in God and believes that this is her destiny. When Isaac and Rebekah meet, the Scriptures tell us, Isaac, who is sad because of his mother's death, is comforted by his new wife. It is in love and tenderness that Rebekah and Isaac begin their married life together.

Rebekah thought that she was not able to conceive. Isaac prayed to God to give them a child. God answered his prayers and renewed Rebekah's faith. It was Rebekah who prayed to God when she became worried about her pregnancy. She believed God when He told her that she was to have twin sons. Rebekah believed, though she did not fully understand, God's prediction that the older son, Esau, would serve the younger one, Jacob. Rebekah's actions from then on were motivated by her faith in God's words. It was the Israelite custom that the firstborn son should inherit the birthright and the blessing. Rebekah believed that in order for God's words to come true, she would have to lend a hand. We learn from the Scriptures that she had great influence over Jacob and Isaac. Rebekah used her influence to accomplish God's will. Her actions were decisive, daring, and bold. There is no denying that Jacob received both the birthright and Isaac's blessing through deception. Yet Rebekah herself received no reward for her efforts. Though she was motivated by faith, she did not completely understand God's will. She sinned, because she knew that deceiving Isaac was wrong. God allowed her to suffer the consequences of her actions. She lost both of her sons.

Rebekah's actions were important because they were concerned with Jacob. It is through Jacob that God continued the promise of the covenant and of a nation that would bear Jacob's new name, Israel. Had it not been for Rebekah's faith, Jacob would not have renewed his own faith in the God of the covenant.

REVIEW QUESTIONS

1. Who was Rebekah?
2. How did Rebekah first show that she was a woman of faith?
3. What did Rebekah do when she was afraid of losing her babies while she was pregnant?
4. What were Rebekah's motives for aiding Jacob in stealing Isaac's blessing from Esau?
5. Why was Rebekah's faith important to the continuance of the covenant?

Rachel, Beautiful and Beloved

The story of Rachel can be found in Genesis 29–31 and 35:16–29.

A Summary of the Story of Rachel

The story of Rachel begins with the arrival of Jacob in Haran. Jacob had been sent to Haran by his mother, Rebekah, to escape the anger of his brother, Esau. He had traveled a long time. He was afraid, and he missed his family. He hoped to find refuge with his uncle Laban. When Jacob arrived in Haran, he asked some shepherds who were assembled near a well if they knew his uncle. They replied that they did and pointed out Rachel, who was approaching the well to water her father's flock of sheep. "As soon as Jacob saw Rachel, the daughter of his uncle Laban, with the sheep of his uncle Laban, he went up, rolled the stone away from the mouth of the well, and watered his uncle's sheep. Then Jacob kissed Rachel and burst into tears" (Gen 29:10–11). Jacob told Rachel who he was, and he was welcomed into Laban's family with open arms.

After only a month, Jacob had fallen in love with Rachel. Rachel was the younger of two daughters. Her sister's name was Leah. "Leah had lovely eyes, but Rachel was well formed and beautiful" (Gen 29:17). Jacob asked Laban for permission to marry Rachel. Laban told Jacob that he would have to work seven years for Rachel. "So Jacob served seven years for Rachel, yet they seemed to him but a few days because of his love for her" (Gen 29:20).

When it came time for Jacob to marry Rachel, Laban tricked Jacob. In the darkness of evening, Laban brought Leah to Jacob's tent, with a veil covering her face. In the morning, Jacob discovered that it was not his beloved Rachel, but her sister, Leah, whom he had married. Jacob was understandably upset and demanded an explanation from Laban. Laban replied that it was the custom for the oldest daughter to marry first. If Jacob still wanted Rachel, he would have to work another seven years. Jacob's love for Rachel was so great that he agreed to his uncle's demands. Finally, Rachel was given to Jacob in marriage, "and he loved her more than Leah" (Gen 29:30).

Rachel, however, suffered the same anxiety and disappointment as Sarah and Rebekah had before her. She thought that she was not able to conceive and bear a son for Jacob. Even though she knew that Jacob loved her, the sorrow of not having a child was almost too hard to bear. Leah, on the other hand, gave birth to four sons. This made it even more difficult for Rachel. Then Rachel, like Sarah, offered her maidservant, Bilhah, to Jacob, so that she could bear a son through her servant. When Bilhah conceived and bore a son, Rachel said, "God has . . . heeded my plea and given me a son" (Gen 30:5–6). Bilhah had two sons by Jacob.

The competition between the two sisters to bear more sons continued. Leah offered her maidservant, Zilpah, to Jacob. Zilpah and Jacob had two sons. Then Leah herself had two more sons and a daughter. Leah had now borne a total of six sons and one daughter, as well as two sons by her servant Zilpah. Rachel herself had not yet conceived, but she had two sons by her servant Bilhah.

"Then God remembered Rachel; he heard her prayer and made her fruitful. She conceived and bore a son, and she said, 'God has removed my disgrace.' So she named him Joseph meaning 'May the LORD add another son to this one for me!'" (Gen 30:22–24). God heard her prayers again, and Rachel conceived and bore another son, Benjamin. Rachel died giving birth to Benjamin. Before she died, however, she was comforted by her midwife, who said to her, "Have no fear! This time, too, you have a son" (Gen 35:17). Joseph and Benjamin were favored by Jacob over all his other sons because of the love he had for Rachel.

How Was Rachel a Woman of Faith?
The beginning of Rachel's story reminds us of the first romantic meeting of Jacob's parents, Rebekah and Isaac. The writer makes clear Jacob's deep love for Rachel. But, almost from the start, their happiness was shattered. Rachel's father tricked Jacob into marrying her sister first. Even though Rachel was aware of the customs of her people, this must have hurt her deeply. Jacob, however, met the challenge set before him and won Rachel's hand in marriage. Rachel's faith in Jacob's love for her was never in question.

The importance of bearing a son, however, caused jealousy and strife between Rachel and her sister, Leah. Here we should recall the significance of bearing sons to this society. The firstborn son inherited the birthright, which included not only property but family and tribal authority, and also the continuance of the covenant. Other sons shared in the inheritance, but to a lesser degree. The birthright was not passed on through daughters. A woman in this society was not on equal terms with a man. The status of a woman, however, was increased by her ability to have sons. Mothers of sons were regarded with high esteem. For Rachel, then, it was extremely important for her to give a son to Jacob. Even though Jacob married Leah first, and Leah had borne him four sons, as well as two through her maidservant, Rachel knew that she was the favored wife. Her faith in Jacob's love for her never wavered. She knew that Jacob, in turn, would love and favor her sons more than Leah's.

For many years, Rachel prayed that God might give her a son. God "heard her prayer and made her fruitful" (Gen 30:22). Rachel's faith in God was rewarded. She bore Jacob two sons, Joseph and Benjamin. These favored sons played a

significant role in the development of the Israelite nation. It was through Joseph that the Hebrew tribes grew numerous in Egypt and could take part in the Exodus from that land. Later, the tribes descended from Benjamin and the sons of Joseph, Ephraim and Manasseh, became the heartland of Israel, while the rest of Israel was ruled by nine of the other brothers and their tribes.

REVIEW QUESTIONS

1. Who was Rachel?
2. From what similar problem did Sarah, Rebekah, and Rachel suffer?
3. When Rachel could not have children, what did she do that showed she was a woman of faith?
4. What significant role did Rachel have in the history of the Israelites?

Miriam, Woman of the Exodus

The story of Miriam can be found in Exodus 15:20–21; Numbers 12:1–15, 20:1; Micah 6:4; and 1 Chronicles 5:29.

A Summary of the Story of Miriam

Although Miriam is not mentioned by name in the biblical story of the young baby Moses, Tradition identifies her as the sister of Moses who watched over him when he was put in a basket among the reeds on the river. When the baby Moses was discovered by Pharaoh's daughter, Miriam stepped out of the rushes and was quick to suggest that a Hebrew woman be found to nurse the child. Moses' own mother was brought to nurse her child. And so Moses and the future nation of Israel were saved by his sister. There is a passage in 1 Chronicles 5:29 that lists Miriam, along with Moses and Aaron, as the children of Amram, a descendant of the tribe of Levi. Thus, Tradition concludes that Miriam was the sister of Moses.

The first scriptural reference to Miriam by name occurs immediately after the miraculous crossing at the Red Sea. Here, Miriam is called a prophetess. "The prophetess Miriam, Aaron's sister, took a tambourine in her hand, while all the women went out after her with tambourines, dancing, and she led them in the refrain: Sing to the Lord, for he is gloriously triumphant; horse and chariot he has cast into the sea" (Ex 15:20–21).

The next scriptural reference to Miriam is found in Numbers 12:1–15. This story, however, was not a happy occasion for Miriam. On this occasion, Miriam and Aaron complained and spoke out against the authority of Moses. "Is it through Moses alone that the Lord speaks? Does he not speak through us also?" (Nm 12:2). Their envy angered the Lord. God told Miriam and Aaron that He spoke to them only in visions or in dreams. "Not so with my servant Moses! Throughout my house he bears my trust: face to face I speak to him, plainly and not in riddles. The presence of the Lord he beholds" (Nm 12:7–8). When the Lord departed, "there was Miriam, a snow-white leper! When Aaron turned and saw her a leper, 'Ah, my lord!' he said to Moses, 'please do not charge us with the sin that we have foolishly committed!'" (Nm 12:10–11). Then Moses prayed to the Lord to heal Miriam. The Lord replied, "Let her be confined outside the camp for seven days; only then may she be brought back" (Nm 12:14). After seven days, Miriam was healed and brought back into the camp.

Miriam is not mentioned in the story of the Exodus again until her death. Miriam died and was buried at Kadesh. Miriam's brother, Aaron, died later on Mount Hor. Neither Miriam nor Aaron ever saw the Promised Land.

How Was Miriam a Woman of Faith?

Miriam was one of the few women in the Old Testament who was given the title "prophetess". A *prophet* was a person chosen by God to speak to His people. Only two other women in the Old Testament were recognized and accepted by their people as prophets, Deborah and Huldah. In the very first scriptural reference to Miriam, in Exodus 15:20, she is called "prophetess". A second source, the prophet Micah, also lists Miriam, along with Moses and

Aaron, as prophets, or ones sent by God. "And I sent before you Moses, Aaron, and Miriam" (Micah 6:4). The Hebrew people must have recognized her faith in the one true God, or they would not have accepted her as His prophet. Miriam was there when the Hebrews left Egypt. She led the festive celebration after the miraculous crossing at the Red Sea. She walked and stood beside her brothers, Moses and Aaron, throughout the crossing of the desert. She believed that God would fulfill His promise of the covenant.

What can be said about Miriam's envy of Moses? Even though Miriam showed her faith in God by acting as His prophet, this does not mean that she was without fault. It was clear to all the Hebrews that Moses was their leader. It was Moses to whom God chose to speak "face to face". Moses was the receiver of the covenant. Miriam was envious of his authority and his superior position with the people. Her envy caused her to become discontented and to complain about Moses to Aaron. Aaron also was drawn into this sin of envy. He suffered the consequences of his sins later, when he was not permitted to enter the Promised Land. God, however, allowed Miriam to suffer the consequences of her sin immediately. Miriam was afflicted with leprosy, a dreaded skin disease. She was banished from the camp for seven days, until she was healed. Her return to the camp can be seen as a foreshadowing of the sacrament of Reconciliation. When we sin, we hurt God, ourselves, and others. God then allows us to suffer the consequences of our sins. The sacrament of Reconciliation restores our relationship with God and the community. It draws us back to Him. So it was with Miriam. After her penance, she was brought back into the camp. She was restored to the community. God did not allow her sin to diminish her faith, but to serve as the occasion to renew it.

The very fact that the writers of this part of Hebrew history mentioned Miriam specifically by name is testament to the significance of the role she played as a woman of faith.

REVIEW QUESTIONS

1. Who was Miriam?
2. How did Miriam save Moses when he was a baby?
3. On what occasion does the Bible first mention Miriam by name?
4. What is a prophet?
5. In what ways did Miriam show she was a woman of faith?
6. Why was Miriam envious of Moses?
7. How was Miriam reconciled with God for her sin of envy?

Deborah, Prophet and Judge

The story of Deborah can be found in Judges 4 and 5.

A Summary of the Story of Deborah

The Israelites, during this period of their history (1250–1050 B.C.), were ruled by judges. The judges were usually military leaders who helped the Israelites to overcome their enemies. The Israelites had offended God by worshiping the false gods of the Canaanites. God allowed the Israelites to suffer the consequences of their sin—they fell into the power of a Canaanite king, Jabin. The general of Jabin's army was named Sisera. For twenty years the Israelites were oppressed by the Canaanites. Finally they called out to God for help.

"At this time the prophetess Deborah, wife of Lappidoth, was judging Israel. She used to sit under Deborah's palm tree, situated between Ramah and Bethel in the mountain region of Ephraim, and there the Israelites came up to her for judgment" (Jgs 4:4–5).

One day, Deborah called for a man named Barak. She told Barak that God wanted him to lead the fight against the Canaanites. He was to gather a large army of footsoldiers on Mount Tabor. Deborah would lead Sisera with his iron chariots and troops to Barak. But Barak answered her, "If you come with me, I will go; if you do not come with me, I will not go" (Jgs 4:8). Deborah agreed to go with him, but warned Barak that he would not receive the glory of the victory, "for the LORD will have Sisera fall into the power of a woman" (Jgs 4:9).

Barak assembled ten thousand men from the tribes of Israel. Sisera met him with nine hundred of his iron chariots and all his forces. Deborah then said to Barak, "Be off, for this is the day on which the LORD has delivered Sisera into your power. The LORD marches before you" (Jgs 4:14). Barak and his men overpowered Sisera's army. "The entire army of Sisera fell beneath the sword, not even one man surviving" (Jgs 4:16). Sisera, in the meantime, fled on foot. He took refuge in the tent of a woman named Jael, whose husband was an ally of the Canaanites. Jael deceived Sisera into thinking that he would be safe in her tent. She offered him a drink and promised to stand guard at the entrance of the tent. "While Sisera was sound asleep, she stealthily approached him and drove the [tent] peg through his temple down into the ground, so that he perished in death" (Jgs 4:21).

On that day Deborah sang a canticle praising God and the deeds of those who fought against Sisera. After that, "the land was at rest for forty years" (Jgs 5:31).

How Was Deborah a Woman of Faith?

During the time of the judges, the majority of the Israelites had forgotten the one true God, the God of the covenant. They had come under the influence of the Canaanite religion and worshiped false gods. One woman, Deborah, did not forget God. She remained faithful to Him. God rewarded her by blessing her with the gift of prophecy. Deborah was accepted by her people not only as a prophetess, but also as a judge. Of the twelve judges recorded during this time of Israel's history, only one was a woman—Deborah. The Israelites thought of Deborah as wise and sought her counsel. She was also brave. Deborah did not hesitate to accompany Barak to the fight against Sisera. It was Barak who hesitated and asked Deborah to accompany him to Mount Tabor. Because this one woman, Deborah, was not afraid to act as an image of God, the Israelites were able to overcome their enemies, and the faith of an entire nation was renewed.

REVIEW QUESTIONS

1. Who was Deborah?
2. Identify these persons who played a part in the story of Deborah: Barak, Sisera, and Jael.
3. How did Deborah show her faith in God?
4. How did the Israelites think of Deborah?
5. What influence did Deborah have on the history of Israel?

Ruth, Loyal and Faithful

The story of Ruth can be found in the Book of Ruth.

A Summary of the Story of Ruth

During the time of the judges there was a famine in Judah, a section of Israel. A certain family decided to migrate from Bethlehem of Judah to the land of Moab. The man's name was Elimelech, and his wife's name was Naomi. They had two sons, Mahlon and Chilion. After arriving in Moab, the two sons married Moabite women, one named Orpah, the other Ruth. Soon after this, Elimelech died; and ten years later both sons died. The three women were left without husbands to support them.

Naomi decided to return to her homeland in Judah. She advised Orpah and Ruth to return to their families. Their own families could provide for them until they married again. Naomi could offer them nothing. "Again they sobbed aloud and wept; and Orpah kissed her mother-in-law good-by, but Ruth stayed with her" (Ru 1:14). Naomi tried to convince Ruth not to come with her. But Ruth insisted, "Do not ask me to abandon or forsake you! For wherever you go I will go, wherever you lodge I will lodge, your people shall be my people, and your God my God. Wherever you die I will die, and there be buried" (Ru 1:16–17). After hearing these words, Naomi accepted Ruth's decision.

The two women traveled to Bethlehem and arrived at the beginning of the barley harvest. Ruth was determined to provide for herself and Naomi. She began working in the fields, gathering whatever the harvesters had left behind. One day the owner of the field, a man named Boaz, came and greeted the harvesters. Boaz asked who Ruth was. The harvesters explained that she was a Moabite and the daughter-in-law of Naomi. They told Boaz that she had been working very hard since early morning, with scarcely any rest. Boaz was impressed with Ruth. He greeted her and gave her permission to work his fields until the end of the harvest. He assured her that no harm would come to her and that her needs would be attended to. Ruth was overwhelmed and asked Boaz why he would treat a stranger in his land with such kindness. Boaz replied, "I have had a complete account of what you have done for your mother-in-law after your husband's death; you have left your father and your mother and the land of your birth, and have come to a people whom you did not know previously. . . . May you receive a full reward from the LORD, the God of Israel, under whose wings you have come for refuge" (Ru 2:11–12).

When Ruth returned home, she told Naomi of her meeting with Boaz. Naomi knew that Boaz was a relative of hers. Under the Israelite law a relative was responsible for the care of a widow in his family and could marry her. Naomi

encouraged Ruth to offer herself in marriage to Boaz. That evening, while Boaz was asleep, Ruth entered his tent and lay down at his feet. Boaz awoke, startled, and asked, "Who are you?" Ruth replied, "I am your servant Ruth. Spread the corner of your cloak over me, for you are my next of kin" (Ru 3:9). This was Ruth's way of asking Boaz to be her protector, by marrying her according to his duty under the Israelite law. Boaz was pleased and touched by Ruth's request. After certain arrangements were made, Boaz married Ruth and also provided for Naomi.

Not long after, Boaz and Ruth had a son. The neighbor women were very excited by the news. They praised the Lord for providing an heir for Naomi's family. "May he become famous in Israel! He will be your comfort and the support of your old age, for his mother is the daughter-in-law who loves you. She is worth more to you than seven sons!" (Ru 4:14–15). They named the boy Obed.

Obed became the father of Jesse, who was the father of David, the famous king of Israel. Ruth, then, was the great-grandmother of King David, from whose family Jesus was born.

How Was Ruth a Woman of Faith?

Three books of the Bible have titles bearing the names of women: the Books of
Ruth, Judith, and Esther. All three books are found in the Old Testament.
Judith and Esther were Jewish, that is, they were from the tribes of Israel.
Ruth, however, was not a descendant from any of the tribes of Israel. She was
from the land of Moab. She was called a Moabite. Hence she was a Gentile, a
person who was not Jewish. The Moabites did not believe in the one true God
of Israel. Like the Canaanites, they worshiped many different gods. Yet, in this
land that did not know God, God called Ruth to become a woman of faith.
Because Ruth acted as an image of God and accepted His call, she became an
example of how faith in God is found in all people, Israelite and Gentile alike.

After the death of her husband, Ruth chose to stay with her mother-in-law,
Naomi, rather than returning to her own family. It would have been much
easier for Ruth to choose to stay, as Orpah did. To remain in her own land and
return to her own family was the logical and most practical choice. Yet Ruth
made the unexpected, the more difficult, choice. In doing so, she took a leap
of faith. "Wherever you go I will go, wherever you lodge I will lodge, your
people shall be my people, and your God my God" (Ru 1:16). Ruth chose to
take the God of Israel as her own.

The remainder of the story tells how Ruth put her faith into action. Ruth took
it upon herself to care for her mother-in-law. When they arrived in Bethlehem,
she worked hard in the fields. Her loyalty, faithfulness, and spirit of self-
sacrifice did not go unnoticed. Boaz, an influential and wealthy Israelite, was
impressed with the faith of this stranger, a Gentile. The kindness Ruth showed
for Naomi was returned through the kindness of Boaz. He cared for her and
loved her. When Ruth became the mother of Obed, she became the great-
grandmother of a king and an ancestress of Jesus.

The Book of Ruth is a message about true faith in God. It does not matter
whether you are a Gentile or a Jew. Faith is what matters. Ruth is remembered
as a woman of faith who acted as an image of God.

REVIEW QUESTIONS

1. Who was Ruth?
2. Identify these persons from the story of Ruth: Naomi, Boaz, Obed.
3. What is a Gentile?
4. How did Ruth prove to be a woman of faith?
5. What effect did Ruth's actions have on the history of the nation of Israel?

Hannah, a Woman of Hope

The story of Hannah can be found in 1 Samuel 1; 2:1–10, 18–21.

A Summary of the Story of Hannah

Once there was a man named Elkanah. "He had two wives, one named Hannah, the other Peninnah; Peninnah had children, but Hannah was childless" (1 Sm 1:2). Elkanah regularly went on a pilgrimage to the city of Shiloh to offer sacrifice and to worship the Lord. During the meal on the day of sacrifice, Elkanah would offer a portion of food to Peninnah and her children, but he would offer a double portion to Hannah because he loved her. Peninnah would then tease and taunt Hannah for not having any children. This made Hannah miserable. She cried and refused to eat. Each time, Elkanah tried to comfort her and said, "Hannah, why do you weep, and why do you refuse to eat? Why do you grieve? Am I not more to you than ten sons?" (1 Sm 1:8).

This happened year after year. Finally, after one such meal, Hannah could bear it no more. She left the table and went to the temple to pray. Eli, who was the priest of the temple, was sitting near the door. Hannah cried and prayed to the Lord for a long time. Then she made this promise to the Lord: "O LORD of hosts, if you look with pity on the misery of your handmaid, if you remember me and do not forget me, if you give your handmaid a male child, I will give him to the LORD for as long as he lives; neither wine not liquor shall he drink, and no razor shall ever touch his head" (1 Sm 1:11). Eli, who was watching her, but could not hear her prayers, thought that she was drunk. He approached her and said, "How long will you make a drunken show of yourself? Sober up from your wine!" (1 Sm 1:14). Hannah was offended that Eli should think such a thing. She told him of her unhappiness and of her prayers to the Lord. Then Eli said, "Go in peace, and may the God of Israel grant you what you have asked of him" (1 Sm 1:17). Then Hannah returned to Elkanah and felt content.

Within the next year Hannah gave birth to a boy, whom she named Samuel. She kept Samuel at home until he was about three years old. Then she took him along on the pilgrimage to the temple in Shiloh. There she presented him to Eli, reminding him of their meeting several years ago. "I prayed for this child, and the LORD granted my request. Now I, in turn, give him to the LORD; as long as he lives, he shall be dedicated to the LORD" (1 Sm 1:27–28). Hannah left Samuel with Eli and then sang a hymn of praise and thanksgiving to the Lord.

Read aloud the "Song of Hannah", 1 Samuel 2:1–10.

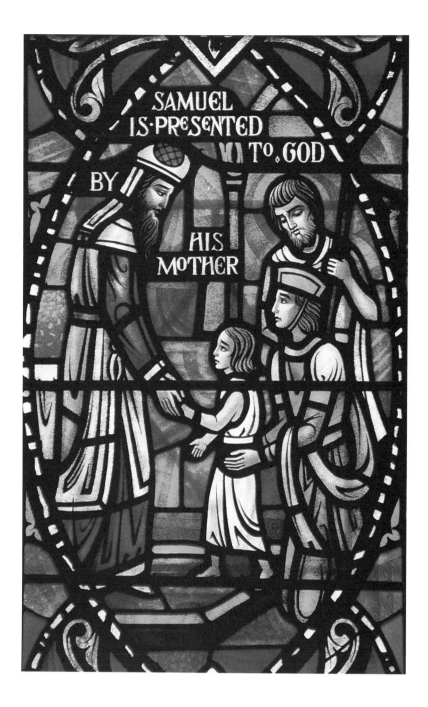

Samuel remained in the service of the Lord under the priest Eli. "His mother used to make a little garment for him, which she would bring him each time she went up with her husband to offer the customary sacrifice" (1 Sm 2:19). "The LORD favored Hannah so that she conceived and gave birth to three more sons and two daughters, while young Samuel grew up in the service of the LORD" (1 Sm 2:21).

How Was Hannah a Woman of Faith?

Hannah was unhappy for many years because she was unable to have children. Even though Hannah knew that Elkanah loved her, she was unhappy because she was not able to give him children, as Peninnah did. What is more, Peninnah teased and taunted her. Rather than despair and become embittered by her inability to have children, Hannah turned to God. Hannah's prayer was an act of faith. The Bible says that, after Hannah prayed, she returned to Elkanah "and no longer appeared downcast" (1 Sm 1:18). This tells us that Hannah had confidence in God's love. She was at peace with herself and hoped in God's kindness and mercy.

Furthermore, Hannah did not forget her promise to God after her prayers were answered. How easy it would have been to rejoice in the birth of her long-awaited son and then selfishly keep Samuel to herself. Hannah, however, was a woman of faith. She believed in the God of the covenant. She had made her own covenant, a promise, with God. She did not forget her promise. When Samuel was old enough, she presented him to Eli, the priest of the temple. She dedicated her son to the service of God. It must have been extremely difficult for Hannah to give up her son. She would be able to visit him only when she came to Shiloh on the regular pilgrimage. Hannah's faith gave her the courage to do what was right, to act as an image of God.

Hannah had no knowledge of the future when she sang her song of praise and thanksgiving to God. In her song, she praised God as the helper of the weak, Who casts down the mighty and raises up the lowly, and Who alone is the source of true strength. Her song ends with an early prophecy about the Anointed One, Jesus Christ. The "Canticle of Hannah" is a source and prototype of the "Magnificat", Mary's song of thanksgiving, recorded in the Gospel of Saint Luke.

As a result of Hannah's faithfulness, not only was she blessed with more children, but the entire nation of Israel was blessed. Samuel became a priest, a prophet, and a judge. He was one of the great leaders of Israel. He drew the Israelites back to God at a time when they often forgot their promise to worship only the one true God of Israel. Samuel was highly respected by the Israelites and also by their enemies. Peace reigned during the time of Samuel. Later, Samuel, under God's direction, chose and anointed the first two kings of Israel, Saul and, after him, David.

REVIEW QUESTIONS

1. Who was Hannah?
2. Why was Hannah unhappy?
3. How did Hannah show her faith in God?
4. How did Hannah's faithfulness affect the nation of Israel?

Judith, Cunning and Courageous

The story of Judith can be found in the Book of Judith 8–16.

A Summary of the Story of Judith

Nebuchadnezzar, King of Assyria, was a very powerful ruler. He was angry with many of the countries of western Asia, including Israel, because they refused to help him in his war against the Medes. He decided to invade and destroy these countries for their refusal to aid him. The king's general was a man named Holofernes. King Nebuchadnezzar ordered Holofernes to build an army of 132,000 men to conquer these countries. Fear spread throughout the land as, one by one, the countries fell under the sword of Holofernes. Soon Holofernes and his army were encamped outside the Israelite city of Bethulia.

The Israelites made themselves ready for battle. First, they prayed and did penance, asking God for His help. Then, they "blocked the mountain passes, fortified the summits of all the higher peaks, and placed roadblocks in the plains" (Jdt 5:1). Holofernes was furious that the Israelites dared to oppose him. He asked his advisors to tell him about the Israelites. A man named Achior, the leader of all the Ammonites, explained to Holofernes that the Israelites were unlike any of the other inhabitants of the land. He told Holofernes that he could not defeat the Israelites unless they had sinned against their God. Because the Israelites had not sinned and had remained faithful to the one, true God, they were confident that God would come to their aid. This information infuriated Holofernes even more. He ordered that Achior be delivered into the hands of the Israelites so that he could die with them in the fall of the city. That same day, Holofernes began the siege of Bethulia. He located the source of water for the city and cut off the water supply. He surrounded the city so that no one could go in or out, cutting off their food supply. Then he waited for the Israelites to surrender out of desperation.

The Israelites, including the women and children, suffered without adequate supplies of food and water for thirty-four days. The Israelites began to lose hope and asked Uzziah and the rulers of the city to surrender to Holofernes, arguing that slavery would be better than watching one another die from hunger and thirst. But Uzziah said to them, "Courage, my brothers! Let us wait five days more for the LORD our God, to show his mercy toward us; he will not utterly forsake us" (Jdt 7:30).

Now, Judith was a woman who was highly respected in Bethulia. She had been a widow for several years. "She was beautifully formed and lovely to behold. Her husband, Manasseh, had left her gold and silver, servants and maids, livestock and fields, which she was maintaining. No one had a bad word to say about her, for she was a very God-fearing woman" (Jdt 8:7–8). When Judith heard that Uzziah and the elders were considering surrender, she summoned them to her house. She argued against surrender, urged them to trust in God, and promised to deliver the city. The elders agreed to follow Judith's plan.

After the elders left, Judith prayed to God. She asked God to give her strength to defeat their enemies. "Your strength is not in numbers, nor does your power depend upon stalwart men; but you are the God of the lowly, the helper of the oppressed, the supporter of the weak, the protector of the forsaken, the savior of those without hope. Please, please, God of my forefather, . . . hear my prayer! . . . Let your whole nation and all the tribes know clearly that you are the God of all power and might, and that there is no other who protects the people of Israel but you alone" (Jdt 9:11–14).

After Judith finished her prayers to God, she began to carry out her plan. She dressed in her finest clothes, put on her most expensive jewelry, and made herself very beautiful. Accompanied only by her maid, she went out of the city gate and walked directly across the valley until she encountered the Assyrian army. She allowed herself to be captured and asked to be brought to Holofernes. ". . . [W]hen Holofernes and his servants beheld Judith, they all marveled at the beauty of her face. She threw herself down prostrate before him, but his servants raised her up" (Jdt 10:23). Holofernes assured her that no harm would come to her. He asked her to explain her intentions. Judith cleverly praised Holofernes. "We have heard of your wisdom and sagacity, and all the world is aware that throughout the kingdom you alone are competent, rich in experience, and distinguished in military strategy" (Jdt 11:8). She told him that the Israelites had sinned against the laws of God. God had revealed to her that the Israelites would soon be punished for disobeying His laws. God would use the hand of Holofernes to punish the Israelites. He had sent Judith to tell Holofernes all these things. Holofernes needed only to wait until God told Judith the time of destruction. Then Holofernes would sit on the judgment seat in the city of Jerusalem. "This was told me, and announced to me in advance, and I in turn have been sent to tell you" (Jdt 11:19).

Holofernes was pleased with these words. He praised not only Judith's beauty, but her wisdom. Then he ordered that a banquet be set for her and invited her "to enjoy drinking wine with us, and to be like one of the Assyrian women who live in the palace of Nebuchadnezzar" (Jdt 12:13). Judith accepted his invitation and entered the banquet dressed in her finest clothes. "The heart of Holofernes was in rapture over her, and his spirit was shaken" (Jdt 12:16). "Holofernes, charmed by her, drank a great quantity of wine, more than he had ever drunk on one single day in his life" (Jdt 12:20). When it grew late, all the

servants and guests "went off to their beds, for they were all tired from the prolonged banquet. Judith was left alone in the tent with Holofernes, who lay prostrate on his bed, for he was sodden with wine" (Jdt 13:1–2). When Judith saw that everyone had left, she asked her maid to keep watch. Then she prayed to God to give her strength to save her people from destruction. After she prayed, she quietly approached the bed of Holofernes. Then she took his own sword and killed him.

Judith and her maid quickly left the sleeping camp, slipped past the guards, and found their way back to Bethulia. All the people assembled to hear her story. Judith told them everything that had happened and then spoke with a loud voice, "Praise God, praise him! Praise God, who has not withdrawn his mercy from the house of Israel, but has shattered our enemies by my hand this very night" (Jdt 13:14). The people rejoiced and praised God for saving them from destruction. Uzziah praised Judith for her courage and blessed her saying, "May God make this redound to your everlasting honor, rewarding you with blessings, because you risked your life when your people were being oppressed, and you averted our disaster, walking uprightly before our God." The people replied, "Amen! Amen!" (Jdt 13:20).

Judith advised the Israelites to take advantage of the situation. She predicted that in the morning, when the Assyrians discovered the body of Holofernes, fear and panic would seize them, and they would run from the camp. The Israelites should make ready to pursue them. Then she asked that Achior the Ammonite be brought before her, so that he would know the power of God. "Now Achior, seeing all that the God of Israel had done, believed firmly in him . . . and he has been united with the house of Israel to the present day" (Jdt 14:10).

Judith's prediction of the Assyrians' reaction to the death of their leader was accurate. Panic and confusion spread through the camp. The Israelites pursued the Assyrians as they fled from the camp. Surrounding tribes joined the Israelites in the defeat of the Assyrians. Their victory over the dreaded King Nebuchadnezzar was complete.

After victory was secured, "All the women of Israel gathered to see her [Judith]; and they blessed her and performed a dance in her honor. She took branches in her hands and distributed them to the women around her, and she and the other women crowned themselves with garlands of olive leaves. At the head of all the people, she led the women in the dance, while the men of Israel followed in their armor, wearing garlands and singing hymns" (Jdt 15:12–13).

Judith's song of thanksgiving is recorded in Judith 16:1–17. It is both a summary of her role in saving the Israelites from their enemy and a testament of her faith in God. "For the rest of her life she was renowned throughout the land" (Jdt 16:21). "During the life of Judith and for a long time after her death, no one again disturbed the Israelites" (Jdt 16:25).

How Was Judith a Woman of Faith?
The message of the Book of Judith is a message of faith. The writer sought to strengthen the faith of his people by reminding them of God's presence among them. He did this through the woman Judith. The story was written to help the reader reflect on the meaning of the yearly Passover observance. Just as God delivered His people during the time of the Exodus by the hand of Moses, so God delivered the Israelites from their enemies by the hand of Judith. Judith,

like Moses, had an extraordinary faith in God. She believed that God would protect the Israelites from destruction. For God is "the God of the lowly, the helper of the oppressed, the supporter of the weak, the protector of the forsaken, the savior of those without hope" (Jdt 9:11). In these words Judith professed her faith. When God called upon Judith to do His will, she responded as an image of God, with faith and courageous action.

The actions of Judith are sometimes judged harshly. Judith lied to Holofernes to gain his trust. She flattered him with her beauty to trick him. Then, with his own sword, she assassinated him. To us, in our present time, these are sinful deeds. Yet, as with all of the characters and events of the Old Testament, they need to be looked at within the context of their own time. Laws and customs, both civil and moral, were different from ours. Christ had not yet come to fulfill their knowledge and understanding of the commandments. All His truths had not yet been revealed. The Israelites and their neighboring countries, both allies and enemies, lived by different rules. So, when the Israelites were threatened with total destruction, Judith accepted without hesitation the challenge to do whatever was necessary, including murdering Holofernes, to save her people. The actions of war, unfortunately, have not changed over the centuries. Death and destruction go hand-in-hand with war. Christ's message of peace has not yet been learned even in modern times.

Judith has been praised for her desire to save her people, not only by the writers of Scripture, but also by the saints in their spiritual writings. She used the gifts God gave her to accomplish her mission. She was cunning, courageous, and, most of all, prudent. *Prudence* is the power that helps us make right choices about what to do or what not to do in specific circumstances. Judith was a woman of faith. She exercised the virtue of prudence when she put her faith into action. She made the right choice about what to do to save her people. She acted as an image of God.

REVIEW QUESTIONS

1. Who was Judith?
2. Identify these persons from the story of Judith: Nebuchadnezzar, Holofernes, Uzziah.
3. How did Judith act as a woman of faith?
4. Why did the author write the story of Judith?
5. How are Judith and Moses similar?
6. What is prudence?

Esther, Resourceful and True

The story of Esther can be found in the Book of Esther.

A Summary of the Story of Esther

At this time, the Israelites were under the rule of King Ahasuerus of Persia. His palace was in the city of Susa. King Ahasuerus was very powerful and wealthy. He "ruled over a hundred and twenty-seven provinces from India to Ethiopia" (Est 1:1). The king decided to hold a feast for his officers and prime ministers. "For as many as a hundred and eighty days, he displayed the glorious riches of his kingdom and the resplendent wealth of his royal estate" (Est 1:4). The beautiful palace was adorned in marble, gold, silver, and colored stones. The king ordered the wine to flow freely. His guests enjoyed themselves without limit. To impress them further, King Ahasuerus ordered his wife, Queen Vashti, to show herself to his guests, for the queen was very beautiful. But she refused to obey his order. "At this the king's wrath flared up, and he burned with fury" (Est 1:13). After consulting with his advisors, the king decided to punish Queen Vashti for disobeying his orders and embarrassing him in front of his guests. He ordered that the crown be taken from her and that she be sent away. His advisors also suggested that a contest be held. The most beautiful girls in the kingdom would be sought for the contest. The girl who was most pleasing to the king would replace Queen Vashti. The king was pleased with this suggestion.

There was a man who served at the king's court who was a Jew. His name was Mordecai. Mordecai had once saved the king's life. He had overheard two court guards plotting to kill the king. Mordecai had investigated their plans and then informed the king. The two guards were questioned, found guilty, and executed. Mordecai's actions were recorded in the king's book of notable events, and Mordecai was appointed to serve at the king's court.

When Mordecai heard of the contest for queen, he thought of his cousin Esther. Esther was an orphan and had come to live with him when she was very young. Mordecai loved Esther as if she were his own daughter. Mordecai was confident that Esther would have a good chance at winning the contest. "The girl was beautifully formed and lovely to behold" (Est 2:7). So Mordecai brought Esther to the palace and entered her in the contest. However, Mordecai gave Esther strict instructions not to reveal her nationality or her family. Esther did as she was told, and no one at the palace knew that she was Jewish or that she was related to Mordecai. Esther quickly won the admiration of all those around her. After many months, it was Esther's turn to be presented to the king. "The king loved Esther more than all other women, and of all the virgins she won his favor and benevolence. So he placed the royal diadem on her head and made her queen in place of Vashti" (Est 2:17).

Mordecai, however, had an enemy at the court. Haman, who was highly regarded by the king, sought to harm Mordecai and his people. Haman was chief of state. As a sign of respect for his high rank, Haman demanded that all the servants kneel and bow down to him. Mordecai, however, would not kneel and bow down. Only the God of Israel deserved this sign of respect. Mordecai's refusal angered Haman tremendously. Haman's hatred and anger would not be satisfied until Mordecai and all like him—meaning the Jews—were destroyed. Haman cleverly planned his vengeance. He even determined the date of the destruction of Mordecai and his people by casting a "pur", or lot (Est 3:7). All the Jews would be destroyed on a single day, the thirteenth day of the twelfth month. In order to accomplish such a terrible deed, Haman knew he would need the approval of the king. Haman told the king that the Jews were the only people in his kingdom who did not obey his laws. The Jews were a bad influence on the other people, he said, and the king should not tolerate their behavior. Haman convinced the king that the Jews should be destroyed. The king gave Haman permission to carry out his plan. Haman quickly wrote the death order in a letter, sealed it with the signet ring of the king, and sent it out to all the royal provinces.

Panic and terror spread throughout the kingdom. "Wherever the king's legal enactment reached, the Jews went into deep mourning, with fasting, weeping, and lament; they all slept on sackcloth and ashes" (Est 4:3). Esther, however, did not know of the decree. Then one of her maids told her that Mordecai was at the palace gates, dressed in sackcloth and ashes. When Esther heard this news, she immediately sent a servant out to Mordecai to discover the meaning of his actions. Mordecai gave the servant a copy of the death letter, with instructions that Esther was to go to the king "to plead and intercede with him in behalf of her people. Invoke the Lord and speak to the king for us: save us from death" (Est 4:9).

Esther must have been horrified when she read the letter and heard Mordecai's request. She sent the servant back to Mordecai with this message: "All the servants of the king and the people of his provinces know that any man or woman who goes to the king in the inner court without being summoned, suffers the automatic penalty of death, unless the king extends to him the golden scepter, thus sparing his life. Now as for me, I have not been summoned to the king for thirty days" (Est 4:11).

Mordecai replied to Esther's fear and hesitation. "Do not imagine that because you are in the king's palace, you alone of all the Jews will escape. Even if you now remain silent, relief and deliverance will come to the Jews from another source; but you and your father's house will perish. Who knows but that it was for a time like this that you obtained the royal dignity?" (Est 4:13–14).

After hearing these words, Esther's faith was stirred to life. She asked Mordecai to tell all the Jews of Susa to pray and fast for three days. She and her maids would do the same. "Thus prepared, I will go to the king, contrary to the law. If I perish, I perish!" (Est 4:16).

On the third day, at the end of her prayers, Esther prepared to meet the king. "She glowed with the perfection of her beauty and her countenance was as joyous as it was lovely, though her heart was shrunk with fear" (Est D:5). When Esther saw the king, she felt faint at the thought of his awesome power. But the king, seeing her beauty and gentle manner, looked kindly on Esther and extended toward her the golden staff, bidding her welcome. Esther came near and touched the tip of the staff. Then the king said to her, "What is it, Queen Esther? What is your request? Even if it is half of my kingdom, it shall be granted you" (Est 5:3). Esther did not reveal the true reason for her presence yet. Instead, she asked the king, along with Haman, to honor her with their presence at dinner. The king accepted. At dinner, the king again asked Esther her request. But again, Esther decided that the timing was not right. She told the king that if he and Haman would come to dinner tomorrow, then she would tell the king of her request.

Haman left the dinner happy and in good spirits. "But when he saw that Mordecai at the royal gate did not rise, and showed no fear of him, he was filled with anger toward him" (Est 5:9). He went home and complained to his wife and friends about Mordecai's insolent behavior. They suggested that Haman have Mordecai hanged as soon as possible. This idea pleased Haman, and he ordered that a gibbet be built for the hanging and decided to ask permission of the king the very next day.

That night, however, the king could not sleep. So he asked that the book of notable events be brought to him. While he was reading, he came upon the passage recording that Mordecai had saved the king's life by uncovering a plot to kill him. When the king remembered that Mordecai had not yet been rewarded for this deed, he summoned Haman. When Haman entered, the king said to him, "What should be done for the man whom the king wishes to reward?" (Est 6:5). Haman was so filled with pride that he immediately thought that he was the man the king wished to reward. So he answered that the man should be dressed in the king's robe and led through the streets on the king's horse, while one of the king's officials shouted before him, "This is what is done for the man whom the king wishes to reward" (Est 6:11). Haman was shocked when the king told him to honor Mordecai according to his own suggestions.

Haman attended dinner that evening with the king and Esther. This time, when the king asked Esther to tell him her request, she replied, "If I have found favor with you, O king, and if it pleases your majesty, I ask that my life be spared, and that you spare the lives of my people. For my people and I have been delivered to destruction, slaughter, and extinction" (Est 7:3–4). "'Who and where', said King Ahasuerus to Queen Esther, 'is the man who has dared to do this?' Esther replied, 'The enemy oppressing us is this wicked Haman'" (Est 7:5–6). Hearing this, Haman was seized with fear. The king was so angry that he ordered Haman to be hanged on the gibbet that had been built for Mordecai.

Esther then told the king of her relationship to Mordecai. Upon hearing this, the king gave Mordecai his signet ring, and thus Mordecai replaced Haman as chief of state. Esther fell at the king's feet, weeping and imploring him to revoke the death letter. Once again the king stretched forth the golden scepter to Esther. Then he gave Esther and Mordecai permission to "write in the king's name what you see fit concerning the Jews and seal the letter with the royal signet ring" (Est 8:8). Mordecai and Esther immediately circulated a letter that instructed the officials in all the provinces to ignore Haman's letter. The letter also gave permission to the Jews to defend themselves against any enemy, which had not been allowed previously.

Esther and Mordecai also encouraged their people to celebrate their deliverance from destruction with the feast of Purim. "They were to observe these days with feasting and gladness, sending food to one another and gifts to the poor" (Est 9:22). "Gathering together with joy and happiness before God, they shall celebrate these days on the fourteenth and fifteenth of the month Adar throughout all future generations of his people Israel" (Est F:10).

How Was Esther a Woman of Faith?

What kind of a woman was Esther? We know, of course, that Esther was a Jew, an Israelite. The Israelites were a conquered people at this time, living under the rule of a Persian king. Although the influence of the pagan Persian religion was great, Esther was a faithful Jew. Her uncle, Mordecai, had raised Esther to worship only the God of Israel. Esther, as can be expected, was also a woman of her times. The biblical text leads us to believe that she was dutiful and obedient to Mordecai. She willingly joined the contest sponsored by the king. She listened and obeyed the counsel of Mordecai and did not reveal her nationality or her relationship to him. We know that Esther was "beautifully formed and lovely to behold" (Est 2:7). Esther's beauty, however, went beyond her physical appearance. The Bible tells us that she soon won the admiration of all those around her. We can assume that the harem of the king was full of beautiful women. Yet Esther's demeanor impressed the other women of the harem and the slaves, as well as the king. "The king loved Esther more than all other women, and of all the virgins she won his favor and benevolence" (Est 2:17). She seemed to be the perfect replacement for his rebellious and disobedient first wife.

How, then, did this gentle and obedient woman find the courage to risk her life for her people? The biblical text tells us that Esther had not been summoned by the king for thirty days. The king had issued a law that forbade anyone, under penalty of death, to approach him without first being called. This law even included his wife, the queen! Esther must have trembled with fear when she first heard Mordecai's request that she ask the king to save her people from destruction. She made her fears and doubts known to Mordecai. But Mordecai showed his own faith in his reply to Esther's hesitation. "Do not imagine that because you are in the king's palace, you alone of all the Jews will escape. Even if you now remain silent, relief and deliverance will come to the Jews from another source; but you and your father's house will perish. Who knows but that it was for a time like this that you obtained the royal dignity?" (Est 4: 13–14). Mordecai's faith encouraged Esther to put her own faith into action. Esther accepted the challenge put before her. After three days of prayer and penance, Esther felt prepared to "go to the king, contrary to the law. If I perish, I perish!" (Est 4:16).

Because Esther acted on her faith, she was able to intercede with the king and save the Israelites from total destruction. People of the Jewish religion continue to celebrate the Feast of Purim today. It is a feast that has been celebrated for more than two thousand years. It is interesting to think that Jesus, Mary, and Joseph must have celebrated this feast with their Jewish friends and relatives. The Catholic Church looks upon Esther as a "type of Mary". Just as Esther interceded for her people with the king, so Mary intercedes for us with her Son, Jesus. We need only remember to pray and put our faith into action, as Esther did.

REVIEW QUESTIONS

1. Who was Esther?
2. Identify these persons from the story of Judith: Ahasuerus, Mordecai, Haman.
3. Describe the characteristics of Esther.
4. Why did Esther hesitate at first when Mordecai asked her to intercede with the king to save her people?
5. What stirred Esther's faith into action?
6. What did Esther do before going to the king?
7. What Jewish feast celebrates God's salvation of the Jews through Esther?
8. Why is Esther a "type of Mary"?
9. What can we learn from the story of Esther?

Susanna, a Woman of Virtue

The story of Susanna can be found in the Book of Daniel 13:1–64.

A Summary of the Story of Susanna

"In Babylon there lived a man named Joakim, who married a very beautiful and God-fearing woman, Susanna, the daughter of Hilkiah; her pious parents had trained their daughter according to the law of Moses" (Dn 13:1–2). Susanna's husband was very rich and was respected by the Jews. He had many visitors, and he often met with them in his garden.

Two men frequently came to visit with Joakim. These men were older and had been appointed judges by the people. They were, however, evil men. The Lord described them saying, "Wickedness has come out of Babylon: from the elders who were to govern the people as judges" (Dn 13:5). When these men came to visit Joakim, they would also see his wife, Susanna. As they watched Susanna walk in the garden, they looked at her with immodest eyes and thoughts. Day after day, they watched Susanna. One day, they admitted to each other that they had these impure thoughts about her. They devised a plan by which they would force her to make love with them.

One day, after Susanna saw that all the guests had left, she decided to bathe in the garden. Susanna did not know that the two old men had hidden themselves in the garden. She sent her two maids for oils and soap and ordered them to shut the garden doors. As soon as the maids left, the two old men ran up to Susanna. They cleverly and shamelessly demanded that she give in to them and let them make love to her. They threatened that, if she refused, they would tell everyone that they saw her send the maids away so she could meet and make love to a young man who was waiting for her in the garden. Susanna was shocked and filled with horror. "'I am completely trapped', Susanna groaned. 'If I yield, it will be my death; if I refuse, I cannot escape your power. Yet it is better for me to fall into your power without guilt than to sin before the Lord'" (Dn 13:22–23). Then Susanna screamed and shouted. The old men ran to open the garden door. As the servants and family members rushed in to see what was the matter, the two old men falsely accused Susanna of adultery. Everyone was in disbelief, "for never had any such thing been said about Susanna" (Dn 13:27). Yet these two men were judges. The elders demanded that she be charged with this sin, whose punishment was death.

The next day Susanna was brought to trial. Her husband, Joakim, and all her friends and relatives were present. Before the entire assembly, the two elders testified to their false story. They told everyone that they had caught Susanna making love to a young man who escaped by a side gate when they revealed their presence and ran after him. "The assembly believed them, since they were elders and judges of the people, and they condemned her to death" (Dn 13:41).

"Through her tears she [Susanna] looked up to heaven, for she trusted in the Lord wholeheartedly" (Dn 13:35). She cried out, "O eternal God, you know what is hidden and are aware of all things before they come to be: you know that they have testified falsely against me. Here I am about to die, though I have done none of the things with which these wicked men have charged me" (Dn 13:42–43).

The Lord heard her prayer, and "God stirred up the holy spirit of a young boy named Daniel" (Dn 13:45). Daniel spoke out in defense of Susanna. He refused to believe that Susanna was guilty and asked to examine the two men separately. The first elder was brought to Daniel. Daniel asked him to tell the story again. Then he asked him, "Now, then, if you were a witness, tell me under what tree you saw them together" (Dn 13:54). The first elder told him: under a mastic tree. (A mastic tree is very small.) Then the second elder was questioned by Daniel in the same manner. "Now then, tell me under what tree you surprised them together" (Dn 13:58). The second elder told him: under an oak tree. (An oak tree is very large.)

Upon hearing this conflicting testimony, the entire assembly "rose up against the two elders, for by their own words Daniel had convicted them of perjury. According to the law of Moses, they inflicted on them the penalty they had plotted to impose on their neighbor: they put them to death" (Dn 13:61–62).

Susanna and all her family and friends rejoiced and praised God "because she was found innocent of any shameful deed. And from that day onward Daniel was greatly esteemed by the people" (Dn 13:63–64).

How Was Susanna a Woman of Faith?

The story of Susanna appears in the Book of Daniel. Daniel was a prophet who lived from approximately 617 to 537 B.C.. During most of this time, the Israelites were under the rule of King Nebuchadnezzar, a Persian king whose capital city was Babylon. God chose Daniel to be His prophet. Daniel was given visions by God, which predicted what would happen to great nations in the future. He was faithful to God and highly respected by his people, as well as by the great leaders of the Persian empire. Susanna's story takes place when Daniel was a young man. Daniel's early show of wisdom helped him to become "greatly esteemed by the people" (Dn 13:64).

The story of Susanna praises not only the virtue of faith, but also the virtues of honor and modesty. In the first passage of Scripture we are told that Susanna was a "God-fearing woman" and had been brought up "according to the law of Moses" (Dn 13:2–3). Susanna knew and lived by the Ten Commandments, given to Moses in the covenant. Susanna loved God and was faithful to His teachings. Because she lived as an image of God, she loved her husband and was faithful to him. When she became the object of the sinful desires of the two elders, she was forced to make a decision that was life-threatening. She knew that the sin of adultery meant death. Yet the biblical text clearly announces her decision to accept death, rather than "to sin before the Lord" (Dn 13:23). Susanna's faith sustained her throughout the humiliation of the trial. She prayed to God in her distress, and her faith was rewarded when "God stirred up the holy spirit of a young boy named Daniel" (Dn 13:45).

The story of Susanna is an inspiration for us even today. It is difficult to remain faithful to the commandments of God. Those who think highly of virtue, modesty, and honor are often laughed at and joked about. Yet God asks us to take this risk. He invites us to act as He acts, to act as images of God. We might all ask ourselves how we would respond if we ever found ourselves in Susanna's situation. Would you act as an image of God?

REVIEW QUESTIONS

1. Who was Susanna?
2. Of what sin was Susanna unjustly accused?
3. How did Susanna show her faith in God?
4. How did Daniel defend Susanna?
5. How did Susanna act as a woman of virtue?
6. Recall the sixth and ninth commandments. Discuss how God asks us to act, both as adults and as sixth graders.

Concepts of Faith

1. What is faith?

Faith is the power that God gives us to enable us to believe in Him.

Vocabulary

grace: God's life.

faith: The power God gives us to enable us to believe in Him.

prophet: A messenger; a person chosen by God to speak to His people.

gentile: A person who is not Jewish.

prudence: The power that helps us make right choices about what to do or what not to do in specific circumstances.

Living the Lesson

Womanhood and the Person of Mary

From the time that you were very young, you have heard stories from the life of Mary, the Mother of Jesus. Can you think of the main events in Mary's life?

Pope John Paul II wrote, "God then manifests the dignity of women in the highest form possible, by assuming human flesh from the virgin Mary." Womanhood could hardly be more greatly honored than it was in and through the Blessed Mother. Through Mary, God became man.

Mary is the connecting link between the Old and the New Testament. She binds together the old and the new People of God. We are the present People of God. In Mary, we can live the unity of Sacred Scripture in its entirety.

How Was Mary a Woman of Faith?

"Behold, I am the handmaid of the Lord. May it be done to me according to your word" (Lk 1:38). When Mary spoke these words to the angel, she showed that she was a woman of faith. Even though she was troubled and did not understand how such a wonderful thing could happen, she said "Yes!" to God's invitation to become the Mother of His Son, Jesus. Mary was probably about fourteen years old at the time. Yet already her faith in God was strong.

Throughout all the events in her life, Mary acted as an image of God. She proclaimed the greatness of the Lord in her hymn of praise, the "Magnificat", also called the "Canticle of Mary".

Mary knew that she would suffer many things in her role as mother of Jesus. The prophet Simeon predicted that a sword would pierce her heart. Mary did not know what this prediction meant at the time, but she chose to continue in her role as mother. She loved her Son as all good mothers love their children. She and her spouse, Joseph, taught him all the things that a Jewish boy should know. When Jesus was "lost" for three days, she feared for Him and anxiously looked for Him. Mary did not understand all that Jesus said to her, yet she silently "kept all these things in her heart. And Jesus advanced [in] wisdom and age and favor before God and man" (Luke 2:51–52). Mary knew that Jesus respected and loved her and would do anything for her because she was His mother. It was at Mary's request that Jesus performed His first miracle, at the marriage feast at Cana. When Jesus was crucified, Mary showed her courage when most of the Apostles hid in fear: she was not afraid to stand under the cross. God rewarded Mary's faithfulness. Mary was present at the birth of the Church at Pentecost. She, along with the Apostles, received the Holy Spirit, Who had been sent by her Son, Jesus. Finally, this woman of faith was taken up to heaven to reign as Queen over all God's creation. As a woman of faith, Mary is still an example for every Christian man and woman.

Questions to Think, Talk, and Pray About

1. How did Mary show that she was a woman of faith?

2. How is the role of women in our society different from the role of women in the Old Testament?

3. Is a job, or career, different from a vocation?

4. How can women act as images of God in the modern world? in the modern Church?

Prayers

"Hail Mary".
"Canticle of Deborah" (Judges 5:1–31).
"Song of Hannah" (1 Samuel 2:1–10).
"Canticle of Mary" (Luke 1:46–56).

Women of Faith Today

Mother Teresa of Calcutta, who serves God in the poor.

Joan Andrews, who works to protect unborn children.

Identifying Women of Faith in the Old Testament

Identify each woman of faith by writing the corresponding letter in front of her name.

_____ 1. Sarah   **A**   Wife of Jacob; mother of Joseph and Benjamin.

_____ 2. Rebekah   **B**   A prophetess and judge; encouraged Barak to fight against Sisera and the Canaanites.

_____ 3. Rachel   **C**   Mother of Samuel, a prophet.

_____ 4. Miriam   **D**   Wife of Abraham; mother of Isaac.

_____ 5. Deborah   **E**   Queen of a Persian king; she saved the Jews from destruction.

_____ 6. Ruth   **F**   Saved the Israelites by killing Holofernes.

_____ 7. Hannah   **G**   Wife of Isaac; mother of Esau and Jacob.

_____ 8. Judith   **H**   A woman of virtue, falsely accused of adultery; defended by Daniel.

_____ 9. Esther   **I**   A Moabite woman who left her homeland and went to Bethlehem with her mother-in-law; an ancestress of Jesus.

_____ 10. Susanna   **J**   Sister of Moses and Aaron; a prophetess during the Exodus.

Other Women of Faith

Women of faith who have influenced the history of the Church

Women of Faith in the New Testament	*Women of Faith in the Church*
Mary, the Mother of Jesus	Lydia
Matthew 1 and 2; 12:46–50; 13:54–58	Acts 16:11–40
Mark 3:31–35; 6:1–6	Priscilla and Aquila
Luke 1:26–56; 2; 8:19–21	Acts 18
John 2:1–12; 19:25–27	Romans 16
Acts 1:14	1 Corinthians 16:19–24
Mary and Martha	2 Timothy 4:19–22
Luke 10:38–42	Phoebe
John 11:1–44; 12:1–11	Romans 16:1–2
Mary Magdalene	Saint Elizabeth of Hungary
Matthew 27:55–28	Saint Hedwig of Germany
Mark 15:40–16:20	Saint Joan of Arc
Luke 8:1–3; 24:1–12	Saint Teresa of Avila
John 19:25–20:18	
The Woman at the Well	
John 4:1–42	

Israel Becomes a Kingdom

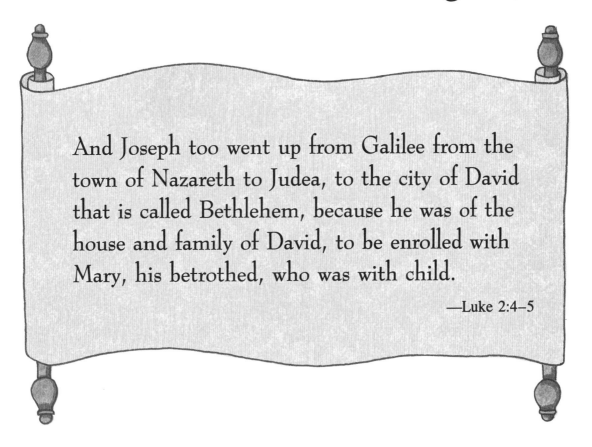

And Joseph too went up from Galilee from the town of Nazareth to Judea, to the city of David that is called Bethlehem, because he was of the house and family of David, to be enrolled with Mary, his betrothed, who was with child.

—Luke 2:4–5

The Prophet Samuel

Samuel was a prophet who played a very important role in the history of Israel. There are two books of the Old Testament whose titles bear his name: 1 Samuel and 2 Samuel. Look at the time-line below. Samuel was born at the end of the rule of Israel by judges. During his lifetime, two kings reigned over Israel. The first king was Saul, anointed in 1030 B.C.; the second was David, anointed in 1010 B.C. The two Books of Samuel record their stories.

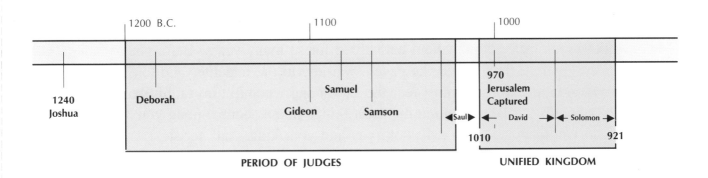

Samuel's mother, Hannah, prayed to God for a son. If God would give her a son, she prayed, she promised to dedicate him to the service of the Lord. God heard Hannah's prayer, and Samuel was born to her. Hannah remembered her promise to God. She took Samuel to the temple at Shiloh, where the temple priest, Eli, cared for Samuel and taught him how to serve the Lord. One evening, while Samuel was asleep, the Lord called to him. At first, Samuel did not understand that it was the Lord calling him. Eli helped Samuel to hear God's call. Finally, Samuel answered the Lord, "Speak, for your servant is listening" (1 Sm 3:10). Then the Lord made him a prophet. "Samuel grew up, and the LORD was with him, not permitting any word of his to be without effect" (1 Sm 3:19).

During this time, the Philistines, an enemy of Israel, grew more powerful. They repeatedly attacked the Israelites. One time, they even stole the Ark of the Covenant. Under the leadership of Samuel, the Israelites were able to defeat the Philistines, and the Ark was returned to them. This experience, however, convinced the Israelites that they needed a king to lead their scattered tribes. Samuel was against this idea. He looked upon their request as a rejection of God, Who should be their only King. The people insisted, however. "Not so! There must be a king over us. We too must be like other nations, with a king to rule us and to lead us in warfare and fight our battles" (1 Sm 8:19–20). God told Samuel to grant their request.

Saul, the First King of Israel

God asked Samuel to anoint Saul as the first king of Israel. To *anoint* means to bless someone with oil. "There was no other Israelite handsomer than Saul; he stood head and shoulders above the people" (1 Sm 9:2). "Then, from a flask he had with him, Samuel poured oil on Saul's head; he also kissed him, saying: 'The LORD anoints you commander over his heritage. You are to govern the LORD's people Israel, and to save them from the grasp of their enemies roundabout'" (1 Sm 10:1).

After Samuel anointed Saul, he presented the new king to the people. By this time, Samuel was an old man. He was also a wise man. He knew the weaknesses of the people whom he had led for so many years. Before he stepped down as their leader, he gave a warning to the Israelites and to Saul, their new king. "But you must fear the LORD and worship him faithfully with your whole heart; keep in mind the great things he has done among you. If instead you continue to do evil, both you and your king shall perish" (1 Sm 12:24–25).

Saul did many good things for the Israelites. He built up a strong army and defeated all the surrounding enemies of Israel. He built a fortress and a palace at a place called Gibeah. Archaeologists have discovered the ruins of Saul's city at Gibeah. From this city Saul reigned over Israel for twenty years. During his reign, Saul had three sons and two daughters. Two of his children, Jonathan and Michal, later played important roles in the life of David, the second king of Israel.

For a while, Saul remembered that his success rested on his faithfulness to the Lord. But soon a weakness in Saul's character began to surface. He was unable to surrender his own will entirely to the will of God. After a while, he chose to disobey God's commands. He forgot that God was responsible for his success. Saul made many wrong choices. As Saul drew himself farther from God's love, he became moody and angry. He was anxious and tense, mistrusting those around him. He lived an unhappy life. One of Saul's servants described his sadness as an "evil spirit" (1 Sm 16:15). He suggested to Saul that the music from a harp might soothe his "evil spirit" and make him feel better. Saul ordered that a skilled harpist be brought to him. The servant replied, "I have observed that one of the sons of Jesse of Bethlehem is a skillful harpist. He is also a stalwart soldier, besides being an able speaker, and handsome. Moreover, the LORD is with him" (1 Sm 16:18) "Thus David came to Saul and entered his service. Saul became very fond of him. . . . David would take the harp and play, and Saul would be relieved and feel better, for the evil spirit would leave him" (1 Sm 16:21, 23).

1. Who was Samuel?
2. Who taught Samuel as a young boy?
3. Why did Samuel object to the Israelites' request for a king?
4. Why did the Israelites want a king?
5. Whom did God ask Samuel to anoint as the first king of Israel?
6. What does it mean to anoint someone?
7. What final words of wisdom did Samuel give to the Israelites before he stepped down as their leader?
8. List some of the accomplishments of Saul during his reign as king.
9. How did Saul draw himself away from God?
10. Describe Saul's "evil spirit".
11. Why was David brought into the service of Saul?

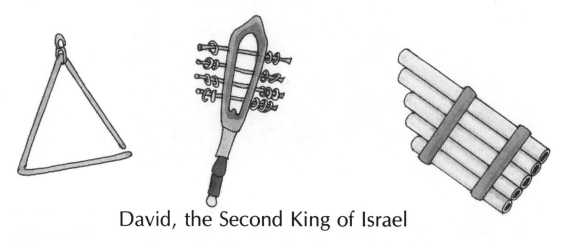

David, the Second King of Israel

Read 1 Samuel 16 for the scriptural account of David's anointing as king of Israel, or read the summary below.

A Summary of David's Anointing

Because Saul had chosen to reject God's love, God chose a new king to lead His people. God told Samuel to go to Bethlehem to the house of Jesse. There he was to anoint one of Jesse's sons as the new king. When Samuel arrived in Bethlehem, Jesse presented his many sons to him. "As they came, he looked at Eliab and thought, 'Surely the LORD's anointed is here before him'. But the LORD said to Samuel: 'Do not judge from his appearance or from his lofty stature, because I have rejected him. Not as man sees does God see, because man sees the appearance but the LORD looks into the heart'" (1 Sm 16:6–7). Seven sons were presented to Samuel, but none of them were chosen. "Then Samuel asked Jesse, 'Are these all the sons you have?' Jesse replied, 'There is still the youngest, who is tending the sheep'" (1 Sm 16:11). Samuel asked that Jesse send for him. "Jesse sent and had the young man brought to them. He was ruddy, a youth handsome to behold and making a splendid appearance. The LORD said, 'There—anoint him, for this is he!' Then Samuel, with the horn of oil in hand, anointed him in the midst of his brothers; and from that day on, the spirit of the LORD rushed upon David" (1 Sm 16:12–13).

The Challenge of Goliath

Not long after David's anointing, he was brought into the service of Saul as his harpist. David tried his best to serve Saul faithfully. Even though David knew that he had been chosen to succeed Saul, he was willing to wait until God was ready to have him take over as king. David remembered that Saul had once been chosen by God, too.

Read 1 Samuel 17:1–51 for the scriptural account of David and Goliath, or read the summary below.

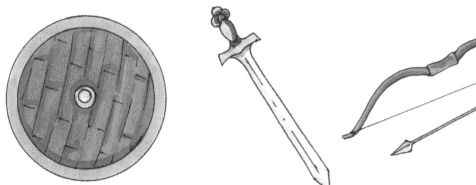

A Summary of David and Goliath

At this time, the Philistines were fighting against the Israelites. The Philistines had a champion named Goliath, who challenged the Israelites to a one-on-one fight. The winner of the fight would win the entire battle for his people. Now, Goliath was a fierce warrior. He was very tall and wore a bronze helmet. His armor, shield, and sword also were made of bronze. The Israelites trembled in fear before him. For forty days the Philistine repeated his challenge. But no one dared to accept it.

Although David was in the service of Saul, he remained at home with his father, Jesse, to tend the sheep. His brothers Eliab, Abinidab, and Shammah had joined Saul in the battle against the Philistines. One day Jesse asked David to check on the welfare of his brothers and to bring them some bread and cheese. David did as his father asked and found them in the battle camp. While he was talking to them, Goliath again shouted his challenge. David asked those around him, "Who is this . . . Philistine . . . that he should insult the armies of the living God?" (1 Sm 17:26). The soldiers told David of Goliath's challenge. They also told David that the King had promised a great reward to the soldier who killed Goliath. Then David spoke to Saul: "Let your majesty not lose courage. I am at your service to go and fight this Philistine" (1 Sm 17:32). Saul did not want David to fight Goliath, for David was too young and inexperienced at fighting. But David insisted. He told Saul of the many times he had protected his sheep from wild animals. He had even killed a lion and a bear. He argued, "The LORD, who delivered me from the claws of the lion and the bear, will also keep me safe from the clutches of this Philistine." Saul replied, "Go! the LORD will be with you" (1 Sm 17:37).

Saul tried to prepare David for the battle. He offered him a complete suit of armor and his own tunic and sword. But David felt awkward in the armor and would not wear any of it. He approached the giant warrior with only his staff, his sling, and five smooth stones.

When Goliath saw that the Israelites had sent only a young boy to fight him, he made fun of David. But David boldly spoke out against the Philistine. "You come against me with sword and spear and *scimitar*, but I come against you in the name of the LORD of hosts, the God of the armies of Israel that you have insulted. Today the LORD shall deliver you into my hand" (1 Sm 17:45–46). These words angered Goliath, and he moved in to meet David. "David put his hand into the bag and took out a stone, hurled it with the sling and struck the Philistine on the forehead. The stone embedded itself in his brow, and he fell prostrate on the ground" (1 Sm 17:49).

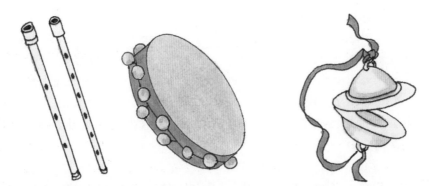

When the Philistines witnessed the power of the God of Israel demonstrated through the young boy, David, they scattered and fled from the battlefield. The Israelites pursued them and were victorious in routing the Philistines. When they returned to Jerusalem, ". . . the women came out from each of the cities of Israel to meet King Saul, singing and dancing, with tambourines, joyful songs, and *sistrums*. The women played and sang: 'Saul has slain his thousands, and David his ten thousands'" (1 Sm 18:6–7).

Saul's Jealousy

David then carried out successfully every mission on which Saul sent him. So Saul put him in charge of his soldiers, and this was agreeable to the whole army, even to Saul's own officers" (1 Sm 18:5). David soon became the favored hero of the people. Saul's jealousy grew with David's popularity. Saul's son, Jonathan, became David's closest friend. "And Jonathan entered into a bond with David, because he loved him as himself" (1 Sm 18:3). David also gained the love of Saul's youngest daughter, Michal, whom he married. Yet even the love that David shared with the people of Israel and with Saul's own family did not heal Saul's jealousy. Saul's jealousy grew into hatred. He plotted against David and even tried to kill him on several occasions. Both Jonathan and Michal pleaded with their father on David's behalf, but to no avail. David was forced to flee for his life.

David was able to build a sizable army of his own while he was a fugitive. He waged his own campaigns against Israel's enemies. On occasion, these campaigns brought him into contact with Saul's armies. Several times, David had the opportunity to kill Saul, but he chose not to. He continued to respect Saul as king. David had faith that God would choose the time for him to take over as the new king of Israel. That time came when Saul chose to reject God totally. Before a battle with the Philistines, Saul sought the advice of a witch, or fortune teller, rather than placing his trust in God. Saul tricked the fortune teller into conjuring up, or summoning, the ghost of Samuel, the prophet who had died several years earlier. The spirit of Samuel told Saul that he would lose the battle to the Philistines because he had been unfaithful to God. Moreover, Saul and his sons would lose their lives, and David would inherit the kingdom. During the next day's battle on Mount Gilboa, Samuel's prediction came true. The Philistines were victorious; Saul's sons—including Jonathan—were killed, and Saul was wounded. Then Saul committed suicide to avoid being mocked by the Philistine soldiers.

While Saul remained faithful to God, he was able to do great things for God, for himself, and for Israel. But when Saul chose to allow his jealousy, his "evil spirit", to turn him away from God, he suffered the consequences. The Israelites suffered, too. The Philistines triumphed over them. The Israelites were again a scattered nation, seeking refuge from their enemies. They had asked God for a king to lead them in war like the other nations, and God had granted their request. Now their king had failed to act as an image of God, and once again the Israelites were reminded of their dependence on God. Throughout all these events, God continued to love His people mercifully. He gave His people a new leader, David, who became a greater king than Saul had been, because he chose to act as an image of God.

1. Whom did Samuel anoint to replace Saul as king?

2. When Samuel was looking among Jesse's sons for the next king, God said these words to him: "Do not judge from his appearance or from his lofty stature, because I have rejected him. Not as man sees does God see, because man sees the appearance but the LORD looks into the heart" (1 Sm 16:7). How can we apply the message of this Bible passage to our own lives?

3. How did David show his faith in God when he chose to fight Goliath?

4. What message does God give us in the story of David and Goliath?

5. Why was Saul jealous of David?

6. Why did David run away from Saul?

7. Why did David continue to respect Saul?

8. What incident showed that Saul had totally rejected God?

9. How did God show His merciful love to the Israelites after Saul's death?

David Becomes King

The Second Book of Samuel begins with a beautiful poem that David sang when he heard that Saul and Jonathan had been killed. David respected Saul and honored his role as king. He loved Jonathan as his brother. The words of David's poem are a beautiful remembrance of the good things that Saul and Jonathan did for the Israelites.

Read 2 Samuel 1:19–27.

After David mourned for Saul and Jonathan, God told David to move his family and all his followers to the cities near Hebron. There David was anointed king by his own tribe, Judah. Look at the map on page 284. The southern tribes who recognized David as their king joined together and named themselves after David's tribe, Judah. The northern tribes, who continued to follow what was left of Saul's supporters, proclaimed Ishbaal, Saul's only surviving son, as their king. The northern tribes called themselves the nation of Israel. There followed a period of conflicts and battles until finally all opposition to David collapsed, and he was anointed king of the North as well as of the South. "David was thirty years old when he became king, and he reigned for forty years: seven years and six months in Hebron over Judah, and thirty-three years in Jerusalem over all Israel and Judah" (2 Sm 5:4–5).

David accomplished many great things during his reign. The chart on the next page lists some of the events that happened during his reign.

The Reign of King David

David is made king of Judah.	2 Samuel 2
David is made king of all Israel.	2 Samuel 5:1–5
David conquers Jerusalem.	2 Samuel 5:6–12
David defeats the Philistines.	2 Samuel 5:17–25
David brings the Ark of the Covenant to Jerusalem.	2 Samuel 6
David is promised the kingdom forever.	2 Samuel 7:8–17
David defeats other enemies of the Israelites.	2 Samuel 8:1–14; 10
David is kind to Jonathan's son.	2 Samuel 9
David sins with Bathsheba and repents.	2 Samuel 11–12:25
David's son Absalom turns against him.	2 Samuel 15:1–12
David composes his "Song of Thanksgiving".	2 Samuel 22
David counts his army.	2 Samuel 24:1–17
David makes Solomon king.	1 Kings 1:11–53

David Makes Jerusalem the Capital City

After David was anointed king of all the tribes, he decided that a new capital city was needed, which would symbolize the union of the North and the South. He chose the city of Jerusalem. It was strategically located and rested high on natural cliffs. It had never been occupied by any of the tribes and so was neutral to all of them. It seemed a perfect site to which he could bring the Ark of the Covenant and to which all the people would periodically gather in unity to worship the Lord. The city, however, was held by a pagan group called the Jebusites. The Jebusites scoffed at the idea of capture. They were so confident that the natural cliffs would deter any enemy that they boasted to David, "You cannot enter here: the blind and the lame will drive you away!" (2 Sm 5:6). Yet David did indeed capture Jerusalem. He made it his capital and moved his family there. And thus what had been called the City of Zion became known as Jerusalem, or the City of David. From his capital city, David waged war on the Philistines and on many other enemies that threatened Israel's borders.

The Ark of the Covenant and the "House" of David

After David had captured Jerusalem, he set up the Meeting Tent and installed the Ark of Covenant in it with great pomp and ceremony. David also had a beautiful palace built for himself and for his many wives and children. He became concerned, however, about the dwelling place of the Ark and said to Nathan the prophet, "Here I am living in a house of cedar, while the ark of

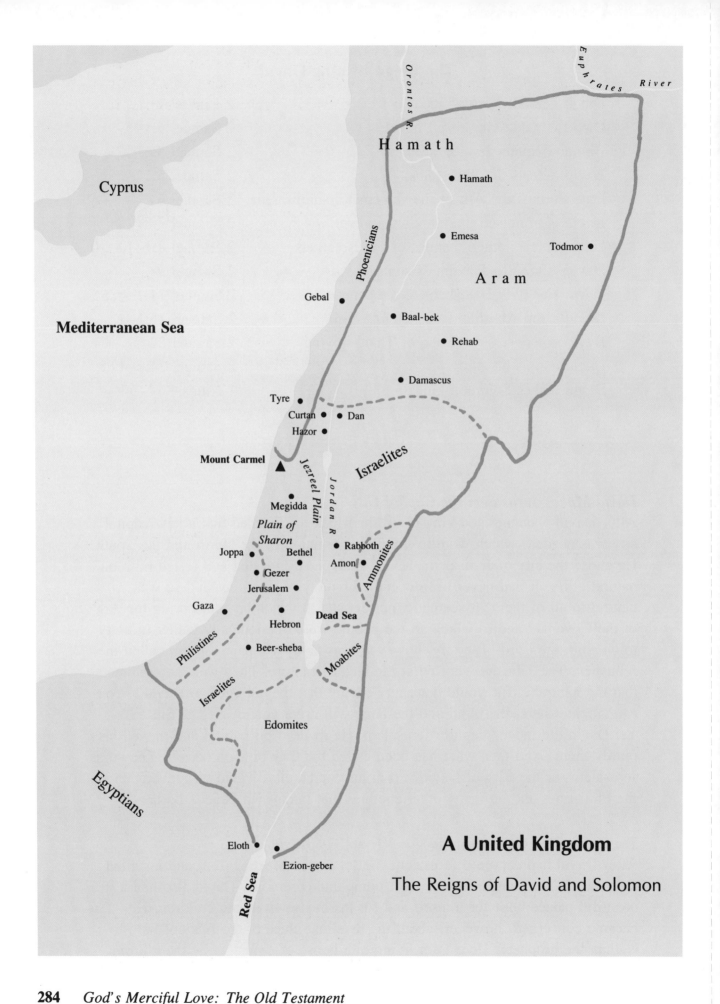

Hamath

● Hamath

● Emesa

● Todmor

A r a m

Phoenicians

Gebal ●

● Baal-bek

● Rehab

Mediterranean Sea

● Damascus

Tyre ●

Curtan ● ● Dan

Hazor ●

Mount Carmel ▲

Israelites

Jezreel Plain

● Megidda

Plain of Sharon

Jordan R.

Joppa ● ● Bethel

● Rabboth

Amon ●

Ammonites

● Gezer

Jerusalem ●

Gaza ●

● Hebron

Dead Sea

● Beer-sheba

Cyprus

Philistines

Israelites

Moabites

Edomites

Egyptians

Eloth ●   ●

Ezion-geber

Red Sea

A United Kingdom

The Reigns of David and Solomon

Orontos R.

Euphrates River

God dwells in a tent!" (2 Sm 7:2). David wanted to build a permanent house for the Lord. But the Lord spoke through Nathan and declined David's offer. Through the prophet Nathan, God revealed a series of wonderful promises to David.

Read 2 Samuel 7:8–17.

The most important of these promises was that God would build a "house" for David. That is, David would be the first of a family line of kings who would rule Israel forever. "Your house and your kingdom shall endure forever before me; your throne shall stand firm forever" (2 Sm 7:16). Upon hearing these words, David prayed a beautiful hymn of thanksgiving, praising God for His greatness. David's prayer is recorded in 2 Samuel 7:18–29.

God's promise to David has been fulfilled in the Person of Jesus, Who, in His human origins, is a descendant of the house of David. In English we still use the word "house" to refer to a royal family. Christ, a true heir of David, is also true God and our eternal King. His reign will endure and last forever, just as God promised to David.

David Sins

David loved the Lord and tried to serve Him faithfully. Unlike Saul, David trusted in God's merciful love and goodness. It was God's merciful love that saved David when he asked God's forgiveness for the terrible sins he committed, sins that hurt God, his neighbor, and himself.

Read the summary below for the story of David's sins; or read 2 Samuel 11; 12:1–25.

One spring, David sent his army to fight against the Ammonites. David decided to stay at home this time. One evening, while he was walking on the roof of his palace, he saw, on the roof of a nearby house, a beautiful woman taking her bath. He found out that her name was Bathsheba and that she was the wife of Uriah the Hittite, one of his faithful soldiers. David knew that Uriah was away at war, so David sent for the woman and then made love to her as if she were his own wife. After a time, Bathsheba knew that she had conceived a child by David. She sent word to David, who devised a plan to cover up his sin. David sent for Uriah from the battlefield. When Uriah arrived at the palace, David questioned him about the progress of the war and the morale of the soldiers. Then David suggested that he spend the night at home with his wife before going back to the battle. But Uriah did not do as David suggested. Instead, he slept at the palace with the other officers. Uriah was a loyal soldier and did not want the comforts of home while his fellow soldiers were encamped on the battlefield. When David found out that Uriah did not go home, he invited him to eat and drink with him, hoping that Uriah would get drunk and then go to his own home. But again, Uriah did not go home. In desperation, David wrote a letter to Joab, the commanding officer. In it he directed: "Place Uriah up front, where the fighting is fierce. Then pull back and leave him to be struck down dead" (2 Sm 11:15). Joab did as he was instructed, and Uriah died on the battlefield the next day. With Uriah out of the way, David was free to marry Bathsheba. Soon after Bathsheba became David's wife, she bore him a son. David thought that he had cleverly covered up his sin, "But the LORD was displeased with what David had done" (2 Sm 11:27).

The Lord sent the prophet Nathan to David with a parable. A *parable* is a short story that teaches a moral or a religious lesson. (Read 2 Sm 12:1–6 for an account of the parable.) By telling David this parable, Nathan was able to help David recognize that he had committed a terrible sin. David immediately showed God that he was sorry for his sin. "He kept a fast, retiring for the night to lie on the ground clothed in sackcloth" (2 Sm 12:16). David prayed for seven days, asking for God's mercy. During this time, David and Bathsheba's baby became very ill and died. This tragedy added to David's sorrow. Throughout all this time, David drew himself closer to God. "Then he went to the house of the LORD and worshiped" (2 Sm 12:20). David returned to the palace knowing that God had forgiven him for his sins. "Then David comforted his wife Bathsheba" (2 Sm 12:24). Later, when David and Bathsheba had another son, "The LORD loved him and sent the prophet Nathan to name him Jedidiah, on behalf of the LORD" (2 Sm 12:24–25). Jedidiah became more popularly known as Solomon.

A Discussion of David's Sins

David's sins are a clear example of the wisdom in choosing to follow God's Ten Commandments. David sinned against the Sixth Commandment, "You will not commit adultery", and the Ninth Commandment, "You will not covet your neighbor's wife". What is more, David's wicked plan to have Uriah killed was a sin against the Fifth Commandment, "You will not kill". How could David do such terrible things?

David is one of the more beloved characters of the Old Testament. We first love him as a youth, so full of faith, so courageous and patient. His love for Saul's son, Jonathan, endears him to us also. Later, the Bible tells us how kind David was to Jonathan's only surviving son, Meribbaal, who was crippled. King David, out of love for Jonathan, took Meribbaal into his own palace and treated him as one of his own family. David often acted as an image of God, openly and joyfully worshiping Him and never forgetting to thank and praise

Him in song. David wrote many songs of praise to God that are recorded in the Book of Psalms. How could this same person choose to commit such grave sins?

David's sins remind us that we are all capable of doing wrong. No human person is without sin. Only Jesus and His Mother, Mary, were without sin. Sometimes we tend to forget this truth about our heroes. Even heroes have their faults. David's greatness lies in the fact that he did not forget that God loved him. At times, David may have forgotten to love God, but God did not forget David. When David sinned, God allowed him to suffer the consequences of his sins. When David acknowledged his sins, he wasted no time in doing penance for them to show God that he was sorry. God forgave David because he was sorry for his sins. God's mercy made it possible for David to draw closer to God. David was then able to love Him once again as an image of God should. Instead of feeling sorry for himself and wallowing in self-pity, David picked himself up and threw himself back into the service of the Lord. David knew that even the unworthy, even sinners, can accomplish great things for God if they allow themselves to accept His merciful love.

David Steps Down As King

The later years of David's reign were spent in ridding Israel of various enemies. Tragically, one of David's enemies was one of his sons, Absalom. Absalom was greedy for the throne and its power. He organized a rebellion against his own father. Rather than fight his son directly, David fled Jerusalem and endured much humiliation from the people because of his flight. When Absalom was killed, David acted as a father should. He mourned and grieved for his son. Even though Absalom had turned against him, David still loved him.

Because Israel was a new and inexperienced nation, the laws of succession to the throne had not yet been established. The will of the ruling king determined succession to the throne. In order to keep peace in the country, David named his successor before he died. On the advice of Nathan the prophet and in the presence of Bathsheba, the king swore, "As the LORD lives, who has delivered me from all distress, this very day I will fulfill the oath I swore to you by the LORD, the God of Israel, that your son Solomon should reign after me and should sit upon my throne in my place" (1 Kings 1:29–30).

Then David gave these last instructions to Solomon. "I am going the way of all mankind. Take courage and be a man. Keep the mandate of the LORD, your God, following his ways and observing his statutes, commands, ordinances, and decrees as they are written in the law of Moses, that you may succeed in whatever you do, wherever you turn, and the LORD may fulfill the promise He made on my behalf when He said, 'If your sons so conduct themselves that they remain faithful to me with their whole heart and with their whole soul, you shall always have someone of your line on the throne of Israel'" (1 Kings 2:1–4).

"David rested with his ancestors and was buried in the City of David [Jerusalem]. The length of David's reign over Israel was forty years: he reigned seven years in Hebron and thirty-three years in Jerusalem" (1 Kings 2:10–11).

REVIEW QUESTIONS

1. Fill in the blanks. After Saul's death, _____ became king of the southern tribes, which called themselves the kingdom of _____. The northern tribes followed Saul's son _____, and called themselves the kingdom of _____. After years of fighting, David became king over both the North and South. This united kingdom became known as _____, and David made _____ the capital city.

2. Why did David want to build a temple for the Lord?

3. What was the most important promise that God gave to David through the prophet Nathan?

*4. How was God's promise to David of a royal "house" that would endure forever fulfilled in the Person of Jesus?

5. List some of the accomplishments of David during his reign as king.

6. Describe some of the good qualities of David's character.

7. What three commandments did David not follow?

*8. How did God show His merciful love to David?

9. What can we learn from David?

10. Who was Absalom?

11. Who succeeded David as king of Israel?

12. What advice did David give Solomon?

Solomon, the Third King of Israel

Solomon's first order of business as king was to secure his throne. Solomon did not hesitate to execute any person who threatened him. His father, David, had warned him he might have to deal with various rivals. Solomon wasted no time in proving himself a decisive and powerful ruler. Having done so, Solomon made various treaties with neighboring kings, thus securing his borders. He took the daughter of the Pharaoh in Egypt for a wife, in order to make peace with the Egyptians. What is more, Solomon organized the new nation of Israel in a manner similar to that of Egypt. The Egyptians had established a powerful empire. Solomon adopted many Egyptian ideas in his governing of Israel.

The Accomplishments of King Solomon

Solomon was able to avoid a major war during his reign. This long period of peace allowed him to attend to other matters. He was responsible for many major building projects. He had a wall constructed around the city of Jerusalem, and ordered the fortification of the cities of Megiddo, Gezer, and Hazor as military bases for his chariot divisions. He created an enormous palace and temple complex north of the City of David on a hill called Zion. The building of this Temple to Yahweh, the Lord, made Solomon a legend in his own time. Because the Temple was to be the central place of worship for all of Israel, Solomon did not spare any expense. The preparations, building, furnishings, and dedication of the Temple and palace are recorded in 1 Kings 5, 6, 7, and 8. The Scripture writers needed four chapters to complete the description! Solomon employed the best architects, artists, and craftsmen from his kingdom. He used the best and most expensive materials: cedar beams, precious stones, bronze, ivory, silver, and gold. The columns, floors, ceilings, walls, and doors were all elaborately decorated. It is estimated that the project took twenty years to complete.

In addition to his building projects, "King Solomon also built a fleet at Ezion-geber, which is near Elath on the shore of the Red Sea in the land of Edom" (1 Kgs 9:26). This is the first recorded mention of sea commerce in the Israelite kingdom. Solomon used his fleet to expand trade with foreign countries. The ships of his fleet brought back much wealth from Arabia, East Africa, Turkey, Egypt, and other Mediterranean countries. In addition, Solomon acquired chariots and the best horses for his army from his trade with Cilicia. Solomon was the first king of Israel to use the chariot as a military weapon. "Solomon collected chariots and drivers; he had one thousand four hundred chariots and twelve thousand drivers; these he allocated among the chariot cities and to the king's service in Jerusalem" (1 Kgs 10:26). Archaeologists have discovered, in the ruins of Megiddo, which was one of Solomon's chariot cities, the stalls for

450 horses; this evidence shows that the figures mentioned in the biblical text are not exaggerated. The Philistines, a conquered nation, were experts in iron-working and chariot-making. Solomon wisely took advantage of their knowledge. With their expertise and the copper and iron mines he possessed in Edom, Solomon's armies were the best-equipped in the world.

The Wisdom of Solomon

The major building projects, his overwhelming wealth, and the strength of his defenses made Solomon a well-known ruler of his time. But Solomon was known for something else: his wisdom. Soon after Solomon became king, he went to Gibeon to pray and offer sacrifice to the Lord. "In Gibeon the LORD appeared to Solomon in a dream at night. God said, 'Ask something of me and I will give it to you'" (1 Kgs 3:5). Solomon thanked God for the favors He had bestowed on his father, David, and on him. However, he doubted his ability to rule God's people and humbly described himself as "a mere youth, not knowing at all how to act" (1 Kgs 3:7). So Solomon asked God, "Give your servant, therefore, an understanding heart to judge your people and to distinguish right from wrong. For who is able to govern this vast people of yours?" (1 Kgs 3:9). God was pleased with Solomon's request. "Because you have asked for this—not for a long life for yourself, nor for riches, nor for the life of your enemies, but for understanding so that you may know what is right—I do as you requested. I give you a heart so wise and understanding that there has never been anyone like you up to now, and after you there will come no one to equal you. In addition, I give you what you have not asked for, such riches and glory that among kings there is not your like. And if you follow me by keeping my statutes and commandments, as your father David did, I will give you a long life" (1 Kgs 3:11–14).

Read 1 Kings 3:16–28 for an example of the wisdom of Solomon.

Solomon showed his wisdom in the many judgments he made as ruler of Israel. He also wrote numerous songs and *proverbs*, which are wise sayings. His wisdom is recorded in the Books of Psalms, Proverbs, Ecclesiastes, Song of Songs, and Wisdom.

Solomon's Temple, his great wealth, and his wisdom became legends in his own time. The Queen of Sheba (present-day Yemen) traveled all the way from Africa to see the great Solomon for herself and to consult with him. She was so impressed with Solomon's wisdom and his wealth that she gave praise to the God of Israel, even though she was a pagan. Her visit is recorded in 1 Kings 10:1–13.

The Sins of Solomon

But Solomon's reign was weakened by the very things that made it great. The wealth that allowed the building of the famous Temple and other projects was funded by heavy taxes. Even though Solomon's extensive trade brought in a tremendous quantity of riches, this wealth was not enough. Solomon's "lifestyle" had become, along with his wealth, too extravagant. He became overindulgent and greedy. The general population was forced to pay for his every desire. The most common tax on the people was forced labor. Although forced labor was commonly used by Egypt and other foreign nations, it was not part of the Hebrew tradition, and the Israelites deeply resented it.

In order to strengthen his military and commercial ties, Solomon had many foreign wives. These foreign wives worshiped pagan gods and brought the worship of their gods to Israel. "When Solomon was old his wives had turned his heart to strange gods, and his heart was not entirely with the LORD, his God, as the heart of his father David had been" (1 Kgs 11:4). Solomon suffered the consequences of this sin against the First Commandment. The strength, prosperity, and unity of Israel lay always in the bond of common worship of the one true God. When the Israelites, led by the example of their king, chose to reject God, they grew weak and fell prey to rebellions both from within and without the kingdom.

When Solomon chose to commit the sin of idolatry, he chose to reject God's love. He broke the covenant that God had made with him. His unfaithfulness cost him his kingdom. Before Solomon died, he saw his kingdom fall apart. Jeroboam, a servant of Solomon, rebelled against him and took possession of Israel, the northern kingdom of ten tribes. Solomon's son and heir, Rehoboam, ruled over what was left of the southern kingdom of Judah. But even the sin of idolatry did not change God's promise to continue the royal line of David's "house" forever.

"The time that Solomon reigned in Jerusalem over all Israel was forty years. Solomon rested with his ancestors; he was buried in his father's City of David, and his son Rehoboam succeeded him as king" (1 Kgs 11:42–43).

The warning of the prophet Samuel to the Israelites held true for Saul, David, and Solomon. "But you must fear the LORD and worship him faithfully with your whole heart; keep in mind the great things he has done among you. If instead you continue to do evil, both you and your king shall perish" (1 Sm 12:24–25).

REVIEW QUESTIONS

1. List some of the accomplishments of Solomon during his reign.
2. What gift did Solomon ask God to give him?
3. How did God react to Solomon's request?
4. In what books of the Bible can we find some of Solomon's wisdom?
5. What is a proverb? Give an example from the Book of Proverbs.
6. What made Solomon a legend in his own time?
7. What were some of Solomon's sins?
8. What were the consequences of Solomon's sin of idolatry?
9. What happened to the united kingdom of Israel?
*10. Name the first three kings of Israel.
11. How did Samuel's words of wisdom recorded in 1 Samuel 12:24–25 affect the first three kings, and what meaning do they have for us today?

Concepts of Faith

1. **Name the first three kings of Israel.**
   Saul, David, and Solomon.

2. **How was God's promise to David, of a royal "house" that would endure forever, fulfilled in the Person of Jesus?**
   Jesus, in His human origins, is a descendant of the house, or royal family, of David. Jesus is also true God and our eternal King.

3. **How did God show His merciful love to David?**
   When David sinned, God allowed him to suffer the consequences. Then, when David showed God that he was sorry for his sins, God forgave him. David was then drawn closer to God and was able to love Him once again as an image of God.

Vocabulary

anoint: Bless with oil.

house of David: David's royal family.

parable: A short story that teaches a moral or a religious lesson.

proverb: A wise saying.

scimitar: A sword with a curved blade.

sistrum: An ancient Egyptian percussion instrument, similar to a tambourine.

Living the Lesson

Present-Day Solomons

"But I tell you, not even Solomon in all his splendor was dressed like one of them." —Luke 12:27

These words are from a parable that Jesus told His disciples. A *parable* is a story that teaches a moral or a religious lesson. There are at least thirty-five parables recorded in the Gospels of the New Testament. There are many more stories that teach religious lessons in the Old Testament. Jesus liked to use parables to teach His disciples and others who came to hear Him speak. Oftentimes, stories help us to remember important things. Jesus, of course, knew this!

Read the parable recorded in Luke 12:22–34, and then discuss the following questions with your family and classmates. Note that some of the questions can have various answers.

1. In the *New American Bible*, the heading "Dependence on God" precedes the parable. Why is this an appropriate title for this parable?

2. What title might you give to this parable?

3. What two examples did Jesus use in His parable to explain the lesson?

4. What are some things that Jesus tells us not to worry about?

5. Jesus tells us to "seek His kingdom" (Lk 12:31). How can we do this?

6. "Provide money bags for yourselves that do not wear out, an inexhaustible treasure in heaven that no thief can reach nor moth destroy" (Lk 12:33). What did Jesus mean by this?

7. "For where your treasure is, there also will your heart be" (Lk 12:34). What kind of treasures are stored in your heart?

8. Why did Jesus mention Solomon in His parable?

9. How did Solomon lose sight of the real treasure?

10. How can we avoid becoming present-day Solomons?

Anointing with Oil

The oil most commonly used throughout the ancient world came from the fruit of the olive tree. The olive tree is one of the few trees that can survive in the harsh desert climate. Olive trees can grow to be very old. There are some that have existed for more than five hundred years. The olive tree is the most common tree found in Palestine, the region that includes the city of Jerusalem. You may remember hearing of a place called the Mount of Olives. The Mount of Olives is mentioned several times in both the Old and the New Testament. It takes its name from the many olive trees that grew on its slopes. The Garden of Gethsemane, on the western slope of the mountain, was the site of the agony and the arrest of Jesus.

Buying and selling olive oil was a big business in the ancient world, as it is today. Olives and olive oil are among the chief exports of modern Greece. During ancient times, the oil was pressed out of the olives by using the weight of large stones. Channels were cut into the rock under the olives so that the oil could run down them and then be collected. Today, you can still see this method of collecting olive oil in many towns of the Middle East. The oil was stored in large pottery jars. These jars, sometimes as tall as an adult, were distributed throughout the country and exported throughout the known world. The oil was then put in smaller bottles or flasks and sold to individuals.

Oil had many uses in the ancient world, just as it has today. It was the most valued product of the land. It is mentioned numerous times in the writings of the Bible. Here are some of the uses of oil that the Bible mentions: to prepare food; to make the face shine; as medicine, to soothe wounds; after a bath; in perfumes; as fuel for lamps; as an export product; for festive and ceremonial occasions; as a sacred sign.

Samuel, the prophet, used oil as a sacred sign when he anointed Saul and David. The purpose of anointing with oil was to make someone or something sacred, or holy. The Old Testament mentions the names of seven kings who were anointed with oil. Priests also were anointed. Various things, such as the Ark of the Covenant, the Tent of Meeting, and the furniture of the Tent, were anointed, too. Anointing with oil was a visible sign of God's blessing.

The birth of Jesus Christ added a deeper meaning to the custom of anointing with oil. In Hebrew, *masiah* means "anointed one". In Greek, *christos* means "anointed one". At the Epiphany, one of the Magi presented Jesus with the gift of myrrh, an expensive perfume that uses olive oil as its base. Jesus Christ, then, is the Messiah, the Anointed One, the eternal King promised by God to David. After the story of the Epiphany, the only time the term *anointing* is used in the New Testament is for the care of the sick.

The Church continues to use anointing as a visible sign of God's blessing. In some of the sacraments, the Church anoints with chrism. Chrism is a mixture of olive oil and balsam, which is consecrated by the bishop on Holy Thursday for use in the sacraments throughout the year. When we are anointed, we receive God's grace and share in His holiness. Jesus instituted the sacraments. He is our King, our High Priest. When we participate in the sacraments, we also share in His Kingship and in His Priesthood. By our acting as images of God, the Kingdom of God will reign in our hearts and in the hearts of others.

Prayers

King David's "Song of Thanksgiving". (Several verses of 2 Samuel 22 could be read aloud. This prayer is also recorded in Psalm 18. Other psalms attributed to David are marked "Of David" in editions of the *New American Bible*.)

Proverbs. (The proverbs attributed to Solomon are found in the Book of Proverbs, Part II, chapters 10–22; Part V, chapters 25–29.)

A United Kingdom:
The Reigns of David and Solomon

Using the map printed in lesson 16, provide the information requested below. Use pencils, crayons, or markers, as appropriate.

1. Cities. Place the following cities on the map by marking a dot and printing the name of the city next to the dot: Bethel, Hazor, Damascus, Hebron, Elath, Jerusalem, Ezion-geber, Joppa, Gezer, and Megiddo.

2. Nations. Using different colors (but not blue), shade in the areas of the following nations and also the boxes of your "color code":

☐ Aram and Hamath ☐ Israelites
☐ Ammonites ☐ Moabites
☐ Edomites ☐ Philistines
☐ Egyptians ☐ Phoenicians

3. Waterways. Use the color blue to mark these waterways: Mediterranean Sea, Red Sea, Dead Sea, Jordan River, and Euphrates River.

4. Important Sites. Draw the following symbols near the sites given:

star:	Jerusalem
mining car:	Ezion-geber
ship:	Joppa
ships:	Elath
ships:	Red Sea
chariot:	Megiddo

5. Outline, in black, the area ruled by David and Solomon.

On the line in front of each numbered item, write the letter that identifies the corresponding person or place.

____ 1. David

____ 2. Jonathan

____ 3. Absalom

____ 4. Jerusalem

____ 5. Samuel

____ 6. Saul

____ 7. Jeroboam

____ 8. Gibeah

____ 9. Rehoboam

____ 10. Jesse

____ 11. Solomon

____ 12. Philistines

____ 13. Michal

____ 14. Goliath

____ 15. Bathsheba

A. Prophet who anointed Saul and David.

B. An enemy of Israel.

C. First king of Israel.

D. City of Saul's palace.

E. Son of Saul, friend of David.

F. Daughter of Saul, wife of David.

G. Second king of Israel.

H. Philistine warrior defeated by David.

I. Father of David.

J. Capital city of David.

K. Wife of Uriah; she sinned with David; mother of Solomon.

L. Betrayed his father, David.

M. Third king of Israel, son of David and Bathsheba.

N. Servant of Solomon who rebelled against him and took possession of the northern kingdom.

O. Son of Solomon who succeeded him as king over the tribe of Judah.

The Prophets: Signs of God's Merciful Love

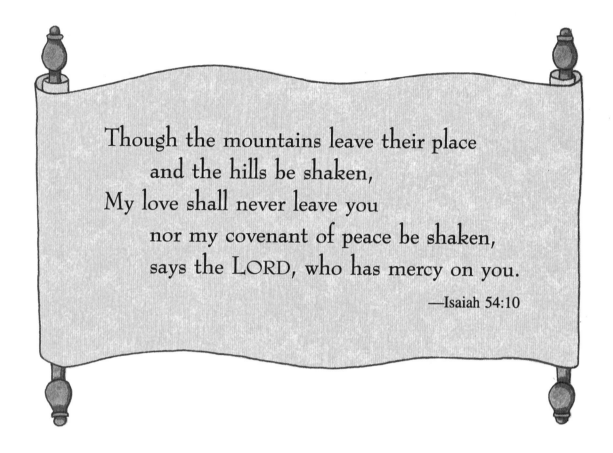

Though the mountains leave their place
and the hills be shaken,
My love shall never leave you
nor my covenant of peace be shaken,
says the LORD, who has mercy on you.

—Isaiah 54:10

What Happened after the Schism?

After King Solomon died, the united kingdom of Israel was split in two. This split or division is known as the *schism*. The northern kingdom kept the name of Israel. The southern kingdom became known as Judah. Judah continued to be ruled by the descendants of David, because of the promise that God had once made to him. But both territories were governed by a long succession of corrupt kings—kings who chose not to act as images of God. These kings encouraged the practice of worshiping pagan gods. The people followed the example of their kings and also chose to reject God's love. They forgot God and the covenant that they had made with Him. Because they chose to sin, they hurt God, themselves, and others. The consequences of their sins were felt for centuries.

Israel and Judah were at war with each other almost constantly during these years. Neighboring countries saw the weakness of the two kingdoms and tried to conquer them. Eventually, Israel was conquered by the Assyrians in 721 B.C., and Judah was conquered by Babylon in 586 B.C.. The city of Jerusalem and the beautiful Temple built by Solomon were destroyed. Both kingdoms were now conquered nations. God's chosen people were taken as captives to Babylon. This period in their history is known as the Babylonian Captivity, or the Exile. Since most of the people taken to Babylon were from the tribe of Judah, the people were called "Jews". The Jews lived in Babylon for almost fifty years.

Then, in 538 B.C., Babylon was defeated by King Cyrus of Persia. Under his reign, the Jews were permitted to return to their land and rebuild the city of Jerusalem and the Temple. Not all of the Jews returned to Jerusalem at the same time, however. It took more than ninety years, until 444 B.C., for all the Jews to return to their homeland. The period from 538 to 333 B.C. is known as the Period of Restoration. Even though the Jews were still under the rule of Persia, they were able to reestablish themselves as a new community and to renew their Covenant with God. Two men, Ezra and Nehemiah, were especially important during the Period of Restoration. Ezra was a priest who was a great religious leader. He tried to teach the people to follow the laws put down in the Torah. The *Torah* includes the laws found in the Pentateuch and in oral tradition. Nehemiah organized the rebuilding of the walls that surrounded and fortified the city of Jerusalem. Nehemiah also introduced many administrative and political reforms. The efforts and accomplishments of these two men can be found in the Books of Ezra and Nehemiah. Still, in spite of the dedicated work of these men, many of the Jews did not act as images of God.

Other nations were exerting their power at this time, too. In 331 B.C., under the leadership of Alexander the Great, Greece defeated Persia. For almost two hundred years the Jews lived under the rule of Greece and were allowed to retain their own culture and religion. But in 168 B.C., a new Greek ruler tried to force the Jews to accept the Greek religion, and he converted the Temple to the worship of the pagan god Zeus. Led by Judas Maccabeus, the Jews revolted against this change. In 165 B.C. Judas recaptured the Temple and restored it to the worship of Yahweh. This important event is remembered by the Jews today in the festival of Hannukah. The brothers of Judas Maccabeus, Jonathan and Simon, continued the revolt and succeeded in winning independence for the Jews. Their story can be found in two historical books of the Bible, 1 and 2 Maccabees. For a short while, the Jews were able to enjoy independence. However, in 63 B.C., the Romans conquered Palestine, the area occupied by the Jews. The Romans allowed the Jews to practice their own religion, as long as they submitted to the political authority of the emperor of Rome. Jesus Christ was born while the Jews were under the domination of Rome.

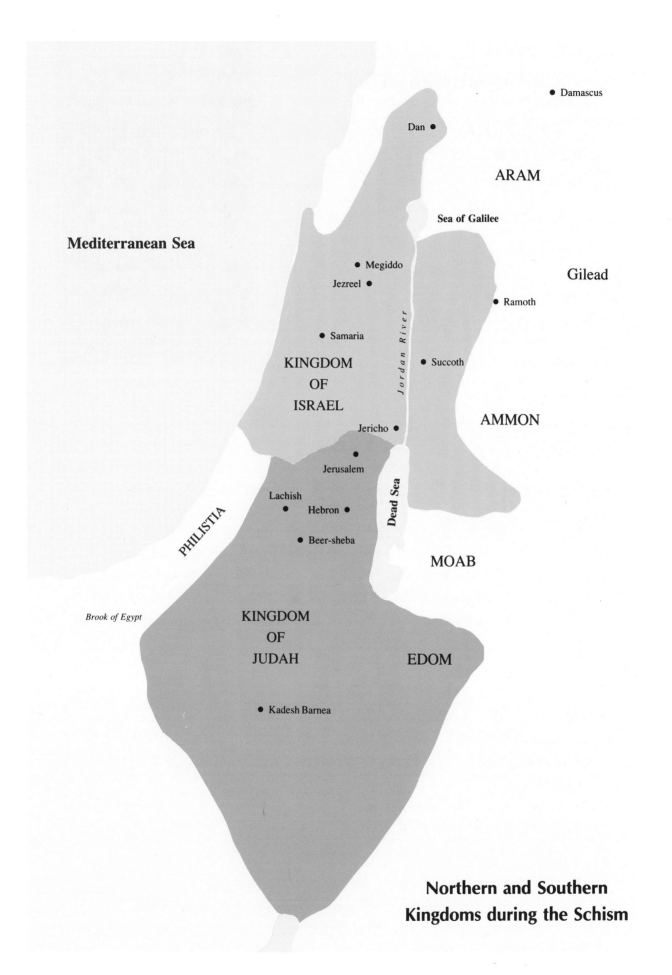

Damascus

Dan

ARAM

Sea of Galilee

Mediterranean Sea

Megiddo

Jezreel

Gilead

Ramoth

Samaria

Jordan River

KINGDOM
OF
ISRAEL

Succoth

AMMON

Jericho

Jerusalem

Dead Sea

Lachish

Hebron

Beer-sheba

MOAB

PHILISTIA

Brook of Egypt

KINGDOM
OF
JUDAH

EDOM

Kadesh Barnea

**Northern and Southern
Kingdoms during the Schism**

During this long period after the schism, God waited patiently for His chosen people to act as images of God. Even though the Israelites continued to reject God's love, God did not reject them.

God showed His people His merciful love by sending messengers to remind them of their promise to act as images of God. These messengers were called prophets.

REVIEW QUESTIONS

1. What was the schism?
2. Describe some of the details of the schism.
3. Who continued to rule the kingdom of Judah?
4. How did the people choose to act after the schism?
5. Who conquered Israel in 721 B.C.?
6. Who conquered Judah in 586 B.C.?
7. What happened to the Chosen People after Judah was conquered?
8. What is this period of Israel's history called?
9. By what new name were God's Chosen People called?
10. Who defeated Babylon in 538 B.C.?
11. Why is the time period from 538–333 B.C., when the Jews were under Persian rule, known as the Period of Restoration?
12. Why were the prophets Ezra and Nehemiah important during the Period of Restoration?
13. Who conquered Persia in 331 B.C.?
14. Who was Judas Maccabeus?
15. What Jewish holiday celebrates this event?
16. Who conquered the Jews in 63 B.C.?
17. How did God show His merciful love during the period of Jewish history from the schism to Jesus Christ?

What Is a Prophet?

What exactly is a prophet? What did a prophet do? How did a person become a prophet? Was a prophet like a fortuneteller, who could see into the future and predict what would happen?

All of these questions come to mind when we hear the word *prophet*. This word comes from the Greek word *prophetes*, which means "one who speaks before others". The prophets, then, were people through whom God spoke to His people. Many of the prophets did foretell the future as part of their message from God. Because they could "see" into the future, the prophets are sometimes referred to as "seers". God's prophets, however, did not predict the future in the same way or for the same reasons as does a fortuneteller at the circus. There were no crystal balls or reading of palms, no tea leaves or horoscopes. The prophets never charged a fee for their prophecies. They did not prophesy for entertainment or amusement. In fact, they were generally not very popular, because their prophecies and advice were often not what their listeners, usually sinners, wanted to hear.

God chose the prophets to do His work when His people were in need. Whenever the people chose to reject God's love and to sin against the covenant and the Ten Commandments, God would send a prophet to warn them of the consequences of their actions. Then, when God's people were suffering as a result of their sins, the prophets would comfort them and give them hope, by reminding them of God's everlasting love. The prophets, then, were visible signs of God's merciful love.

Who Were the Prophets?

You have already read about some of the prophets of the Old Testament. Miriam, the sister of Moses, is called a prophet in the Book of Exodus. Moses is also referred to as a prophet. Samuel and Nathan were prophets during the time of King Saul and King David.

In this lesson you will learn about some of the prophets who lived after King Solomon and before the time of Saint John the Baptist, the prophet who announced the coming of Jesus. Look in your Bible at the list of books of the Old Testament. Find the Book of Isaiah. All the books of the Old Testament that follow Isaiah, except for the Books of Lamentations and Baruch, are named after prophets. Therefore, they are referred to as books of prophecy or the prophetic books. Isaiah, Jeremiah, Ezekiel, and Daniel are considered major prophets, because their books are longer than those of the other prophets. The other twelve prophets are sometimes called minor prophets.

*1. What is a prophet?
 2. How were the prophets different from fortunetellers?
 3. How were the prophets signs of God's merciful love?
*4. Name the four major prophets.

In the chart below are listed the places where the prophets did God's work, along with suggested scriptural references, and a brief description of their message.

The Prophets and Their Messages

Major Prophets	Place	Scripture	Message Summary
Isaiah	Judah	Is 9:1–6	Prophecy of the Messiah. Repent.
Jeremiah	Judah	Jer 31:31–34	Prophecy of New Covenant. Repent.
Ezekiel	Babylon	Ez 10; 34:25–30; 37:1–14	Destruction of Jerusalem. Salvation for Israel. Vision of the Dry Bones.
Daniel	Babylon	Dn 3, 6, 7	Protection of God. Son of Man. Visions of the future.

Minor Prophets			
Hosea	Israel	Hos 14:2–10	Remain faithful to God. Love only Him.
Joel	Judah	Jl 2:12–18	Repent, for the day of the Lord is coming.
Amos	Israel	Am 2:4–6; 9:14	Repent. Care for the poor. Hope for Israel.
Obadiah	Israel	Ob 17–21	Judah shall be restored.
Jonah	Nineveh*	Jon 1–4	Repent. God is merciful and loves all people.
Micah	Judah	Mi 6:8	Do what is right. Love goodness.
Nahum	Judah	Na 22:10	Prophesy of destruction of Nineveh.
Habakkuk	Judah	Hb 3:16–19	The wicked will be punished. The just will have salvation.
Zephaniah	Judah	Zep 3:1–2; 16–17, 20	Sinners will suffer. God will show mercy to the faithful.
Haggai	Judah**	Hg 1:8–8; 2:19	Rebuild the Temple. Obey God and be blessed.
Zechariah	Persia**	Zec 9:9–10	Promise of the Messiah.
Malachi	Judah**	Mal 3:16–18	Sinners will suffer. Mercy to those who love God.

*Capital of Assyria.   **Under Persian rule.

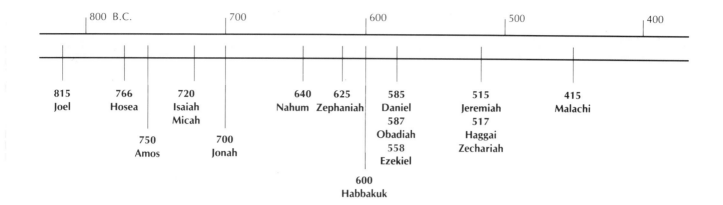

800 B.C.	700	600	500	400

815
Joel

766
Hosea

720
Isaiah
Micah

640
Nahum

625
Zephaniah

585
Daniel
587
Obadiah
558
Ezekiel

515
Jeremiah
517
Haggai
Zechariah

415
Malachi

750
Amos

700
Jonah

600
Habbakuk

Who Were Elijah and Elisha?

There are two important prophets whose names are not on the chart, because they do not have a book of the Bible named after them. They are the prophets Elijah and Elisha. The biblical account of their work can be found in the historical books 1 and 2 Kings; specifically, 1 Kings 17 through 2 Kings 13. Their time period begins about fifty years after the schism, from approximately 874 B.C. to 782 B.C., in the northern kingdom of Israel. At that time, Israel was ruled by the wicked and powerful King Ahab and his wife, Jezebel. Ahab was a strong military ruler who made the city of Samaria his capital. Ahab was much influenced by his foreign wife, and the two of them introduced the worship of the pagan god Baal to the people of Israel.

Elijah was the prophet chosen by God to battle against the worship of Baal and the evil practices of this false religion. God worked many miracles through His prophet Elijah. Some of these miracles are listed in Worksheet 1. Through miraculous signs Elijah proved that Yahweh was the true God and that Baal was a false god. None of these signs, however, convinced Ahab and Jezebel. They continued to commit sins against God and the people they ruled. Both Elijah and Elisha warned them of the consequences of their evil ways, and the words of the prophets came true. The deaths of these two rulers who were unfaithful to God are recorded in 1 Kings 22:29–38 and 2 Kings 9:30–37.

Elijah was faithful in his service to God and was taken up alive into heaven by a whirlwind. Read 2 Kings 2:1–12 for the biblical account of this dramatic event.

Elijah's friend and faithful companion, Elisha, continued God's work of prophecy in Israel. As with Elijah, God worked many miracles through the prophet Elisha. Worksheet 1 lists the biblical references for many of the miracles performed by Elijah and Elisha. You may wish to choose several of them to read about. In response to the preaching of these prophets, some of the Israelites chose to act as images of God. But many of them hardened their hearts against the truth and continued their sinful ways.

1. Who was Elijah?
2. Who ruled Israel during the time of Elijah?
3. How did Elijah prove that Yahweh was the one, true God?
4. How was Elijah taken up to heaven?
5. What prophet continued the work of Elijah?

Assyrian Empire

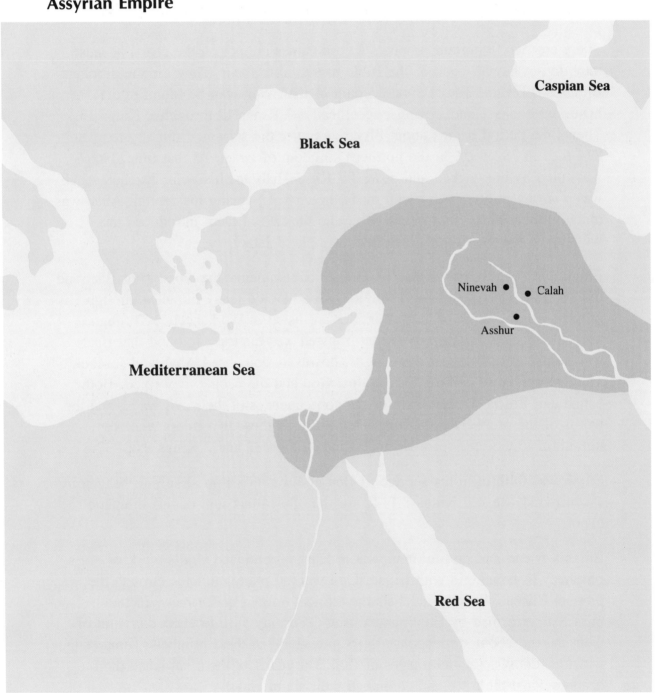

The Prophet Isaiah

Isaiah is one of the Bible's great prophets. He did God's work in the southern kingdom of Judah. Isaiah received the call from God to act as His prophet in 742 B.C., the same year as the death of King Uzziah, one of the few good kings who ruled Judah. Isaiah was in the Temple of Jerusalem when he saw a vision of the Lord, which is described in Isaiah 6:1–13. Isaiah was overwhelmed with the glory of the Lord. The words of the Seraphim angels to announce the presence of the Lord are used in the liturgy of the Mass today: "Holy, holy, holy is the LORD of hosts!" they cried out to one another. "All the earth is filled with his glory!" (Is 6:3). When the Lord asked, "Whom shall I send? Who will go for us?", Isaiah accepted the call by answering, "Here I am, send me!" (Is 6:8). From that moment, Isaiah began his prophetic mission.

Isaiah's words of prophecy were heard throughout the reigns of three kings: King Jotham, the son of Uzziah; Jotham's son, King Ahaz; and his son, King Hezekiah. Jotham and Hezekiah were good kings. But King Ahaz and Isaiah often disagreed on what was best politically for Judah. King Ahaz made alliances with foreign powers, such as Assyria. Ahaz thought that these nations would help protect Judah from enemies. Isaiah tried to persuade the King to put his trust in God, rather than in foreign powers. In 721 B.C., Assyria conquered the northern kingdom of Israel, which made the people of the southern kingdom of Judah very nervous. Then King Hezekiah came to power. Although Hezekiah tried to be a good ruler and to bring the people back to the worship of the one true God, he, too, made alliances with foreign and pagan nations, such as Egypt. Once again Isaiah advised against alliances with these nations. "Trust in the Lord, depend on Him, have faith in the one true God!" was the message that Isaiah preached. But the King did not listen. Assyria attacked Judah and the capital city of Jerusalem in 701 B.C. With Isaiah's support, Hezekiah successfully defended the city. But the land of Judah was devastated and the nation greatly weakened. After this event, Isaiah died.

Throughout this period of Judah's history, Isaiah's voice could be heard. He spoke of many things. Most of Isaiah's prophecies concerned four topics: (1) the greatness of God; (2) the coming of Jesus, the Messiah; (3) the consequences of Judah's sins and the need for repentance; and (4) God's merciful love.

The Greatness of God

Isaiah hoped to persuade the people of Judah to choose God and change their sinful ways by reminding them of the greatness of God. Many of the scriptural verses in the Book of Isaiah are descriptions of the Lord. Isaiah names Him the Lord of hosts and the only God. For more of Isaiah's descriptions of the greatness of God, see Worksheet 2.

The Coming of Jesus, the Messiah

Isaiah lived seven hundred years before the birth of Jesus, yet he often spoke about the coming of the Messiah. "The virgin shall be with child, and bear a son, and shall name him Immanuel" (Is 7:14). The Gospel writers recognized that Isaiah's prophecies about the Messiah were fulfilled in the Person of Jesus. Several of them quoted Isaiah when they wrote their account of the life of Jesus. The words of Isaiah are so beautiful that they are used in the liturgies for Advent, Christmas, and Lent. Many of the verses have also been set to music in Christmas hymns and in the well-known oratorio by G. F. Handel, *The Messiah*.

The Consequences of Judah's Sins and the Need for Repentance

During this period of Judah's history, the people drew away from God. They chose to disobey the laws of the Covenant and did not act as images of God. Many of the people and their kings chose to reject the love of God, and they worshiped false gods. As the people drew away from God, they forgot how to love themselves and others as images of God should. For example, the pagan religions of the time included the evil practice of human sacrifice. Murder, dishonesty, adultery, and neglect of the poor and the suffering were common.

God, however, continued to show the Chosen People His merciful love. One of the reasons God chose Isaiah and the other prophets was to remind the people of their promise to live according to the Ten Commandments and the other laws set down in the Torah. Isaiah warned the people often of the consequences of their sins. Some of the people listened and changed their evil ways. But the nation as a whole continued to reject God's love. The people ultimately suffered the consequences of their sins when the kingdom of Judah became a conquered nation.

God's Merciful Love

"Though the mountains leave their place and the hills be shaken, / My love shall never leave you nor my covenant of peace be shaken, says the LORD, who has mercy on you" (Is 54:10).

Even though the people continued for a long time to reject God, God never abandoned them. The prophet Isaiah spoke many words of hope and comfort to the suffering nation of Judah. His words have been remembered throughout countless generations of sinners. They are used today in the liturgies and prayers of the Church to offer us the same hope of salvation that God promised to the faithful people of Judah centuries ago.

REVIEW QUESTIONS

1. Where did Isaiah work?
2. When were the words of the "Holy, holy, holy", used during the liturgy of the Mass, first used?
3. Why did Isaiah object to the alliances of Judah with foreign powers?
4. What are the four topics of Isaiah's prophecies?

Greek Empire

Caspian Sea

Black Sea

KINGDOM OF SELECUS

Mediterranean Sea

KINGDOM
OF
PTOLEMY

Red Sea

Babylonian Empire

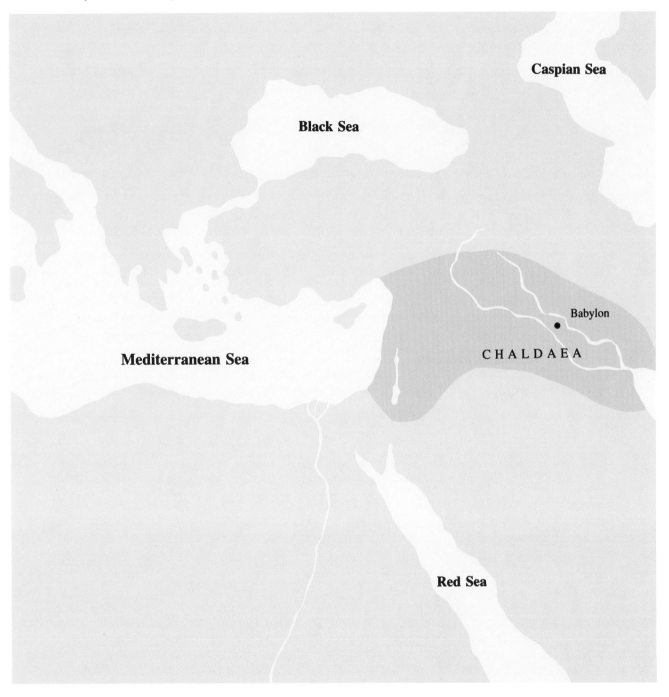

Caspian Sea

Black Sea

Mediterranean Sea

CHALDAEA

Babylon

Red Sea

Persian Empire

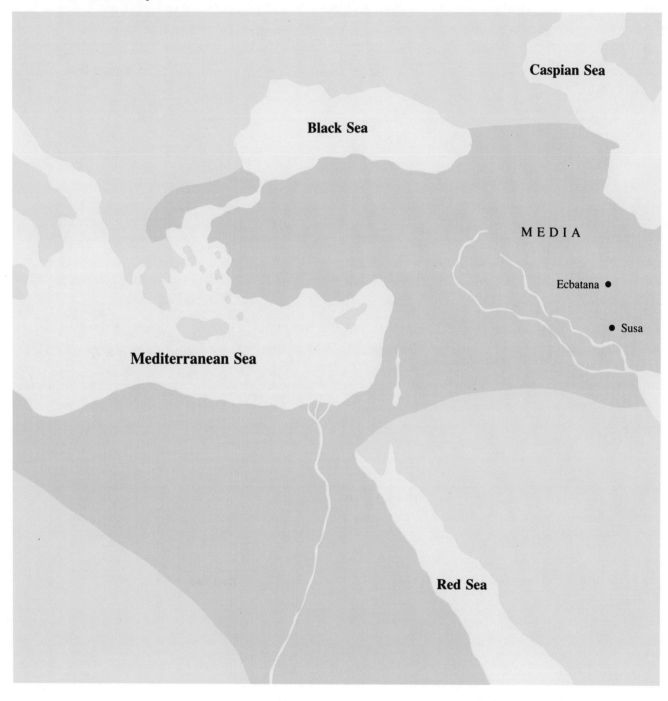

Caspian Sea

Black Sea

MEDIA

Ecbatana ●

● Susa

Mediterranean Sea

Red Sea

Conclusion

The prophets were visible signs of God's merciful love. God was able to speak to His people through them. All the prophets, though they lived at different times and worked in different places, relayed similar messages to the people. They reminded the people that they had been made in God's image. They reminded them that God had chosen them to become more like Him. They could become more like God by living according to the laws of the covenant. The Ten Commandments and other laws written in the Torah taught the people how to act as images of God. The prophets reminded the people of their promise to God. They warned them about the consequences of rejecting God's love. They reminded them that God would never abandon them and that He would show them mercy and forgiveness when they repented of their sins. They promised that God would send them a Messiah Who would save them and help them act as images of God.

The prophets relayed God's message through preaching, through working miracles, and through their writings. God's word was handed down through the generations and comes to us today in the prophetic books of the Old Testament. The message that the prophets gave to the people so long ago is similar to the one we hear in the New Testament. We are images of God. God loves us and wants us to return His love. We can return His love by choosing to follow His Commandments and the teachings of the Church established by His Son, Jesus. When we choose to act this way, we return God's love and become better images of Him.

REVIEW QUESTIONS

1. List some of the messages the prophets gave to the people.
2. How did the prophets relay God's message?
3. How does the message of the prophets apply to us?

Concepts of Faith

1. What is a prophet?

A prophet is a messenger, chosen by God, to speak to His people.

2. Name the four major prophets.

Isaiah, Jeremiah, Ezekiel, and Daniel.

Vocabulary

schism: A split, or division.

Torah: The laws found in the Pentateuch and in Jewish oral tradition.

Living the Lesson

Mary, Queen of the Prophets

You have learned in this lesson that a prophet is a person through whom God spoke to His people. Mary has played the role of prophet many times throughout the history of the Church. Whenever Mary appeared, she had an important message from God to give to the people. Like the messages of the prophets of the Old Testament, Mary's message was directed to the people of that particular time and place. And also like the messages of the prophets of the Old Testament, Mary's message always encouraged the people to repent of their sins, to increase their prayers to God, and to act as images of God.

Below is a list of four of the many appearances of Mary where she acted as a prophet. Choose one appearance and write a brief description of the account and of the message that God sent to us through Mary, Queen of the Prophets.

1. Our Lady appears to Bernadette at Lourdes.
2. Our Lady of Fatima.
3. Our Lady of Guadalupe.
4. Our Lady of the Rosary.

Prayers

"Hail Mary". (Discuss how this traditional and scriptural prayer is also a prophetic one.)

Psalms 50, 75, and 82. (These are often called prophetic psalms.)

The Miracles of Elijah and Elisha

God worked many miracles through the prophets Elijah and Elisha. This worksheet lists some of the wondrous events in which these prophets played a part.

Look up the following biblical references and write a short description of the miracle described in each.

Elijah

1. 1 Kings 17:1 _____

2. 1 Kings 17:7–16 _____

3. 1 Kings 17:17–24 _____

4. 1 Kings 18:16–40 _____

5. 1 Kings 18:41–45 _____

6. 2 Kings 1:9–12 _____

7. 2 Kings 2:6–9 _____

Elisha

1. 2 Kings 2:13–14 _____

2. 2 Kings 3:9–19 _____

3. 2 Kings 4:1–7 _____

4. 2 Kings 4:18–37 _____

5. 2 Kings 4:42–44 _____

6. 2 Kings 5:1–19 _____

7. 2 Kings 6:1–7 _____

WORKSHEET 2
The Prophecies of Isaiah

The prophet Isaiah spoke of many things. This worksheet groups Isaiah's words under four headings. Follow the directions under each heading.

The Greatness of God

Look up each scriptural reference and write the words Isaiah uses to name or describe God.

1. Isaiah 5:16 _____

2. Isaiah 6:3 _____

3. Isaiah 44:6 _____

4. Isaiah 12:2 _____

5. Is 40:11 _____

The Consequence of Sin and the Need for Repentance

The Book of Isaiah contains 66 chapters. Most of these chapters describe the sins of the people of Judah and the consequences they will suffer because of their sins. Isaiah warns the people to repent and to live their lives according to the laws of the covenant.

Read Isaiah 1:1–31. Then list some of the sins described in the verses, the consequences the people will suffer, and what Isaiah tells the people to do.

Sins.

_____

_____

Consequences.

_____

_____

What should the people do?

_____

_____

The Coming of the Messiah

Choose one of these activities to do.

1. Read these two scriptural verses: Isaiah 9:1–6 and Isaiah 53:1–12.

2. Sing one of these hymns: "Comfort, Comfort Ye, My People"; "Lo, How a Rose E'er Blooming".

3. Listen to one of these selections from the oratorio *The Messiah*, by G. F. Handel: "Comfort ye my people" (No. 1), "Every valley" (No. 2), "And the glory of the Lord" (No. 3), "Behold a virgin" (No. 7), "O thou that tellest good tidings to Zion" (Nos. 8–9), "The people that walked in darkness" (Nos. 10–11), "For unto us a Child is born" (No. 12), or "Then shall the eyes of the blind be opened; He shall feed His flock" (No. 17).

God's Merciful Love

Even though most of Judah chose to sin, God continued to show the people His merciful love. God promised many blessings upon those who chose to return His love and act as images of God should.

*There are two scriptural references listed below. Choose **one**. Find the verse in your Bible and list some of the blessings promised by God through His prophet Isaiah.*

Isaiah 35:1–10　　　　　　　　　**Isaiah 60:1–22**

_____　　_____

_____　　_____

_____　　_____

_____　　_____

_____　　_____

_____　　_____

The Wisdom Books

My son, if you receive my words
    and treasure my commands,
Turning your ear to wisdom,
    inclining your heart to understanding;
Yes, if you call to intelligence,
    and to understanding raise your voice;
If you seek her like silver,
    and like hidden treasures search her out:,
Then will you understand the fear of the LORD;
    the knowledge of God you will find;
For the LORD gives wisdom,
    from his mouth come knowledge and understanding;
He has counsel in store for the upright,
    he is the shield of those who walk honestly,
Guarding the paths of justice,
    protecting the way of his pious ones.

Then you will understand rectitude and justice,
    honesty, every good path;
For wisdom will enter your heart,
    knowledge will please your soul,
Discretion will watch over you,
    understanding will guard you.

—Proverbs 2:1–11

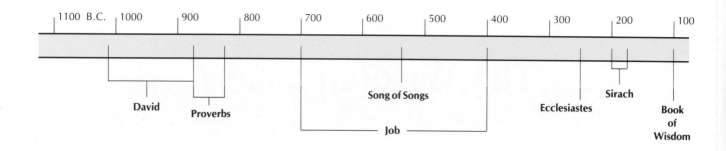

In Lesson 1 you learned that the Bible was written in a variety of literary forms. *Literary forms* are different types of writing. The Old Testament literary forms include history, law, prophecy, prayer, and wisdom. You have already read and studied many of the books of the Old Testament. Can you name a book of the Old Testament for each of these literary forms?

In this lesson you will read about seven books of the Old Testament that are *Wisdom books*. The purpose of the Wisdom books is to teach people how to make right choices about moral behavior so that they may become better images of God. These Wisdom books give insight or common sense about human life and our actions toward each other and toward God. They include the Books of Job, Proverbs, Ecclesiastes, Song of Songs (Canticle of Canticles), Wisdom, and Sirach (Ecclesiasticus). The Book of Psalms, although most often referred to as a prayer book, is also considered one of the Wisdom books.

What Is Wisdom?

"What is wisdom?" is a question whose answer has been sought since the beginning of time. A person who is wise may know many things. Yet wisdom means more than knowledge. A person who is wise may act prudently, that is, with sound reason or common sense. Yet having common sense is not enough to define wisdom. A person who is wise may exhibit good judgment, like King Solomon. Yet even Solomon did not possess sufficient wisdom to remain faithful to God all his life. We know that wisdom is something that everyone wants to possess. But how can we possess wisdom when it is so difficult even to define it?

Wisdom is knowledge so perfect that it guides us to act as images of God. Let's take a closer look at this definition. First of all, it states that wisdom is knowledge. We must study and learn as much as we can about God. Second, this knowledge has to be almost perfect. Third, what we know must be so perfect that we will choose to act as images of God. Wisdom, then, is a quality that every person who acts as an image of God possesses. As we grow in wisdom, we reflect God more clearly, more perfectly.

How Do We Grow in Wisdom?

The Gospel of Saint Luke tells us that when Jesus was twelve years old He went with Mary and Joseph to Jerusalem to celebrate the Passover. On the return journey, Mary and Joseph discovered that Jesus was not with their friends and relatives. They returned to Jerusalem to look for Jesus and found Him preaching to the elders and priests of the Temple. They all were astounded at the knowledge and understanding of the young boy. Then Jesus returned to Nazareth with His mother and father. "And Jesus advanced [in] wisdom and age and favor before God and man" (Lk 2:52).

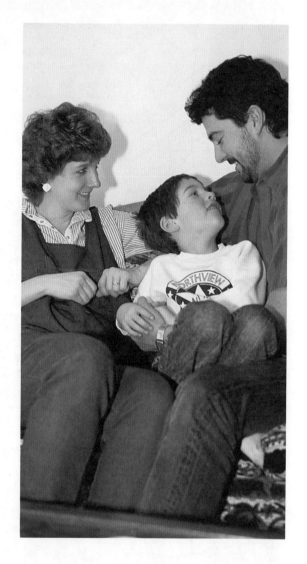

This Scripture passage teaches us that the attainment of wisdom takes time. Even the boy Jesus, Who was both God and man, needed to grow up before He could advance in wisdom. In addition to time, wisdom needs to be nurtured by actions. It is with these actions that the Wisdom books of the Bible are concerned. The Wisdom literature is full of practical, everyday suggestions on how to live as an image of God. These books are like maps. They can guide us through a variety of alternate routes so that we might live as images of God here on earth and someday live with God forever in heaven.

REVIEW QUESTIONS

1. What are some of the literary forms of the books of the Old Testament?
*2. What is the purpose of the Wisdom books of the Bible?
3. Name the seven Wisdom books of the Old Testament.
*4. Define wisdom.
5. How can the Wisdom books help us to become better images of God?

A Summary of the Wisdom Books

The Book of Job

Why do bad things happen to good people? Why does God, Who is all-good and all-loving, allow His people to suffer? Many writers from different cultures, both past and present, have attempted to answer these questions. The Book of Job is one writer's attempt to explain the mystery of suffering. This writer, however, was inspired by God.

We do not know who the human writer of the Book of Job was. Bible experts tell us, however, that the story was composed sometime between the seventh and fifth centuries B.C. The Book of Job is one of the more beautifully written texts of the Old Testament. Many consider it a literary masterpiece. The book is written in the style of a dramatic poem. The main characters are God, Job, and Job's three friends. The story unfolds through a series of speeches and dramatic dialogues.

The story is set during the days of the patriarchs. Job, like Abraham, was a wealthy and prosperous man, whose riches were counted by the number of his wives and children and by the number of his herds and flocks. Job was "a blameless and upright man . . . who feared God and avoided evil" (Job 1:1). Job's goodness was verified by his wealth. Wealth and success were considered God's rewards to those who were faithful to Him. If you were good and remained obedient to God's laws, then good things would happen to you. But if you chose to reject God, then bad things would happen to you. This was the accepted thinking of Job's day. We should remember that the people of this time did not know the teachings of Jesus Christ, for He had not yet been born. Christ was the most "blameless and upright man". Yet, even He, the Son of God, suffered greatly. Many people today still believe that all sufferings are sent by God as a punishment for sin. The story of Job was written to teach the Hebrews and us that that is simply not true.

The first section of the Book of Job describes the terrible sufferings that he had to endure. You will discover the details of Job's sufferings in Worksheet 1, later in this lesson. Job lost everything that was of value to him: his family, his wealth, his health, and his self-esteem.

The next section of the book is an attempt by Job and his three friends to try to understand why these things happened to him. Job knew that he was living a good life. Yet his friends were convinced that God must be punishing Job for some wrongdoing. For 34 chapters the debate continued. At first Job humbly accepted God's will. But as the sufferings increased, Job became depressed and disillusioned: "Perish the day on which I was born" (Jb 3:3). His friends were not much help. Rather than comfort Job and offer him hope, they tried to convince him that he must have done something wrong. By the end of this long section of dialogue, Job's acceptance of God's will gave way to frustration and self-pity. Job could not understand why God would allow him to suffer like this. After all, why should he, "a blameless and upright man", have to suffer at all?

At this point in the story, God takes over as the main speaker. However, God does not answer Job's questions. Rather God said, "Who is this that obscures divine plans with words of ignorance? . . . I will question you, and you tell me the answers!" (Jb 38:2–3). God's speech to Job, recorded in chapters 38 through 41, is a long list of questions whose purpose is to humble Job. "Where were you when I founded the earth? Tell me, if you have understanding. Who determined its size; do you know?" (Jb 38:4–5). The questions continue. Do you know this? Do you know that? Where were you when I did this? Have you done this? Can you do that? Who are you that you should question my ways? And on and on. By the end of this humbling speech, Job finally understood God's message.

Read Job 42:1–6.

Job came to see that he could never completely understand God. Job had allowed his sufferings to cloud his thinking. In his misery, he had forgotten that God could do all things. Job had forgotten that God loved him always and would never abandon him. Job had forgotten that God loved him mercifully. After Job was reminded of these things, he turned his heart toward God. He again acknowledged God as his own. Then Job asked God to forgive him. "I had heard of you by word of mouth, but now my eye has seen you. Therefore I disown what I have said, and repent in dust and ashes" (Jb 42:5–6). God in His merciful love accepted Job's prayers of repentance. Then, "The LORD blessed the latter days of Job more than his earlier ones" (Jb 42:12).

The questions raised in the Book of Job are still asked today. Suffering, especially of those who are innocent, is difficult to accept and to understand. God's answer to Job does not quite leave us satisfied, either. God really does not answer Job's question, "Why me?" Rather, God changes the question to "Why *not* you?" We have an advantage over Job, his friends, and the early readers of this book. We know more of God's wisdom and mercy than they did. God revealed Himself to us through His Son, Jesus. When we look at the sufferings that Jesus endured for love of us, we can make our sufferings work for our own good and the good of others. Through our sufferings and the comfort we can bring to others who are suffering, God gives us an opportunity to share in His Son's sufferings. We can, in a sense, share His pain. We can be drawn closer to Him. Could this be God's message to us?

*1. What did the writer of the Book of Job try to explain?

2. What is the literary form and style of the Book of Job?

3. How does Job 1:1 describe Job?

4. How did the people of Job's day think about the effects of good and bad behavior?

5. Who was the most "blameless and upright man"?

6. Do people who choose to love God sometimes suffer?

7. What was Job's reaction to his many sufferings?

8. What was God's purpose in questioning Job?

9. What did Job forget about in his relationship with God?

10. Did Job ever come to understand God completely? Can we?

11. How did Job respond to God in the end?

*12. How did God show Job His merciful love?

13. What can we learn from the Book of Job?

The Book of Psalms

The Book of Psalms is one of the more familiar books of the Old Testament. Even if you have not read the Psalms yourself from the Bible, you most probably have prayed or sung the Psalms in some way. For instance, did you know that the verses of several Psalms are used throughout the liturgy of the Mass? There are four places in the Mass where the Psalms can be heard: (1) during the entrance procession; (2) after the first Scripture reading; (3) during the preparation of the gifts; and (4) at Communion time. You may have heard a song leader, or *cantor*, at church ask the congregation to sing or say together the *Responsorial Psalm* after the first reading. The Responsorial Psalm, sometimes called an *antiphon*, is usually one verse from the Psalm of the day that the congregation says or sings as a response to other verses of the Psalm that are read or sung. Singing the Psalms is a natural way to pray them. In fact, that is the definition of a Psalm. A *psalm* is a sung prayer. The Book of Psalms, then, is a collection of sung prayers.

Who Wrote the Psalms?

History records that King David was a musician and a composer. You may remember that, as a young boy, David was asked to comfort King Saul by singing Psalms and playing his lyre, or harp. Both Christian and Jewish traditions accept David as the main writer of the Book of Psalms. Other writers also contributed to the Book of Psalms. Moses, Solomon, Heman, and Ethan are recorded as writers of one Psalm each. There are other Psalms whose writers are described as "the sons of Korah" and "the sons of Asaph". These were small groups of temple singers. About one-third of the Psalms have no author's name.

How Are the Psalms Organized?

There are 150 Psalms, which have been organized into five "books", or sections. Some scholars believe that they were organized this way in imitation of the five books of the Pentateuch.

Every Psalm is written in the form of a poem. The poems, however, do not rhyme, nor do they have a steady rhythm. The Hebrew people wrote their own kind of poetry. Their poetry put thoughts together, rather than rhyming words. This has made it easier to translate the Psalms into many languages.

What Do the Psalms Talk About?

Like all prayers, the Psalms speak to God. They may take the form of praise; thanksgiving; *petition*, or asking God for something; and *contrition*, or telling God we are sorry. Some of the Psalms are historical; they tell what God has done for His people. Some Psalms speak of our relationship with God—His love for us and our response to Him. These Psalms are sometimes called *confidence* Psalms. When we place our confidence in someone, we trust that person. Such a person is often a friend. God is our most perfect Friend. He shows us His love, and we respond to His love by placing our confidence, our trust, in Him. Sometimes these confidence Psalms are also referred to as friendship Psalms. Many other Psalms predict the coming of Jesus, the Messiah, and are therefore known as Messianic Psalms. A chart listing some of the Psalms and their subject matter follows.

Types of Psalms

Praise	Psalms 19, 29, 33, 47, 93, 96–99, 139, 146–150
Thanksgiving	Psalms 34, 65, 66, 103, 124, 136
Petition	Psalms 3, 5, 6, 7, 13, 22, 26, 31
Contrition	Psalms 6, 25, 32, 38, 51, 102, 130, 143
Historical	Psalms 77, 78, 105, 106
Confidence	Psalms 23, 27, 121, 131
Messianic	Psalms 2, 8, 16, 22, 45, 72, 89, 110, 118, 132

Why Are the Psalms Popular?

The Psalms cover a wide range of human emotions. They give praise to God in times of joy and cry out to Him in times of deepest sorrow. People of every age have found in them the perfect expression of their own mood for every occasion. We, too, can use the Psalms as another way of praying to God.

REVIEW QUESTIONS

1. What is a Psalm?
*2. What is the Book of Psalms?
3. List the four places in the Mass where the Psalms can be heard.
4. What is another name for the Responsorial Psalm?
5. What is the Responsorial Psalm, and how is it often used during the Mass?
6. Who is the main writer of the Book of Psalms?
7. How many Psalms are there?
8. How are the Psalms different from our poetry?
9. Name some of the types of Psalms.
10. What do we do in a Psalm, or prayer, of petition?
11. What do we do in a Psalm, or prayer, of contrition?
12. What do confidence Psalms express?
13. What do Messianic Psalms express?
14. Why are the Psalms so popular?

The Book of Proverbs

A *proverb* is a wise saying. The Book of Proverbs is a collection of wise sayings that cover many different areas of everyday life. Israel was naturally influenced by its neighboring countries. You know from your past studies that Egypt influenced the development of Israel in both good and bad ways. The Egyptians were fond of writing different types of literature, and the writing of proverbs was one of them. Scholars have discovered that the proverbs in the Bible are similar to many proverbs recorded by the Egyptians. The writers of the Book of Proverbs include King Solomon, two men named Agur and Lemuel, and others who were simply known as the wise ones. These writers, unlike the Egyptian writers, were inspired by God.

Proverbs were written as a way of instructing people, especially the young, to think about what is important in life. We are asked to make choices throughout our entire lives. Sometimes the choice between good and evil is very clear and easy to decide. But more often we are asked to make choices that are not so "black and white". We have to try to make the best choice. We need to learn to choose wisely. For example, a student may say, "When I grow up I want to be rich." This is not a bad thing, assuming that the wealth is earned in an honest way. The three proverbs below, however, remind us that there are things more important than material wealth.

> A good name is more desirable than great riches, and high esteem, than gold and silver.
> —Proverbs 22:1

> Rich and poor have a common bond: the LORD is the maker of them all.
> —Proverbs 22:2

> The reward of humility and fear of the LORD is riches, honor and life.
> —Proverbs 22:4

The Book of Proverbs is a wonderful and rich source of wisdom. Its sayings are easily read and remembered. Like the young boy Jesus, we, too, need to "grow in wisdom". This Wisdom book can help us.

REVIEW QUESTIONS

1. What is a proverb?
*2. What is the Book of Proverbs?
3. Name one of the writers of the Book of Proverbs.
4. Why were proverbs written?

The Book of Ecclesiastes

The writer of the Book of Ecclesiastes was a teacher of wisdom. He gives us his name in Ecclesiastes 1:12–13: "I, Qoheleth, was king over Israel in Jerusalem, and I applied my mind to search and investigate in wisdom all things that are done under the sun." Because Qoheleth is called "David's son, . . . king in Jerusalem" (Eccl 1:1), many believed that Ecclesiastes was the wisdom of King Solomon, who used the name Qoheleth as a literary name. Bible scholars have determined, however, that this Wisdom book was written in approximately 250 B.C. History records that Solomon lived from 970 to 931 B.C. The inspired writer of Ecclesiastes used Solomon's name because of the legendary wisdom of this king. The writer knew that more people would learn God's message if they believed that its author was the wise King Solomon.

The message of Ecclesiastes is often described as pessimistic or depressing. Here are two passages from this Wisdom book that reflect a pessimistic mood.

> I have seen all things that are done under the sun, and behold, all is vanity and a chase after wind.
> —Ecclesiastes 1:14

> For in much wisdom there is much sorrow, and he who stores up knowledge stores up grief.
> —Ecclesiastes 1:18

The writer then continues to give examples of how every action is worthless. No matter how good a person is, no matter how wise a person is, no matter how hard a person works, in the end he will die, and all his goodness, all his wisdom, and all his labor will have been for nothing. Isn't this depressing? What is wrong with this conclusion? What has been left out? Why is such a depressing book in the Bible? What is God trying to tell us through this writer?

You must read the very last verse of Ecclesiastes to find the "hidden" meaning in this Wisdom book.

> The last word, when all is heard: Fear God and keep his commandments, for this is man's all; because God will bring to judgment every work, with all its hidden qualities, whether good or bad.
> —Ecclesiastes 12:13–14

In the end, Ecclesiastes looks forward to a reward greater than that which can be found on earth. This longing was satisfied in the teachings of Jesus Christ, Whose Person was not revealed for another three hundred years.

1. What literary name did the writer of Ecclesiastes use?
2. Was King Solomon the author of Ecclesiastes?
3. Why did the inspired writer of Ecclesiastes use Solomon's name?
4. Why is the message of Ecclesiastes often described as pessimistic or depressing?
5. What is God's real message in this Wisdom book?

The Song of Songs

This Wisdom book of the Bible is also known by two other names, Canticle of Canticles and the Song of Solomon. Because of the style of this poem, Bible scholars think that it was written probably sometime after the Babylonian Exile in 538 B.C. Hence, as with the Book of Ecclesiastes, Solomon could not have been the author. God inspired another unknown poet to compose this masterpiece.

This biblical book is a beautiful love song. The text has many different meanings. Some have interpreted this poem as an expression of ideal married love. Some read it as a representation of the relationship between God and Israel. Others see it as a foreshadowing of the union between Christ and the Church, and so this book is used as a source of the Church's liturgical texts for feasts of the Blessed Virgin Mary.

1. What are two other names for the Song of Songs?
2. Did King Solomon write this book of wisdom?

The Book of Wisdom

The Book of Wisdom is also known as the Wisdom of Solomon. Like several of the other Wisdom books attributed to Solomon, it was written by another inspired author. The unknown author wrote this book about a hundred years before Christ was born. At that time there was a large Jewish community living at Alexandria, in Egypt. During this period of history, the civilization of Greece was the world's leader in learning and philosophy. The Greek culture, like other cultures in the past, had a strong influence on the Jewish people. Many of the Jews, impressed with other aspects of Greek culture, began to accept the pagan religion of Greece. The author's purpose in writing the Book of Wisdom was to warn the Jews that their faith was in danger and to remind them of the wisdom of remaining faithful to the one, true God.

The first and last verses of the Book of Wisdom summarize its intent.

> Love justice, you who judge the earth; think of the LORD in goodness, and seek him in integrity of heart.   —Wisdom 1:1

> For every way, O LORD! you magnified and glorified your people; unfailing, you stood by them in every time and circumstance.
> —Wisdom 19:22

The Book of Sirach

The Book of Sirach is also known as Ecclesiasticus, which means "Church book". The author wrote this text between 200 and 175 B.C., around the same time as the Book of Wisdom was written.

Its purpose, as with all the Wisdom books, is to teach people how to make right choices, especially in their moral behavior. The writer chose to discuss the wisdom of remaining dutiful to God and parents; the wisdom of practicing the virtues of humility, justice, and sincerity; and the wisdom of giving alms to the poor. The writer includes advice for the good conduct of both family and public life. This inspired writer also offers advice concerning relationships and even on how to choose a friend.

Conclusion

The Wisdom books of the Bible continue to be a source of God's merciful love. These books helped the people of the Old Testament to prepare for and look forward to the coming of the Messiah. Through these writings and the teachings of Jesus, we can become better images of God, Who is Wisdom.

REVIEW QUESTIONS

1. What is another name for the Book of Wisdom?
2. Did Solomon write this book?
3. What culture strongly influenced the Hebrews at this time?
4. Why was the author inspired by God to write this book?
5. What is another name for the Book of Sirach?
6. What specific topics of behavior are discussed in this Wisdom book?
*7. What is the purpose of the Wisdom books of the Bible?

Concepts of Faith

1. **What is the purpose of the Wisdom books of the Bible?**
   To teach people how to make right choices about moral behavior so that they may become better images of God.
2. **What is wisdom?**
   Wisdom is knowledge so perfect that it guides us to act as images of God.
3. **What did the author of the Book of Job try to explain?**
   The mystery of suffering.
4. **How did God show Job His merciful love?**
   God accepted Job's prayers, blessed him, and restored his good fortune.
5. **What is the Book of Psalms?**
   A collection of sung prayers.
6. **What is the Book of Proverbs?**
   A collection of wise sayings.

Vocabulary

literary forms: Different types of writing.

Wisdom books: Books of the Old Testament that give insight or common sense about human life and our actions toward each other and toward God.

wisdom: Knowledge that is so perfect that it guides us to act as images of God.

cantor: Song leader.

antiphon, or Responsorial Psalm: One verse from a Psalm that the congregation says or sings.

psalm: A sung prayer.

petition: A prayer that asks God for something.

act of contrition: A prayer that tells God we are sorry.

confidence: Trust.

proverb: A wise saying.

Living the Lesson

Live and Up Close: An Interview with a Wise Person

You are employed by a local TV station. The station has been doing a special report entitled "The Wise Ones". One segment of the show explored the meaning of wisdom. Another segment researched the history of wisdom by relating the stories of wise people of the past. Your assignment is to bring this topic up to date. You have been told to interview several local residents who are known to possess wisdom and present a "Live and Up Close!" segment for the closing segment of the special report.

Here are some suggestions:

(1) Determine in your own mind what qualities determine a "wise one".

(2) Compile a list of questions you might want to ask. The questions should be adaptable to various age groups.

(3) Choose several different types of persons (both male and female) who qualify as "wise ones" (an adult, an adolescent, a child, persons from different occupations and vocations).

(4) Take notes during the interview so that you will not misquote anyone. Be sure to ask permission to quote or to tape the interview.

(5) Choose a format for your segment. For example:
> Brief review of the previous segments;
> Introduction to the "Live and Up Close!" segment;
> The names of the persons to be interviewed and a
>   brief summary of who they are;
> The actual interviews;
> Closing statements.

(6) You may wish to videotape or tape-record the interview or to bring the "wise ones" into the classroom. Or the class could get together in small groups and present an interview using students in the various roles of interviewer and "wise ones".

Prayers

Ecclesiastes 3:1–15—"There is an appointed time for everything . . . ." (This wonderful passage can be read aloud prayerfully in alternating verses. Take time to reflect on its timeless wisdom.)

Psalms. (Pray selected verses from the Book of Psalms.)

Jesus and the Apostles quoted the Book of Proverbs to emphasize their teachings. Read the following passages during prayer time: John 7:34; Romans 12:20; and James 4:6. (Compare 1 Peter 4:8 and James 5:20 with Proverbs 10:12.)

Find these passages in the Book of Job and write a brief summary of Job's sufferings, or of his *response* to his suffering, described in each passage.

1. Job 1:14–15 _____

   _____

2. Job 1:16 _____

   _____

3. Job 1:17 _____

   _____

4. Job 1:18–19 _____

   _____

5. Job 2:7 _____

   _____

6. Job 2:9 _____

   _____

7. Job 1:21 _____

   _____

8. Job 2:10 _____

   _____

Cantor: The Responsorial Psalm is *Teach me your laws, O LORD.*

Response: *Teach me your laws, O LORD.*

Cantor: *Teach me your laws, O LORD.*

Teach me wisdom and knowledge,
for in your commands I trust.

R: *Teach me your laws, O LORD.*

Cantor: You are good and bountiful;
teach me your statutes.

R: *Teach me your laws, O LORD.*

Cantor: Let your kindness comfort me
according to your promise to your servants.

R: *Teach me your laws, O LORD.*

Cantor: Let your compassion come to me that I may live,
for your law is my delight.

R: *Teach me your laws, O LORD.*

Cantor: Never will I forget your precepts,
for through them you give me life.

R: *Teach me your laws, O LORD.*

Cantor: I am yours; save me,
for I have sought your precepts.

R: *Teach me your laws, O LORD.*

Look at the chart entitled "Types of Psalms", earlier in this lesson. Choose *one* Psalm from each of the seven categories. Read the Psalm. Write one or two verses from the Psalm that illustrate the type of Psalm it is, as shown in the following example.

Petition: *Heed my call for help, my king and my God! (Psalm 5:3).*

Type of Psalm   *Psalm Verse*

Praise: _____

_____

Thanksgiving: _____

_____

Petition: _____

_____

Contrition: _____

_____

Historical: _____

_____

Confidence: _____

_____

Messianic: _____

_____

Family Proverbs

Part One

Look up the following five passages in the Book of Proverbs. Write each proverb on the lines following the Scripture reference. Then, continue with Part Two of the worksheet.

1. **Proverbs 1:8:** _____

    _____

2. **Proverbs 10:1:** _____

    _____

3. **Proverbs 13:24:** _____

    _____

4. **Proverbs 20:7:** _____

    _____

5. **Proverbs 23:24:** _____

    _____

Part Two

Choose one of the five proverbs and explain what wisdom it can offer to you today.

_____

_____

_____

_____

_____

The Church Year

There is an appointed time for everything,
and a time for every affair under the heavens.
A time to be born, and a time to die;
a time to plant, and a time to uproot the plant.
A time to kill, and a time to heal;
a time to tear down, and a time to build.
A time to weep, and a time to laugh;
a time to mourn, and a time to dance.
A time to scatter stones, and a time to gather them;
a time to embrace,
and a time to be far from embraces.
A time to seek, and a time to lose;
a time to keep, and a time to cast away.
A time to rend, and a time to sew;
a time to be silent, and a time to speak.
A time to love, and a time to hate;
a time of war, and a time of peace.

—Ecclesiastes 3:1–8

The *Church year* is sometimes called the liturgical year or the ecclesiastical year. All three names refer to the same cycle of events. The Church year is similar to a calendar. However, the Church's year does not begin in January on New Year's Day. Instead, it begins in November or December, four Sundays before Christmas, on the first Sunday of Advent. Just as the calendar year has seasons, so the Church year has seasons. There are six liturgical seasons in the Church year—Advent, Christmas, Lent, Easter Triduum, Easter, and Ordinary Time. The Holy Days of obligation and the feast days honoring Jesus, Mary, the angels, and the saints are included throughout the seasons of the Church year. Various liturgical colors are associated with the seasons of the Church year: white, red, violet, green, and black. (Black is an optional color and may be used at funeral Masses and on All Souls' Day.) The color of the vestments worn by the priest and deacons and the color of the altar and church decorations reflect the "mood" of the liturgical season or feast day.

Within the cycle of a year the Church unfolds the whole mystery of Christ, from His Incarnation and birth to His death, Resurrection, and Ascension and the day of Pentecost. Along with the story of Christ is mingled the history of the Church. These events are made known to God's people through the Old and New Testament readings assigned to each day of the Church year. It is important for us to hear these readings because they reveal God's merciful love. Because it would be almost impossible to include all the texts from the Bible in one year, there are three cycles of Sunday readings. These cycles are called Year A, Year B, and Year C.

REVIEW QUESTIONS

*1. What are the six liturgical seasons of the Church year?

*2. When does the Church year begin?

3. What liturgical colors are used throughout the Church year?

*4. What cycle of events takes place during the Church year?

5. How do the people learn of these events?

6. How many cycles of Sunday readings are there?

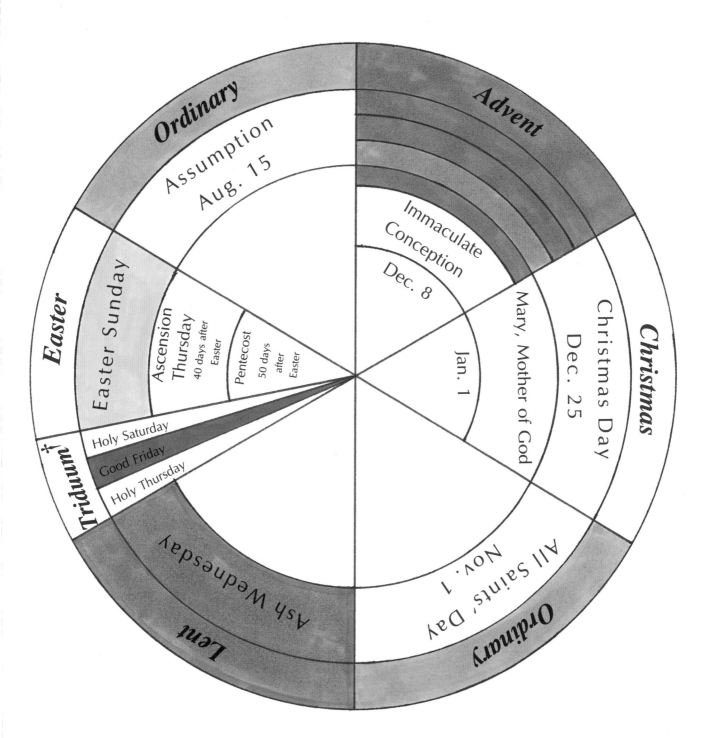

The Church Year

†*Note: The Triduum is from Holy Thursday night to Easter Sunday night.*

The Season of Advent

The word *advent* means "coming". The season of Advent celebrates the three comings of Christ—past, present, and future. First, Advent celebrates the historical coming of Christ about two thousand years ago. We wait for the prophecies foretelling the birth of the Messiah to be fulfilled at His birth. Second, Advent reminds us that Jesus comes to us and is present before us right now. Christ is with us always. He comes to us through grace, through His Church, and through the sacraments. Above all, He comes to us whenever we receive the Holy Eucharist. Third, Advent celebrates the future and final coming of Christ on the last day of the present world.

The season of Advent includes the four Sundays before Christmas. The first Sunday of Advent begins the Church year. The liturgical color for Advent is violet. This color reflects the purpose and mood of the season. It is a time of preparation, of making our hearts ready to receive the long-awaited Messiah. Prayer and penance are two ways to prepare for the coming of Christ. Many other customs, such as the Advent wreath and the Advent calendar, are also reminders to help us prepare for the coming of Jesus.

Below is a list of some of the feast days that may be celebrated during the Advent Season. The liturgical color used for feast days is white or red.

November 30	Saint Andrew
December 3	Saint Francis Xavier
December 6	Saint Nicholas
December 7	Saint Ambrose
December 8	**Immaculate Conception** (Holy Day of obligation)
December 12	Our Lady of Guadalupe
December 13	Saint Lucy
December 14	Saint John of the Cross

REVIEW QUESTIONS

1. What does the word *advent* mean?
2. What three comings of Christ does Advent celebrate?
3. How many Sundays are included in Advent?
4. What is the liturgical color of Advent?
*5. Describe the purpose of Advent.
6. What Holy Day of obligation is celebrated during Advent?

The Christmas Season

The Christmas Season celebrates the birth of Jesus and reminds us of His early childhood years at Nazareth. It begins on Christmas Eve, continues through the Epiphany, and ends with the baptism of Jesus. The liturgical color of this season is white. There are countless religious customs that help us celebrate this joyous and festive season. The Church often mingles local and national customs with her liturgical rites.

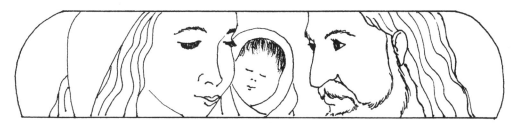

Below is a list of some of the feast days that may be celebrated during the Christmas season.

December 25	**Christmas Day** (Holy Day of obligation)
December 26	Saint Stephen
December 27	Saint John the Apostle
December 28	Feast of the Holy Innocents (Mt 2:13)
December 29	Saint Thomas Becket
December 30	Holy Family
December 31	Saint Sylvester
January 1	**Mary, Mother of God** (Holy Day of obligation)
January 2	Saints Basil the Great and Gregory Nazianzen
January 4	Saint Elizabeth Ann Seton (in U.S.)
January 5	Saint John Neumann (in U.S.)

Sunday between January 2 and January 8
Epiphany
Sunday after the Epiphany (usually)
Baptism of our Lord

REVIEW QUESTIONS

*1. What does the Christmas season celebrate?

2. When does the Christmas season begin and end?

3. What is the liturgical color of the Christmas season?

4. Discuss some of the customs used to celebrate Christmas.

5. What Holy Days of obligation are celebrated during the Christmas season?

The Season of Lent

The Lenten season focuses on the Passion and death of Christ. The biblical readings of this season remind us of the need to follow Christ through the crosses we are called upon to carry. The season of Lent, like the season of Advent, is a time of preparation. As Advent prepares us for Christmas, so Lent prepares us for Easter. But Lent is a more penitential season because of the events in Christ's life that we celebrate during Lent. The liturgical color of violet is used to reflect this solemn mood.

There are three forms of penance that the Church asks us to practice during the season of Lent. One form of penance is fasting. Fasting is eating less food, usually one main meal a day and two smaller meals. Adults between the ages of 21 and 59 are asked to fast on Ash Wednesday and Good Friday. Abstinence is another type of fasting. Lenten abstinence means to refrain from eating meat on certain days of Lent. These days include Ash Wednesday and all Fridays of Lent. Persons over the age of 14 are asked to abstain from eating meat on these days. Fasting and abstinence help bring us closer to the sufferings of Christ and to those among us who are less fortunate. A second form of penance is private and liturgical prayer. The Church asks us to increase our personal prayers and to receive the sacraments frequently, especially the sacraments of Reconciliation and Holy Eucharist. Meditating on the Stations of the Cross is one form of liturgical prayer that is practiced during Lent. The third form of penance that the Church asks us to practice during Lent is charity toward our neighbor. When we practice the virtue of charity, we give of ourselves. We love our neighbor as Jesus taught us. Christ loved us so much that He gave His very life for us. The Church asks us to imitate Christ's love in whatever way we can.

Lent begins with Ash Wednesday, continues for six Sundays, and ends on Holy Thursday evening with the celebration of the Lord's Supper. The sixth Sunday of Lent is called either Palm Sunday, because it celebrates Christ's triumphant entrance into the city of Jerusalem, or Passion Sunday, because it marks the beginning of Holy Week.

Below is a list of feast days sometimes celebrated during the season of Lent.

February 14	Saints Cyril and Methodius
February 22	Chair of Peter
March 7	Saints Perpetua and Felicity
March 17	Saint Patrick
March 19	Saint Joseph
March 25	The Annunciation
April 7	Saint John Baptist de la Salle
April 13	Saint Martin
April 21	Saint Anselm

*1. What does the season of Lent celebrate?

2. For what does the season of Lent prepare us?

3. What liturgical color reminds us of the penitential mood of Lent?

4. What three forms of penance does the Church ask us to practice during Lent?

5. When does Lent begin?

6. When does Lent end?

7. What special week does Passion Sunday begin?

The Easter Triduum

The Easter Triduum is the shortest and the most important of the liturgical seasons. During the Easter Triduum we celebrate Christ's Passion, death, and Resurrection.

The Triduum begins on the evening of Holy Thursday with the celebration of the Lord's Supper. At the Last Supper, Jesus instituted the sacraments of Holy Eucharist and Holy Orders. The Triduum continues through Good Friday, which commemorates the Passion and death of Our Lord. The Triduum reaches its high point on Holy Saturday during the Easter Vigil. The word *vigil* means "to keep watch". During this most holy night, when Christ rose from the dead, the Church watches and waits for this miracle by celebrating the sacraments. The Easter Vigil has four main parts: the Service of Light, the Liturgy of the Word, the Liturgy of Baptism, and the Liturgy of the Eucharist. The Easter Triduum closes with evening prayer on Easter Sunday. The colors of this three-day season change from white on Holy Thursday evening, to red on Good Friday, and back again to white on Holy Saturday.

*1. Why is the Easter Triduum the most important of the liturgical seasons?

*2. What three days make up the Easter Triduum?

3. What sacraments did Christ institute on Holy Thursday at the Last Supper?

4. What do we remember on Good Friday?

5. What important event is celebrated during the Easter Vigil service on Holy Saturday night?

6. What two liturgical colors are used during the Easter Triduum?

The Easter Season

The Easter season relives the Resurrection and Ascension of Christ and the coming of the Holy Spirit on Pentecost. It begins on Easter Sunday and ends on Pentecost Sunday. The word *pentecost*, from the Greek, means "fifty days". The Easter season is fifty days long. During the season of Easter, the theme is resurrection from the death of sin to a life of grace. The Church uses the liturgical color white to remind us of the hope that we all have in the Resurrection. The last ten days of the season, Ascension Thursday through Pentecost, focus on the promise of the presence and power of the Holy Spirit. Just as the Apostles were called to spread the "Good News", so too, we are encouraged to be witnesses to the teachings of Christ. During this season a special emphasis is placed on the sacraments of Baptism, Confirmation, and the Eucharist to help us carry on our responsibility to the teaching of Christ. The Church has asked us to attend Mass on all Sundays of the year to encourage us to become witnesses to the message of the Resurrection.

The Easter season, appropriately, occurs in the spring, a time of new life. Unlike Christmas Day, which is always celebrated on December 25, the feast of the Resurrection, Easter Sunday, is a movable feast—that is, its date changes. Easter Sunday is always the first Sunday after the vernal equinox, which occurs between March 22 and April 25. The vernal equinox is the time in spring when the sun crosses the equator at a point that makes the length of day and of night equal. The Church chooses this time of year for Easter in order to give us a visual reminder of the New Life we find in the risen Lord. Christ conquers the darkness of sin and gives us the light of eternal life.

Below is a list of the some of the feast days often celebrated during the Easter season.

April 7	Saint John Baptist de la Salle
April 13	Saint Martin
April 21	Saint Anselm
April 25	Saint Mark
April 29	Saint Catherine of Siena
May 1	Saint Joseph the Worker
May 2	Saint Athanasius
May 3	Saints Philip and James
Forty Days after Easter	**Ascension Thursday** (Holy Day of obligation)
Fifty days after Easter	Pentecost Sunday

REVIEW QUESTIONS

*1. What does the Easter season celebrate?

2. When does the Easter season begin and end?

3. How long is the Easter season?

4. What is the theme of the Easter season?

5. What liturgical color is used during the Easter season?

6. What is the focus of the days from Ascension Thursday to Pentecost?

7. What are we encouraged to do during the Easter season?

8. What sacraments are emphasized during the Easter season to help us be witnesses to Christ?

9. During what time of year does the Easter season occur and why?

10. What Holy Day of obligation is celebrated during the Easter season?

Ordinary Time

Ordinary Time occurs twice during the Church year. The first period of Ordinary Time occurs before Lent. It begins the Monday after the Baptism of our Lord, or the Monday after January 7, and ends on the Tuesday before Ash Wednesday. The second period of Ordinary Time occurs after the Easter season. It begins on the Monday after Pentecost and continues until the end of the Church year, the Saturday before the first Sunday of Advent. The liturgical color of Ordinary Time is green.

Together, these two periods of Ordinary Time comprise thirty-three to thirty-four weeks of the Church year. Unlike the other seasons of the year, which celebrate specific events in the life of Christ, this season has salvation history as its main theme. During this season, the long history of God's merciful love is reviewed. The readings remind us of the continuing love and care God showed to His chosen people, from the time of Abraham to the coming of Jesus Christ. The emphasis is on the covenant relationship that God offers to us and on our response to this offer.

Below is a list of some of the feast days that may be celebrated during the two periods of the season of Ordinary Time.

Special Sundays during Ordinary Time:

Trinity Sunday—the Sunday after Pentecost

Body and Blood of Christ (Corpus Christi)—the Sunday after Trinity Sunday

Christ the King—the last Sunday of the Church year

January 17	Saint Anthony
January 21	Saint Agnes
January 24	Saint Frances de Sales
January 25	Conversion of Saint Paul
January 26	Saints Timothy and Titus
January 28	Saint Thomas Aquinas
January 31	Saint John Bosco
February 2	Presentation of the Lord
February 5	Saint Agatha
February 6	Saint Paul Miki and Companions
February 10	Saint Scholastica

May 14	Saint Matthias
May 26	Saint Philip Neri
May 31	The Visitation
June 1	Saint Justin
June 3	Saint Charles Lwanga and Companions
June 5	Saint Boniface
June 11	Saint Barnabas
June 13	Saint Anthony of Padua
June 24	Birth of John the Baptist
June 29	Saints Peter and Paul
July 3	Saint Thomas the Apostle
July 11	Saint Benedict
July 15	Saint Bonaventure
July 22	Saint Mary Magdalene
July 25	Saint James
July 26	Saints Joachim and Ann (parents of Mary)
July 29	Saint Martha
July 31	Saint Ignatius of Loyola
August 4	Saint John Vianney
August 6	Transfiguration
August 8	Saint Dominic
August 10	Saint Lawrence
August 11	Saint Clare
August 15	**Assumption** (Holy Day of obligation)
August 24	Saint Bartholomew
August 27	Saint Monica
August 28	Saint Augustine
September 3	Saint Gregory the Great
September 8	Birth of Mary
September 9	Saint Peter Claver
September 13	Saint John Chrysostom
September 14	Triumph of the Cross
September 16	Saints Cornelius and Cyprian
September 21	Saint Matthew
September 27	Saint Vincent de Paul
September 29	Archangels Michael, Gabriel, and Raphael
September 30	Saint Jerome

October 1	Saint Theresa of the Child Jesus
October 2	Guardian Angels
October 4	Saint Francis of Assisi
October 7	Our Lady of the Rosary
October 15	Saint Teresa of Avila
October 17	Saint Ignatius of Antioch
October 18	Saint Luke
October 28	Saints Simon and Jude
November 1	**All Saints' Day** (Holy Day of obligation)
November 2	All Souls' Day
November 4	Saint Charles Borromeo
November 9	Dedication of St. John Lateran
November 10	Saint Leo the Great
November 11	Saint Martin of Tours
November 12	Saint Josaphat
November 13	Saint Frances Xavier Cabrini
November 17	Saint Elizabeth of Hungary
November 21	Presentation of Mary
November 22	Saint Cecilia
November 30	Saint Andrew

REVIEW QUESTIONS

1. When does Ordinary Time occur in the Church year?

2. What liturgical color is used during Ordinary Time?

*3. What main theme is expressed in the readings during Ordinary Time?

4. What two Holy Days of obligation are celebrated during Ordinary Time?

5. On what days do we celebrate the Resurrection of Christ and are therefore obligated to attend Mass?

6. List all the Holy Days of obligation celebrated throughout the Church year in the United States.

Concepts of Faith

1. **What are the six liturgical seasons of the Church year?**
   Advent, Christmas, Lent, Easter Triduum, Easter, and Ordinary Time.

2. **When does the Church year begin?**
   First Sunday of Advent.

3. **What cycle of events takes place during the Church year?**
   The story of the life of Christ and the history of the beginnings of the Church.

4. **Describe the purpose of Advent.**
   Advent is a time of waiting and preparation for the coming of Christ.

5. **What does the Christmas season celebrate?**
   The birth and early childhood years of Jesus.

6. **What does the season of Lent celebrate?**
   The Passion and death of Jesus.

7. **What three days make up the Easter Triduum?**
   Holy Thursday evening to Easter Sunday evening.

8. **Why are the three days of the Easter Triduum the most important in the Church's year?**
   During the Easter Triduum, we celebrate Christ's Passion, death, and Resurrection.

9. **What does the Easter season celebrate?**
   The Resurrection and Ascension of Christ, and the coming of the Holy Spirit on Pentecost.

10. **What is the main theme of Ordinary Time?**
    Salvation history.

Vocabulary

Church year: Liturgical year, ecclesiastical year, cycle of events.

advent: coming.

Living the Lesson

Get into It!

A parish priest was asked to visit a religion class one day to give a talk about the sacrament of Holy Eucharist and the Mass. A discussion followed on the importance of going to Mass every Sunday. One of the students complained, "I don't get anything out of going to Mass, so why should I go?" The priest replied, "Perhaps you don't get anything out of it because you don't put anything into it!"

"Get into it!" "Intense!" "The more you give, the more you get." "No pain, no gain!" We have all heard these sayings in one form or another. And we have heard them applied to many different situations, including going to church, participating in sports, and doing homework.

The Church year offers us endless opportunities to "Get into it!" As each season approaches, discuss with your classmates the many ways you can make that particular season more meaningful.

Advent

The "O" Antiphons

During the last week of Advent, the Church assigns one special prayer for each day of the week to help us prepare for the coming of Jesus. These prayers were originally taken from the Scriptures and sung during evening prayer, called Vespers. The tune, or melody, of the antiphon is based on Gregorian chant and dates back to the 9th century. The familiar hymn "O Come, O Come, Emmanuel" is based on these antiphons.

After each antiphon, write a short explanation of the meaning of the verse.

December 17: *O Wisdom*

Wisdom, O holy Word of God, you govern all creation with your strong yet tender care. Come and show your people the way to salvation.

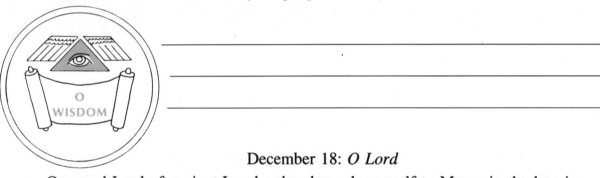

December 18: *O Lord*

O sacred Lord of ancient Israel, who showed yourself to Moses in the burning bush, who gave him the holy law on Sinai mountain: come, stretch out your mighty hand to set us free.

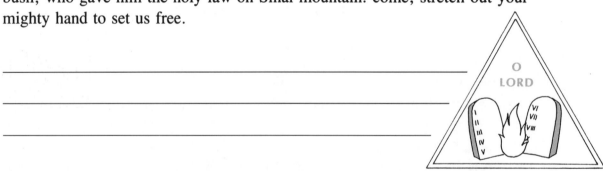

December 19: *O Flower of Jesse*

O Flower of Jesse's stem, you have been raised up as a sign for all peoples; kings stand silent in your presence; the nations bow down in worship before you. Come, let nothing keep you from coming to our aid.

December 20: *O Key of David*

O Key of David, O royal Power of Israel controlling at your will the gate of heaven: come, break down the prison walls of death for those who dwell in darkness and the shadow of death; and lead your captive people into freedom.

December 21: *O Radiant Dawn*

O Radiant Dawn, splendor of eternal light, sun of justice: come, shine on those who dwell in darkness and the shadow of death.

December 22: *O King*

O King of all the nations, the only joy of every human heart; O Keystone of the mighty arch of man, come and save the creature you fashioned from the dust.

December 23: *O Emmanuel*

O Emmanuel, king and lawgiver, desire of the nations, Savior of all people, come and set us free, Lord our God.

Christmas

Keeping Christ in Christmas

It is often difficult to keep Christ at the center of Christmas amid the hustle and bustle of shopping. Discuss the following questions with your classmates and family.

1. Why do we give gifts at Christmas time?

2. When did this custom first begin?

3. What type of gifts (that cannot be bought) can we give to those we love?

4. If you were one of the shepherds who came to see the newborn Baby Jesus, what gift would you bring to Him?

The Christmas Story

Read the Christmas story with your family. Perhaps your class could do a dramatic reading of the story, with costumes and hymns. Here is an outline of the Scripture verses that tell the Christmas story, along with some suggested hymns for various parts of the Christmas story.

The Annunciation	Luke 1:26-38	"Angels We Have Heard on High"
The Visitation	Luke 1:39-56	"Away in a Manger"
The Nativity	Luke 2:1-20	"Silent Night"
Presentation in the Temple	Luke 2:21-24	"Joy to the World"
The Coming of the Magi	Matthew 2:1-12	"We Three Kings of Orient Are"
The Prophecy of Simeon and Anna	Luke 2:25-40	"The First Noel"

Lent

Lent is a time to prepare ourselves for the joy and new life of Easter. One way to prepare for Easter is to do various acts of penance. An act of penance is a sacrifice, something difficult to do, which we offer to God. We do this to show God that we love Him and that He is most important to us. God sacrificed His only Son for us to show us His love. We should want to show God our love for Him.

Below are listed three forms of Lenten penance that the Church suggests. Discuss with your classmates and family various sacrifices or activities that you might make or do during Lent to prepare you for Easter.

1. Fasting and Abstinence.

2. Prayer.

3. Acts of Charity.

Stained Glass Windows

Materials needed: several sheets of black construction paper; ruler; pattern; cardboard desk-protectors; tissue paper in assorted colors; white glue; scissors.

Directions:

1. Choose a pattern.

2. With your ruler, draw a 1/2″ frame around an 8″ x 12″ piece of black construction paper.

3. Trace the pattern in the center of the black paper.

4. With your ruler, draw "rays" connecting the pattern with the edge of the frame you have drawn around the paper. Draw the rays in various angles. Make each of the rays about 1/2″ wide so that tissue paper can be glued to the back of the ray.

5. With a scissors, cut out the shapes of the rays. (Use a piece of thick cardboard underneath the paper to protect the surface of the desk.)

6. Cut small pieces of tissue paper in various colors, each large enough to cover one of the "ray" openings.

7. Glue the various pieces of tissue paper onto the back of the black paper, over the openings.

8. Mount the finished Stained Glass Windows on the classroom's windows for display and viewing.

Easter Season

The Easter Season celebrates the Resurrection and Ascension of Jesus and the coming of the Holy Spirit on Pentecost.

Scripture Narratives of the Resurrection. All four Gospel writers—Matthew, Mark, Luke, and John—tell the story of the Resurrection. Read the four narratives and compare them:

> Matthew 28:1–10 Luke 24:1–11
> Mark 16:1–8 John 20:1–9 (10–18)

Activity. The Psalm assigned for Easter Sunday is Psalm 118:1-2,15-24. Read the Psalm aloud.

Verse 24 reads: "This is the day the Lord has made; let us be glad and rejoice in it". List several reasons why we should "be glad and rejoice". Be sure to think about all the signs of spring that remind us of "New Life". Make an Easter collage of pictures and drawings that reflect your list.

Ascension Thursday

In a letter to his friend Theophilus, Saint Luke tells the story of Christ's Ascension into heaven.

Read Acts 1:1-11.

1. How many days had Jesus been with the Apostles since His resurrection?

2. Jesus asks the Apostles to stay in Jerusalem and wait for "the promise of the Father". What is the "promise of the Father"?

3. What will the Holy Spirit help the Apostles do?

4. What message is in the Ascension story for us?

Pentecost

The word *pentecost* comes from Greek words meaning "fiftieth day". The period of fifty sacred days after Easter Sunday ends on Pentecost Sunday. The "promise of the Father" given to the Apostles by Jesus before His Ascension is fulfilled on this day.

Read Acts 2:1-41 for Saint Luke's account of the descent of the Holy Spirit.

Saint Luke tells how Saint Peter and the other Apostles began to tell all the people gathered outside that Jesus had risen from the dead, that He was indeed the Messiah. Many heard the message of Peter and the Apostles. "Those who accepted his message were baptized, and about three thousand persons were added that day" (Acts 2:41). This event marked the beginning of the first community of Christians. The Apostles and the first Christians used the gifts that God had given them to continue Christ's work on earth. They "served the Lord". Their service included preaching the Good News, visiting and healing the sick, and sharing their wealth with the poor. The Church grew, and new Christian communities began to spring up throughout the land. Pentecost, for that reason, is sometimes referred to as the "Birthday of the Church".

Activity. Discuss the many ways that you and your class could spread the Good News by being of service to your community. Plan a project and carry it through.

REVIEW QUESTIONS

1. What signs announced the appearance of the Holy Spirit?
2. What occurred when the Apostles were filled with the Holy Spirit?
3. What message does the feast of Pentecost bring to us?

Calendar Activity (Worksheet 1)

Fill in the blank spaces with the correct calendar dates. Then add the names of various feast days celebrated during the month. Lightly color the blanks with the appropriate liturgical color of the season.

Easter Candle Activity (Worksheet 2)

The white Easter candle represents our risen Lord shining with the light and splendor of His resurrection. He is the new "pillar of fire" leading redeemed Israel out of the bondage of sin into the promised land of heaven. Inscribed on the candle are an outline of the Cross, the first and last letters of the Greek alphabet (alpha and omega), and the numerals of the current year. These emblems on the candle teach us that the risen Christ, the Lord of all ages, should shine in our lives during this current year of grace.

In the rite of preparation of the Easter candle, the priest places these emblems on the candle in eight steps:

1. *Christ yesterday and today* [tracing the vertical beam of the cross]
2. *The beginning and the end* [tracing the horizontal beam]
3. *Alpha* [placed above the cross]
4. *and Omega* [below the cross]
5. *All time belongs to Him* [placing the first numeral of date]
6. *And all the ages* [the second numeral]
7. *To Him be glory and power* [the third numeral]
8. *Through every age and for ever. Amen.* [the fourth numeral]

When the priest finishes these steps, he may insert five grains of incense in the candle, in the form of a cross, while saying:

1. *By His holy*
2. *And glorious wounds*
3. *May Christ our Lord*
4. *Guard us*
5. *And keep us. Amen.*

Using crayons or markers, color the picture of the Easter candle, using red for the Cross and the Alpha and Omega.

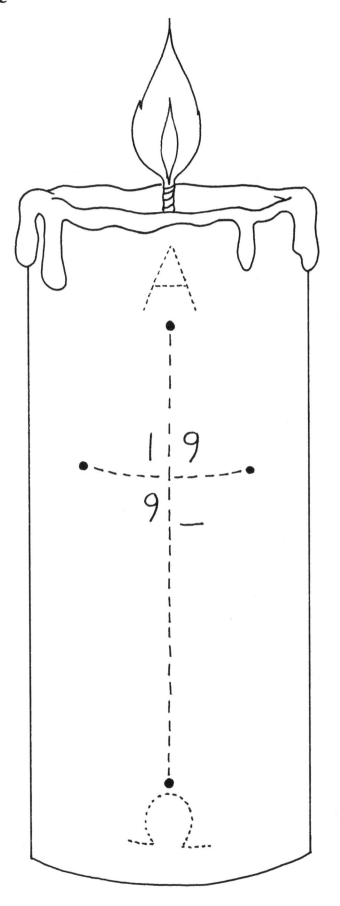

Prayers to Know

Our Father

Our Father, Who art in heaven,
hallowed be Thy name;
Thy kingdom come;
Thy will be done on earth as it is in heaven.
Give us this day our daily bread;
and forgive us our trespasses as we forgive those who trespass against us;
and lead us not into temptation, but deliver us from evil.
Amen.

Apostles' Creed

I believe in God, the Father almighty,
    Creator of heaven and earth.
I believe in Jesus Christ, His only Son, our Lord.
    He was conceived by the power of the Holy Spirit
        and born of the Virgin Mary.
    He suffered under Pontius Pilate,
        was crucified, died, and was buried.
    He descended to the dead.
    On the third day He rose again.
    He ascended into heaven,
        and is seated at the right hand of the Father.
    He will come again to judge the living and the dead.
I believe in the Holy Spirit,
    the holy Catholic Church,
    the communion of saints,
    the forgiveness of sins,
    the resurrection of the body,
    and the life everlasting.
Amen.

Glory Be

Glory be to the Father, and to the Son, and to the Holy Spirit,
as it was in the beginning, is now, and ever shall be, world without end.
Amen.

Hail Mary

Hail, Mary, full of grace, the Lord is with thee.
Blessed art thou among women, and blessed is the fruit of thy womb, Jesus.
Holy Mary, Mother of God, pray for us sinners now and at the hour of our death.
Amen.

Hail, Holy Queen

Hail, holy Queen, Mother of mercy,
   our life, our sweetness and our hope.
To you do we cry, poor banished children of Eve.
To you do we send up our sighs,
   mourning and weeping in this vale of tears.
Turn then, most gracious advocate,
   your eyes of mercy toward us,
   and after this exile
   show to us the blessed fruit of your womb, Jesus.
O clement, O loving, O sweet Virgin Mary.
   V. Pray for us, O holy Mother of God.
   R. That we may be made worthy of the promises of Christ.

Angelus

The angel of the Lord declared unto Mary:
And she conceived by the Holy Spirit.
   Hail, Mary, . . .
Behold the handmaid of the Lord:
Be it done to me according to Your word.
   Hail, Mary, . . .
And the Word was made flesh:
And dwelt among us.
   Hail, Mary, . . .
Pray for us, O holy Mother of God:
That we may be made worthy of the promises of Christ.
   Pour forth, we beseech You, O Lord, Your grace into our hearts, that we to whom the
   Incarnation of Christ, Your Son, was made known by the message of an angel, may
   by His Passion and Cross be brought to the glory of His resurrection. Through Christ
   our Lord. Amen.

Memorare

Remember, O most gracious Virgin Mary,
    that never was it known
    that anyone who fled to your protection,
    implored your help,
    or sought your intercession,
    was left unaided.
Inspired by this confidence,
    I fly unto you, O Virgin of virgins, my Mother.
To you do I come, before you I stand, sinful and sorrowful.
O Mother of the Word Incarnate,
    despise not my petitions,
    but in your mercy hear and answer me.
Amen.

Act of Contrition

My God,
I am sorry for my sins with all my heart.
In choosing to do wrong and failing to do good,
I have sinned against You,
    Whom I should love above all things.
I have hurt myself and others.
I firmly intend, with Your help,
    to do penance, to sin no more,
    and to avoid whatever leads me to sin.
Our Savior Jesus Christ suffered and died for us.
In His name, my God, have mercy.
Amen.

Morning Offering

O Jesus, through the Immaculate Heart of Mary,
I offer You my prayers, works, joys, and sufferings of this day
in union with the Holy Sacrifice of the Mass throughout the world.
I offer them for all the intentions of Your Sacred Heart:
the salvation of souls,
reparation for sin,
the reunion of all Christians.
I offer them for the intentions of our bishopsand of all Apostles of Prayer,
and in particular for those recommended by our Holy Father this month.
Amen.

—Apostleship of Prayer

Grace before Meals

Bless us, O Lord, and these Thy gifts,
which we are about to receive from Thy bounty.
Through Christ our Lord.
Amen.

Grace after Meals

We give Thee thanks for all Thy gifts, almighty God.
You live and reign forever.
Amen.

An Act of Faith

O my God, I firmly believe that You are one God in three Divine Persons,
    Father, Son, and Holy Spirit.
I believe that Your Divine Son became man and died for our sins,
    and that He will come to judge the living and the dead.
I believe these and all the truths which the holy Catholic Church teaches,
    because You have revealed them, Who can neither deceive nor be deceived.
Amen.

An Act of Hope

O my God, relying on Your infinite goodness and promises,
    I hope to obtain pardon of my sins,
    the help of Your grace,
    and life everlasting,
    through the merits of Jesus Christ,
        my Lord and Redeemer.
Amen.

An Act of Love

O my God, I love You above all things,
    with my whole heart and soul,
    because You are all-good and worthy of all my love.
I love my neighbor as myself for the love of You.
I forgive all who have injured me,
    and ask pardon of all whom I have injured.
Amen.

NOTES

NOTES